Microsoft®
Excel 2010:
Level 1 of 3

SANDRA RITTMAN
Long Beach City College

LABYRINTH
LEARNING™

El Sobrante, CA

Microsoft Excel 2010: Level 1
by Sandra Rittman

Copyright © 2011 by Labyrinth Learning

LABYRINTH
LEARNING™

Labyrinth Learning
P.O. Box 20818
El Sobrante, California 24820
800.522.9746
On the web at lablearning.com

President:
Brian Favro

Product Development Manager:
Jason Favro

Managing Editor:
Laura A. Lionello

Production Manager:
Rad Proctor

eLearning Production Manager:
Arl S. Nadel

Editorial/Production Team:
Pamela Beveridge, Belinda Breyer, Everett
Cowan, Alec Fehl, Sandy Jones,
PMG Media

Indexing: Joanne Sprott

Interior Design:
Mark Ong, Side-by-Side Studios

Cover Design:
Words At Work

ITEM: 1-59136-313-6
ISBN-13: 978-1-59136-313-2

Manufactured in the United States of America.

10 9 8 7 6 5 4 3 2 1

Table of Contents

Quick Reference Tables

Preface

Microsoft® Excel 2010: Level 1 provides thorough training of Excel 2010 introductory skills. This course is supported with comprehensive instructor resources and our eLab assessment and learning management tool. And, our new work-readiness exercises ensure students have the critical thinking skills necessary to succeed in today's world. After completing the course, students will be able to successfully face the challenges presented in the next book in this series, *Microsoft Excel 2010: Level 2*.

Visual Conventions

This book uses many visual and typographic cues to guide students through the lessons. This page provides examples and describes the function of each cue.

Type this text	Anything you should type at the keyboard is printed in this typeface.
	Tips, Notes, and Warnings are used throughout the text to draw attention to certain topics.
Command→ Command→ Command, etc.	This convention indicates how to give a command from the Ribbon. The commands are written: Ribbon Tab→Command Group→Command→ Subcommand.
FROM THE KEYBOARD Ctrl+S to save	These margin notes indicate shortcut keys for executing a task described in the text.

Exercise Progression

The exercises in this book build in complexity as students work through a lesson toward mastery of the skills taught.

- **Develop Your Skills** exercises are introduced immediately after concept discussions. They provide detailed, step-by-step tutorials.
- **Reinforce Your Skills** exercises provide additional hands-on practice with moderate assistance.
- **Apply Your Skills** exercises test students' skills by describing the correct results without providing specific instructions on how to achieve them.
- **Critical Thinking and Work-Readiness Skills** exercises are the most challenging. They provide generic instructions, allowing students to use their skills and creativity to achieve the results they envision.

Exploring Excel 2010

LESSON OUTLINE

LEARNING OBJECTIVES

After studying this lesson, you will be able to:

- Explain ways Excel can help your productivity
- Navigate around the Excel window and issue commands
- Enter text and numbers into cells
- Distinguish between a text and a number entry in a cell
- Save, "save as," and close workbooks

In this lesson, you will develop fundamental Excel skills. This lesson will provide you with a solid understanding of Excel so you are prepared to master advanced features later. You will learn how to navigate around a worksheet, enter various types of data, and select cells.

Building a Basic Spreadsheet

Welcome to Green Clean, a janitorial product supplier and cleaning service contractor to small businesses, shopping plazas, and office buildings. Green Clean uses environmentally friendly cleaning products and incorporates sustainability practices wherever possible, including efficient energy and water use, recycling and waste reduction, and reduced petroleum use in vehicles. In addition to providing green cleaning services, the company also sells its eco-friendly products directly to customers.

You will follow the steps with Green Clean employees as they use essential Excel features to complete tasks and projects.

Nicole Romero works as a payroll assistant at Green Clean. She needs to create a list of hours that cleaning service employees worked during the weekend (Friday through Sunday). Nicole's manager has asked her to compile the data from employee time sheets and report hours on a daily basis. Nicole decides that Excel is the right tool for this task and proceeds to organize the data in a worksheet, shown in the following illustration.

	A	B	C	D	E
1	Service Employees Weekend Hours Worked				
2					
3	Alton Mall		Friday	Saturday	Sunday
4		Barnes	6	6	6
5		Chau	8	8	8
6		Lee	4	0	4
7		Olsen	4	3	0
8		Total Hrs			
9	Century Bank				
10		Garcia	3	5	0
11		Kimura	3	4	0
12		Tan	3	5	0
13		Total Hrs			
14	Newport Medical				
15		Kowalski	8	6	8
16		Silva	6	6	0
17		Wilson	5	2	5
18		Total Hrs			

Notice that Excel makes it easy for you to organize your data in columns and rows. The "Total Hrs" rows have been included in the example, although you will not learn how to create formulas to calculate totals in this lesson.

1.1 Presenting Excel 2010

Video Lesson labyrinthelab.com/videos

Microsoft Office Excel is an electronic spreadsheet program that allows you to work with numbers and data much more efficiently than the pen-and-paper method. Excel is used in virtually all industries and many households for a variety of tasks such as:

- Creating and maintaining detailed budgets
- Keeping track of extensive customer lists
- Performing "what-if" scenarios and break-even analyses
- Determining the profitability of a business or sector
- Creating tables to organize information
- Tracking employee information
- Producing detailed charts to graphically display information
- Creating invoices or purchase orders
- Determining the future value of an investment, the present value of an annuity, or the payment for a loan
- Working with reports exported from small business accounting software programs such as Intuit's QuickBooks®

As you can see from this list, Excel is not just used to crunch numbers. It is a very powerful program that is used not only to work with numbers but also to maintain databases. If you have started a database in Excel, you can even import it into Microsoft Access (the program in the Microsoft Office Suite that is specialized for working with databases). Many people may use Excel to track their databases rather than Access because of its ease of use and because Access is not included in all of the Microsoft Office editions. If you are tracking multiple databases that you wish to include in reports and data queries, you will want to consider utilizing Access, though, as it really is designed to work with multiple tables of data.

Throughout the Excel lessons, the terms *spreadsheet* and *worksheet* will be used interchangeably.

1.2 Starting Excel

The method you use to start Excel depends in large part on whether you intend to create a new workbook or open an existing workbook. A workbook is a file containing one or more worksheets. To create a new workbook, use one of the following methods. (The item names in the menus may vary depending on your Windows version.) Once the Excel program has started, you can begin working in the new workbook that appears.

- Click the Start ⊞ button, choose the Microsoft Office folder from the All Programs menu, and choose Microsoft Office Excel 2010. (Depending on your installation of Microsoft Office, Microsoft Office Excel 2010 may appear on the All Programs menu.)
- Click the Microsoft Office Excel 2010 🗗 button on the taskbar located to the right of the Start button. (This button may not appear on all computers.)

Use one of the following methods if you intend to open an existing Excel workbook. Once the Excel program has started, the desired workbook will open in an Excel window.

- Navigate to the desired document using Windows Explorer or Computer and double-click the workbook.
- Click the Start ⊞ button and point to Recent Items. You can choose the desired workbooks from the documents list, which displays the most-recently used documents.

Start Excel

In this exercise, you will start the Excel program.

1. **Start** your computer, if necessary, and the Windows Desktop will appear.
2. Click the **Start** ⊞ button and choose **Programs** (or All Programs).
3. Choose the **Microsoft Office** folder from the menu, and then choose **Microsoft Office Excel 2010**.
   After a pause, the Excel program loads and the Excel window appears.
4. **Maximize** ⬚ the window, if necessary.

1.3 Exploring the Excel Program Window

Video Lesson   labyrinthelab.com/videos

When you launch Excel, you will see a blank workbook displayed. The window is filled with many objects and a space for you to create your spreadsheet. Using the figures that follow, you will have an opportunity to learn the names of some of the objects that you can see on your screen.

Quick Access Toolbar   Tabs   Title Bar

Home Ribbon

Name Box

Active Cell

Worksheet Area   Formula Bar

Status Bar

Numbered Sheet Tabs   New Sheet Tab   View Buttons   Zoom Slider

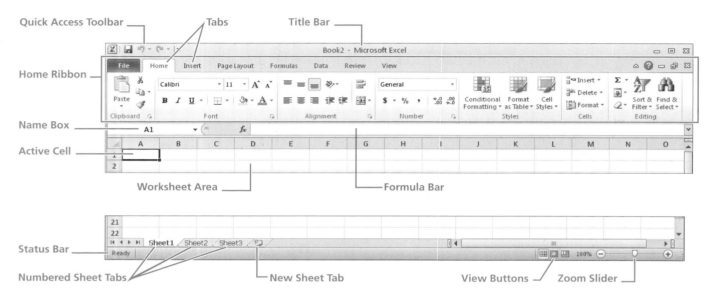

Using Worksheets and Workbooks

Excel displays a blank workbook the moment you start the program. A workbook is composed of worksheets. A workbook is similar to a paper notebook with several sheets of paper. You enter text, numbers, formulas, charts, and other objects in worksheets. By default, Excel displays three worksheets in a new workbook, each accessible by a separate tab at the bottom of the screen. The maximum number of worksheets you can insert is limited only by the amount of memory available on your computer.

In this example, the sheet tabs are named so that you can organize data for each season as well as track annual information.

A worksheet has a grid structure with horizontal rows and vertical columns. A new worksheet has 16,384 columns and 1,048,576 rows. However, at any given time only a small number of the rows and columns are visible in the worksheet window. The intersection

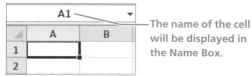

The name of the cell will be displayed in the Name Box.

of each row and column is a cell. Each cell is identified by a reference. The reference is the column letter followed by the row number. For example, A1 is the reference of the cell in the top-left corner of the worksheet. So, this is called cell A1.

Mousing Around in Excel

The shape of the mouse pointer will change as you move it around the Excel window. The shape of the pointer will let you know what will happen if you click over that spot.

Mouse Pointer Shape	Function
✛	Click to select a cell. Click and drag to select multiple cells.
✛	The fill handle pointer; dragging this pointer will copy the cell contents or the next values in a data series to adjacent cells.
↖	Allows you to perform a variety of tasks when clicked, such as issue a command from the Ribbon or select a new tab.
⊹	The move pointer; if you drag with this, it will move cell contents from one location to another.
↕ ⇔ ↘	The resize pointers; dragging one of these pointers will allow you to change the height, width, or both dimensions of objects such as pictures, shapes, or charts.
→ ↓	Select a row or column.
I	Click with the I-beam pointer to enter text, such as in the Formula Bar.

Scrolling Along in a Worksheet

There are two scroll bars visible in the Excel window, both vertical and horizontal. They allow you to see other areas of the worksheet without changing which cell is active. There are three ways to use the scroll bars to view other areas of your spreadsheet.

Click between an arrow and the scroll box to move one "screen view" at a time.

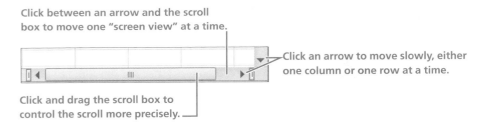

Click an arrow to move slowly, either one column or one row at a time.

Click and drag the scroll box to control the scroll more precisely.

Navigating in a Worksheet

When you have a cell selected, it is surrounded by a thick line, which indicates that it is the active cell. You can change the active cell by clicking in another cell or by using the keyboard. This is important because data is entered into the active cell. The vertical and horizontal scroll bars let you navigate through a worksheet; however, scrolling does not change which cell is active. After scrolling, you will have to select which cell is to be active, either by clicking or using one of the keystrokes listed below.

You may type a cell reference in the Name Box and then tap ⬚Enter⬚ to navigate to that cell.

Keystroke(s)	How the Highlight Moves
→ ← ↑ ↓	One cell right, left, up, or down
Home	Beginning of current row
Ctrl + Home	Home cell, usually cell A1
Ctrl + End	Last cell in active part of worksheet
Page Down	Down one visible screen
Page Up	Up one visible screen
Alt + Page Down	One visible screen right
Alt + Page Up	One visible screen left
Ctrl + G	Displays Go To dialog box—enter cell reference and click OK

DEVELOP YOUR SKILLS 1.3.1

Move the Selection and Explore the Excel Window

In this exercise, you will practice selecting the active cell in a worksheet so that you can become comfortable enough with the program to begin to create a worksheet.

Navigate with the Mouse

1. Slide the **mouse pointer** over the screen and notice the thick **cross shape** ✛ when it is in the worksheet area.
   If you click with this pointer shape, you will select a cell.

2. Click the **cross-shaped pointer** on any cell and notice that the cell becomes active.

3. Move the selection five times by **clicking** in various cells.

Navigate with the Keyboard

Now that you have practiced using the mouse, it is time to learn how to use the keyboard to move about a worksheet. You should use the keys on your keyboard that are between the main part and the numeric keypad on the far right.

4. Use the →, ←, ↑, and ↓ keys to position the highlight in **cell F10**.

5. **Tap** the Home key and see that the highlight moves to cell A10.
   The Home key always makes the cell in column A of the current row active.

6. **Press** Ctrl + Home to make A1 the active cell.

7. **Tap** the Page Down key two or three times.
   Notice that Excel displays the next 25 or so rows (one "visible" screen's worth) each time you tap Page Down.

8. **Press** and **hold down** the ↑ key until A1 is the active cell.

Use the Scroll Bars

The scroll bars allow you to see other areas of the Excel worksheet area without changing which cell is active.

9. Click the **Scroll Right** ▶ button on the horizontal scroll bar until columns AA and AB are visible.
   Excel labels the first 26 columns A–Z and the next 26 columns AA–AZ. A similar labeling scheme is used for the remaining columns out to the final column, XFD.

10. Click the **Scroll Down** ⏷ button on the vertical scroll bar until row 100 is visible.
    Notice that the highlight has not moved. To move the highlight, you must click in a cell or use the keyboard.

11. Take a few minutes to practice **scrolling** and **moving** the selection.

Use the Go To Command

As you learned in the preceding keystroke navigation table, you can use Ctrl + G *to display the Go To box, where you can go to a specific cell by entering the desired cell reference in the Reference box and clicking OK. You can use* Ctrl + Home *to select cell A1.*

12. **Press** Ctrl + G to display the Go To dialog box.

13. Type **g250** in the Reference box and click **OK**.
    Notice that cell references are not case sensitive.

14. Use the **Go To** command to move to two or three different cells.

15. **Press** Ctrl + Home to return to cell A1.

Navigate with the Name Box

16. Click the **Name Box** at the left of the Formula Bar.

17. Type **ab9** and **tap** Enter .

18. **Press** Ctrl + Home to return to cell A1.

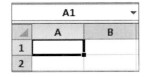

Explore the Excel Window

Now that you have learned how to select cells and move around in the window, it is time to explore the Excel window a bit further.

19. Follow these steps to explore the Excel window:

Ⓐ Click the **Sheet2** tab and notice that a different blank worksheet appears. The number of worksheets you can have is limited only by the amount of available memory in the computer.

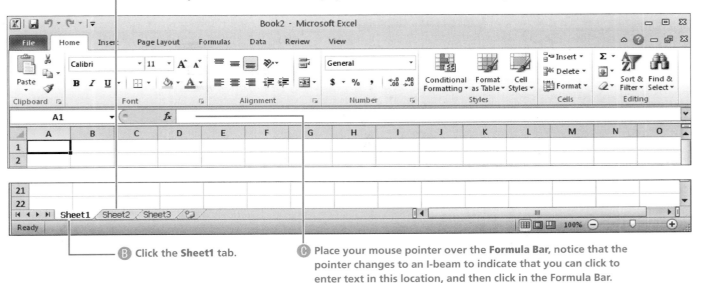

Ⓑ Click the **Sheet1** tab.

Ⓒ Place your mouse pointer over the **Formula Bar**, notice that the pointer changes to an I-beam to indicate that you can click to enter text in this location, and then click in the Formula Bar.

20. Select any cell **other than** A1, the currently active cell, to exit the Formula Bar.

21. Select **cell A1**.
    Leave the Excel window open.

1.4 Working with Tabs and Ribbons

Video Lesson   labyrinthelab.com/videos

In Microsoft Office 2010, Excel does not have the traditional menu and toolbars with which computer users are familiar. You are able to access the commands that will allow you to effectively utilize Excel through the tabs, ribbons, and Office button located at the top of the window.

The Quick Access Toolbar

The Quick Access Toolbar is located at the top-left corner of the window and contains commands that you use frequently. This toolbar can be customized using the Customize Quick Access Toolbar button. If

Quick Print and Open commands added

Customize Quick Access Toolbar button

you regularly use the Quick Print and Open commands, you may wish to add them to the Quick Access toolbar, as shown.

Displaying Tabs and Working with Ribbons

The tabs at the top of the Excel window organize the commands into eight categories. The commands appear on ribbons displayed across the screen. In order to view a different tab, you simply need to single-click it. The commands on the Ribbon can be chosen by a single-click as well.

Excel's Home Ribbon

The standard tabs along with the Ribbon are displayed in the preceding illustration. Additional contextual tabs will become visible as necessary. For instance, if you are working with a picture, a picture tab will appear.

The Ribbon with a contextual tab displayed. When a picture is selected, a special Picture Tools Format tab appears. All of the commands on this ribbon deal with the formatting of the picture.

Point to the Ribbon and slowly roll the mouse wheel to browse from one tab to another.

The File Tab

The File tab on the Ribbon, when clicked, accesses a menu that allows you to issue file-management commands. File management simply means working with Excel on the level of the "file"—such as creating new files, opening existing files, saving the file you are working on, and printing the file.

The following illustration shows a special group of tabs on the menu, Info through Help. When one of these tabs is selected, the Backstage view displays a large window pane containing the various options. Some panes contain help for using the options.

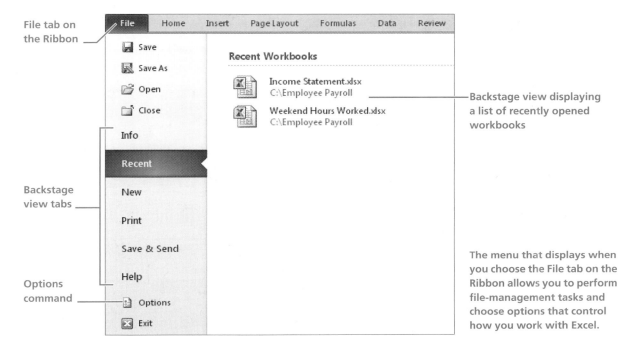

File tab on the Ribbon

Backstage view displaying a list of recently opened workbooks

Backstage view tabs

Options command

The menu that displays when you choose the File tab on the Ribbon allows you to perform file-management tasks and choose options that control how you work with Excel.

Customizing the Ribbon

Microsoft Office users now may easily customize the Ribbon. The Customize Ribbon category in Excel Options allows you to rearrange the tab order, create a new tab, add a new group to an existing tab, add or remove commands, and export all customizations for use on other computers. The built-in tabs cannot be removed, but they may be hidden. An individual tab or all tabs and the Quick Access toolbar may be reset to their original default items.

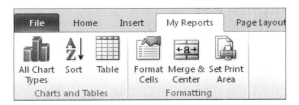

A custom tab added to the Ribbon with commands grouped according to the user's preference and workflow

ScreenTips

A ScreenTip is a little window that appears to describe the function of the object at which you are pointing. ScreenTips appear when you rest your mouse pointer over an option on a ribbon, the Quick Access toolbar, or the Office button. Enhanced ScreenTips appear for some of the commands. An Enhanced ScreenTip is a larger window that is more descriptive than a ScreenTip and provides a link to an Excel help topic.

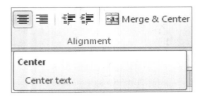

When you place your mouse pointer over an object on the Ribbon, a ScreenTip appears.

Sometimes you will see an Enhanced ScreenTip when you place your mouse pointer over an object. In this case, you receive an Enhanced ScreenTip explaining the function of the Margins command with a link to a help topic.

Dialog Box Launchers

Many of the groups on the Ribbon have dialog box launchers ▣. Clicking on the dialog box launcher will open a window that allows you to issue additional commands.

Clicking the dialog box launcher in the Font area of the Home ribbon will open the Format Cells dialog box with the Font tab displayed.

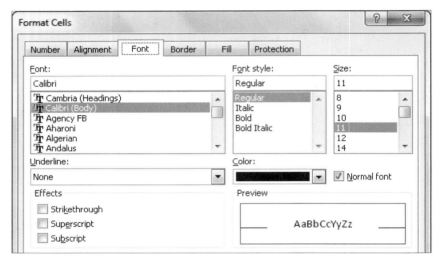

The Font tab of the Format Cells dialog box allows you to make changes to how the font appears in the selected cell(s).

Hiding the Ribbon

There may be times when you do not want the Ribbon displayed at the top of the window. In order to hide it, simply click the Minimize the Ribbon button at the upper-right corner of the window, shown to the right. The button changes to become Expand the Ribbon. To display the Ribbon to issue a single command, click on the tab you wish to view. Once you have issued the command, the Ribbon will be hidden. To display the Ribbon permanently once again, click the Expand the Ribbon button.

DEVELOP YOUR SKILLS 1.4.1

Explore the Tabs, Ribbons, and the Quick Access Toolbar

In this exercise, you will have the opportunity to explore the tabs and Ribbon at the top of the Excel window. In addition, you will add a button to the Quick Access toolbar that you believe is important to always have readily available.

Display the Page Layout Ribbon

In the next few steps you will display the Page Layout tab of the Ribbon and open the Page Setup dialog box.

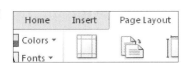

1. Click the **Page Layout tab** at the top of the window.
   The Page Layout tab is displayed.

2. Click the **dialog box launcher** at the bottom-right corner of the Page Setup group of the Ribbon.
   The Page Setup dialog box appears.

3. Click the **Cancel** button at the bottom of the dialog box to close it.

4. Move your **mouse pointer** over various commands on the Page Layout tab of the Ribbon to display their ScreenTips and explore what will occur if you choose to click them.

Add a Button to the Quick Access Toolbar

In this section, you will add a button to the Quick Access toolbar that will allow you to easily open another workbook.

5. Follow these steps to add Open to the Quick Access toolbar:

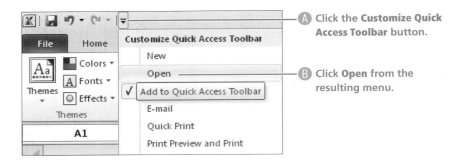

Ⓐ Click the **Customize Quick Access Toolbar** button.

Ⓑ Click **Open** from the resulting menu.

Notice the ScreenTip that displays below the mouse pointer when you point at a menu option, explaining what will occur if you choose that option. The Open button will appear on the Quick Access toolbar.

The new button appears on the Quick Access toolbar.

Remove a Button from the Quick Access Toolbar

In order to remove the Open button from the Quick Access toolbar, you will repeat the steps you took to add it.

6. Click the **Customize Quick Access Toolbar** button.

7. Choose **Open** from the resulting menu.
Excel will essentially "remove the checkmark" from the Open option and remove the button from the toolbar. Leave the Excel window open, as you will continue to work with it in the next exercise.

1.5 Entering Data in Excel

Video Lesson labyrinthelab.com/videos

You can begin entering data the moment Excel is started. Data is entered into the active cell (the cell with the thick line around it). Text and numbers are used for different purposes in a worksheet. For instance, text entries cannot be used in calculations, whereas number entries can. Text is used for descriptive headings and entries that require alphabetic characters or a combination of alphabetic and numeric characters and spaces. Numbers can be entered directly or can be calculated using formulas. Excel recognizes the data you enter and decides whether the entry is text, a number, or a formula that performs a calculation.

Data Types

Entries are defined as one of two main classifications: constant values or formulas. Constant values can be text, numeric, or a combination of both. The one thing that makes an entry constant is that the value does not change when other information changes. Conversely, formula entries display the results of calculations, and a result can change when a value in another cell changes.

f_x 1263

This entry is a constant value; it will not change as other cells are updated.

f_x =SUM(C5:C8)

When a formula entry is used, it will refer to one or more cells and will change as the indicated cells are updated.

Completing Cell Entries

Text and numbers are entered by positioning the highlight in the desired cell, typing the desired text or number, and completing the entry. You can use Enter, Tab, or any of the arrow keys (→, ←, ↑, ↓) to complete an entry. The position of the active cell following a cell entry depends on the method by which you complete the entry.

Entry Completion Method	Where the Active Cell Will Appear
Enter	It will move down to the next cell.
Tab	It will move to the next cell to the right.
→ ↑ ↓ ←	It will move to the next cell in the direction of the arrow key.
Esc	The entry will be deleted and the current cell will remain active.

The Enter and Cancel Buttons

The Enter ✓ and Cancel ✗ buttons appear on the Formula Bar whenever you enter or edit an entry. The Enter button completes the entry and keeps the highlight in the current cell. The Cancel button cancels the entry, as does the Esc key.

The Cancel and Enter buttons appear when an entry is being entered or edited.

	A1 ▾	✗ ✓ f_x	Service Employees Weekend Hours Worked					
	A	B	C	D	E	F	G	H
1	Service Employees Weekend Hours Worked							

Deleting and Replacing Entries

You can delete an entire entry after it has been completed by clicking in the cell and tapping Delete. Likewise, you can replace an entry by clicking in the cell and typing a new entry. The new entry will replace the original entry.

Long Text Entries

Text entries often do not fit in a cell. These entries are known as long entries. Excel uses the following rules when deciding how to display long entries:

- If the cell to the right of the long entry is empty, then the long entry displays over the adjacent cell.

- If the cell to the right of the long entry contains an entry, then Excel shortens, or truncates, the display of the long entry.

Keep in mind that Excel does not actually change the long entry; it simply truncates the display of the entry. You can always widen a column to accommodate a long entry.

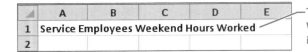 The entry, Service Employees Weekend Hours Worked, is a long entry. The entire phrase is entered in cell A1, although it displays over cells A1-E1.

DEVELOP YOUR SKILLS 1.5.1
Enter Text

In this exercise, you will enter text into your worksheet.

Type a Long Entry

First, you will have the opportunity to see how text can flow over empty cells to the right of its "home" cell.

1. Make **cell A1** active by clicking the **mouse pointer** ✚ in it.

2. Type **Service Employees Weekend Hours Worked** and **tap** Enter.
   The text is entered in the cell and the highlight moves down to cell A2. Excel moves the highlight down when you tap Enter *because most people enter data column by column. Notice that the entry displays over cells B1, C1, D1, and E1. The long entry would not display over these cells if they contained data.*

3. Click **cell A1** and note the appearance of the Formula Bar.

Notice that the Formula Bar displays the name of the active cell (A1) as well as its content. In this example, the cell's content is the title, Service Employees Weekend Hours Worked. The title is a long entry because it is wider than cell A1. Cells B1-E1 are empty so the long entry is displayed over them. Keep in mind, however, that the entire entry belongs to cell A1. This concept will be demonstrated in the next few steps.

Verify that the Entry Belongs to Cell A1

4. **Tap** the → key to make cell B1 active.

5. Look at the **Formula Bar** and notice that cell B1 is empty.
   The long entry belongs to cell A1 even though it is displayed over cells A1–E1.

Type Additional Text Entries

6. Click in **cell C3**.

7. Type **Friday** and **tap** → once.
   Notice that the entry is completed and the highlight moves to cell D3. You can always use the arrow keys to complete an entry and move the highlight in the desired direction.

8. Type **Wednesday** in cell D3 and **tap** → .

9. Type **Sunday** in cell E3 and **tap** ← .
   Notice that the display of Wednesday *is shortened, or truncated. However, the Wednesday entry is still contained in its entirety in cell D3. A long entry is always truncated when the cell to the right contains text, a number, or a formula.*

Friday	Wednesd	Sunday

10. Type **Saturday** in cell D3 and **tap** Enter .
    The new entry in cell D3 replaces the previous entry.

11. **Enter** the remaining text entries shown in the following illustration.
    If Excel proposes any entries for you as you type, simply continue typing. Leave the workbook open for the next exercise.

	A	B	C	D	E
1	Service Employees Weekend Hours Worked				
2					
3	Alton Mall		Friday	Saturday	Sunday
4		Barnes			
5		Chau			
6		Lee			
7		Olsen			
8		Total Hrs			
9	Century Bank				
10		Garcia			
11		Kimura			
12		Tan			
13		Total Hrs			
14	Newport Medical				
15		Kowalski			
16		Silva			
17		Wilson			
18		Total Hrs			

1.6 Working with Numbers

Video Lesson   labyrinthelab.com/videos

Number entries can contain only the digits 0–9 and a few other characters. Excel initially right-aligns numbers in cells, although you can change this alignment. The following table lists characters that Excel accepts as part of a number entry.

Valid Characters in Number Entries
The digits 0–9
The following characters: + – ( ) , / $ % . *

Entering numbers using the numeric keypad is very quick. The keypad is designed like a calculator. It includes its own decimal point and an Enter key.

Number Formats

It isn't necessary to type commas, dollar signs, and other number formats when entering numbers. It's easier to simply enter the numbers and use Excel's formatting commands to add the desired number format(s). You will not format numbers in this lesson.

Decimals and Negative Numbers

You should always type a decimal point if the number you are entering requires one. Likewise, you should precede a negative number entry with a minus (–) sign or enclose it in parentheses ( ).

DEVELOP YOUR SKILLS 1.6.1
Enter Numbers

In this exercise, you will practice entering numbers and canceling entries before completion.

Use the Enter Button

1. Position the highlight in **cell C4**.

2. Type **6** but don't complete the entry.

3. Look at the Formula Bar and notice the **Cancel** ☒ and **Enter** ☑ buttons.
   These buttons appear whenever you begin entering or editing data in a cell.

4. Click the **Enter** ☑ button to complete the entry.
   Notice that the highlight remains in cell C4. You can use the Enter button to complete entries, though it is more efficient to use the keyboard when building a worksheet. This is because the highlight automatically moves to the next cell. The Enter button is most useful when editing entries.

Use the Cancel Button and the Esc Key

5. Position the highlight in cell C5 and type **8**, but don't complete the entry.

6. Click the **Cancel** ✕ button on the Formula Bar to cancel the entry.

7. Type **8** again, but this time **tap** Esc on the keyboard.

   The Esc key has the same effect as the Cancel button.

8. Type **8** once again, and this time **tap** ↓ .

   Notice that Excel right-aligns the number in the cell.

9. **Enter** the remaining numbers shown in the illustration at right.

TIP

To use the numeric keypad to enter numbers, the number lock light must be on. If it's not, press the Num Lock key on the keypad.

◢	A	B	C	D	E
1	Service Employees Weekend Hours Worked				
2					
3	Alton Mall		Friday	Saturday	Sunday
4		Barnes	6	6	6
5		Chau	8	8	8
6		Lee	4	0	4
7		Olsen	4	3	0
8		Total Hrs			
9	Century Bank				
10		Garcia	3	5	0
11		Kimura	3	4	0
12		Tan	3	5	0
13		Total Hrs			
14	Newport Medical				
15		Kowalski	8	6	8
16		Silva	6	6	0
17		Wilson	5	2	5
18		Total Hrs			

10. Take a minute to verify that you have correctly entered all the numbers.

    It is so important for you to be accurate when you are entering data into Excel. Learning how to use complex formulas and functions will not do you any good if your original data is inaccurate!

1.7 Understanding Save Concepts

Video Lesson labyrinthelab.com/videos

One important lesson to learn is to save your workbooks early and often! Power outages and careless accidents can result in lost data. The best protection is to save your workbooks every 10 or 15 minutes or after making significant changes. Workbooks are saved to file storage locations such as a USB drive, the Documents folder, a shared network drive, and websites on the Internet.

Storing Your Exercise Files

Throughout this book, you will be referred to files in your "file storage location." You can store your exercise files on various media, such as on a USB flash drive, in the Documents folder, or to a network drive at a school or company. While some figures may display files on a USB flash drive, it is assumed that you will substitute your own location for that shown in the figures. See Storing Your Exercise Files for additional information on alternative storage media. Storing Your Exercise Files is available on the student web page for this book at labyrinthelab.com/excel10.

NOTE

In Windows XP, the folder is called My Documents. In Windows Vista and Windows 7, it is called Documents. Throughout this book we will use the word Documents when referring to this folder.

If you have not yet copied the student exercise files to your local file storage location, follow the instructions in Storing Your Exercise Files, located on the student web page for this book.

The Save Command

The Save 🖫 button on the Quick Access toolbar or the File tab on the Ribbon initiates the Save command. If a document has been saved previously, Excel replaces the original version with the new, edited version. If a document has never been saved, Excel displays the Save As dialog box. The Save As dialog box lets you specify the name and storage location of the document. You can also use the Save As dialog box to make a copy of a document by saving it under a new name or to a different location. Your filenames can have up to 255 characters, including spaces. Your filenames, however, should be descriptive but brief enough to manage your files and share them on networks and the Internet effectively.

Save As Options

In Excel, you are given multiple options as to how to save your workbook. How you save a workbook depends on how it will be used and who will be using it. If you are collaborating with someone who has a version earlier than Excel 2007 installed, you will need to save the file in the Excel 97-2003 Format. If you wish to publish your workbook and do not wish for others to make changes to it, you may save it as a PDF file for viewing in the Adobe Reader program. The default format is the Excel Workbook format, which is great to use if everyone who will be utilizing the file has Excel 2010 or 2007 installed.

The Save As command allows you to save a spreadsheet or entire workbook in various formats to use data in earlier versions of Excel or other applications.

File	Hom
🖫 Save	
📰 Save As	

Excel Workbook
Excel Macro-Enabled Workbook
Excel Binary Workbook
Excel 97-2003 Workbook
XML Data
Single File Web Page
Web Page
Excel Template
Excel Macro-Enabled Template
Excel 97-2003 Template
Text (Tab delimited)
Unicode Text
XML Spreadsheet 2003
Microsoft Excel 5.0/95 Workbook
CSV (Comma delimited)
Formatted Text (Space delimited)
Text (Macintosh)
Text (MS-DOS)
CSV (Macintosh)
CSV (MS-DOS)
DIF (Data Interchange Format)
SYLK (Symbolic Link)
Excel Add-In
Excel 97-2003 Add-In
PDF
XPS Document
OpenDocument Spreadsheet

Locating Workbooks

The Save As dialog box lets you locate workbooks on your local drives and in network locations. The Documents folder in the hard drive of your local computer usually is the default location for saving a workbook. You must change the location if you do not want to save there. Once you save to or open a workbook from a different location, the default changes to that location. Always check the Save As dialog box for the current drive and folder before finishing the save.

Issuing Commands from the Keyboard

There are many times when it is more convenient to issue a command from the keyboard than to chase it down with your mouse. These commands are termed keyboard shortcuts and can help you to be more efficient as you can enter these commands "on the fly" without removing your fingers from the keyboard. In this book, you will see keyboard shortcuts displayed in a special feature called From the Keyboard. Whenever you issue a keyboard command, you will first hold down the shortcut key (Ctrl ,

FROM THE KEYBOARD
Ctrl + S to save

$\boxed{\text{Alt}}$, or $\boxed{\text{Shift}}$) and then tap the additional key to issue the command. This approach is similar to holding down the $\boxed{\text{Shift}}$ key and then tapping a letter to make it capital. Throughout this book, you will be asked to use $\boxed{\text{Ctrl}}+\boxed{\text{S}}$ to save your worksheet.

Key Tips

While not every command has a keyboard shortcut assigned, you still can use the keyboard to choose any command on the Ribbon or Quick Access toolbar. When you tap the $\boxed{\text{Alt}}$ key, numbered key tips display over buttons on the Quick Access toolbar and alphabetic key tips display over the Ribbon tabs. For example, the sequence for choosing the Save As command is $\boxed{\text{Alt}}$, $\boxed{\text{F}}$, $\boxed{\text{A}}$. You may wish to memorize your most frequently used commands.

FROM THE KEYBOARD
$\boxed{\text{Alt}}$, $\boxed{\text{F}}$, $\boxed{\text{S}}$ or $\boxed{\text{F12}}$
to save as

Tapping $\boxed{\text{Alt}}$ and then $\boxed{\text{F}}$ (or using $\boxed{\text{Alt}}+\boxed{\text{F}}$) will display the File tab.

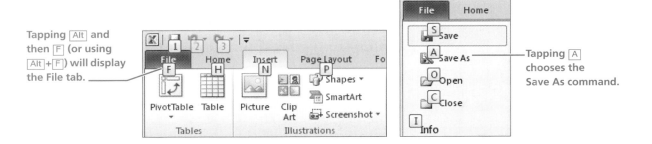

Tapping $\boxed{\text{A}}$ chooses the Save As command.

AutoSave

If your computer suddenly stops working, you may be able to recover some of your work. When switched on, the AutoSave feature saves your workbook to a default file storage location every ten minutes or at the interval you set. This is *not* the location where you save your workbooks. An autosave is performed only if you edited the workbook during the interval. If your computer freezes or loses power, the Document Recovery pane should display when you restart the computer and Excel. The pane contains one or more document versions you may recover. If you wish to keep a version other than the "Original" one you saved, you should then save it to your file storage location. Some of Excel's save options are shown in the following illustration.

Option that automatically creates a workbook recovery file at the specified interval

Option to allow you to recover the last autosave if you did not issue a save command

File storage location for autosaved file versions

File storage location that displays when you save a workbook for the first time

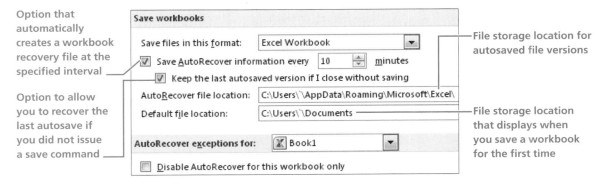

Use the Save command often for the best possible chance of recovering your most recent changes to a workbook. Changes made after the last autosave cannot be recovered.

Managing Workbook File Versions

When the Keep the Last Autosaved Version If I Close Without Saving option is switched on, Excel maintains the last autosaved version for four days. The Info and Recent tabs in Backstage view allow you to recover autosaved versions or the unsaved version of a workbook after you close it.

Autosaved workbook versions displayed in the Info tab of Backstage view

QUICK REFERENCE	SAVING A WORKBOOK AND MANAGING WORKBOOK FILE VERSIONS
Task	**Procedure**
Save for the first time	▪ Click Save 💾 on the Quick Access toolbar.
	▪ Name the workbook and choose the location in which to save it.
	▪ Click Save.
Save changes in the workbook	▪ Click Save 💾 on the Quick Access toolbar.
Save in a new location or with a new name	▪ Choose File→Save As 🖫.
	▪ Change the name of the workbook, the file storage location, or both.
	▪ Click Save.
Save the workbook in the Excel 97-2003 Format	▪ Choose File→Save As 🖫.
	▪ Enter the filename and navigate to the desired file storage location.
	▪ Choose Excel 97-2003 from the Save as Type list.
	▪ Click Save.
Use key tips to choose a command	▪ Tap the Alt key to display key tips.
	▪ Tap the letter or number key that corresponds to the desired tab on the Ribbon or Quick Access toolbar button.
	▪ Tap the letter(s) in the key tip for the desired command on the Ribbon.

Task	Procedure
Set autosave options	■ Choose File→Options 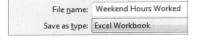, and choose the Save category at the left in the Excel Options dialog box.
	■ Place a checkmark next to Save AutoRecover Information Every, and type the desired number in the Minutes box.
	■ Place a checkmark next to Keep the Last Autosaved Version If I Close Without Saving.
Recover an autosaved workbook version	■ With the workbook file open, choose File→Info.
	■ In the Info tab of Backstage view, click the version that displays the desired date and time.
Recover an unsaved workbook	■ Perform one of the following:
	◆ Choose File→Info. In the Info tab of Backstage view, click the Manage Versions menu ▼ button, and choose Recover Unsaved Workbooks.
	or
	◆ Choose File→Recent. Choose Recover Unsaved Workbooks at the lower-right corner of the Recent tab of Backstage view.
	■ In the Open dialog box, display the files in Details view.
	■ Double-click the file displaying the desired filename, date, and time.
	■ Click Save As in the message area above the worksheet, enter a filename, and choose your file storage location.

DEVELOP YOUR SKILLS 1.7.1
Save the Workbook

In this exercise, you will save the workbook created in the previous exercises to your file storage location. You will also use key tips to select a command on the Ribbon and view Excel's options for saving workbooks.

Before You Begin: Navigate to the student web page for this book at labyrinthelab.com/excel10 and see the Downloading the Student Exercise Files section of Storing Your Exercise Files for instructions on how to retrieve the student exercise files for this book and to copy them to your file storage location.

Use the Mouse to Save

1. Click the **Save** 🖫 button on the Quick Access toolbar.
   The Save As dialog box appears because this is the first time you are saving the workbook.

2. Notice that the proposed name Book1 is highlighted in the File Name box.
   The name may be Book2 or something similar. You may need to select the name to highlight it if you clicked elsewhere in the dialog box.

3. **Type** the name **Weekend Hours Worked** and it will replace the proposed name.

File name:	Weekend Hours Worked
Save as type:	Excel Workbook

4. Choose the Lesson 01 folder in your file storage location by **navigating** to the correct drive and folder.
   See the online document, Storing Your Exercise Files, for specific instructions for your operating system.

5. Click **Save** or **tap** Enter.
   Notice that the filename appears in the Title Bar of the window to indicate that the workbook is saved.

6. **Tap** the Alt key.
   Key tips display on the Quick Access toolbar and Ribbon.

7. **Tap** the F key.
   The File tab displays.

8. **Tap** the A key.
   The Save As dialog box displays.

9. **Tap** Esc to cancel the dialog box without saving.

Explore Save Options

10. Choose File→Options 📋.

11. Choose the **Save** category at the left of the Excel Options dialog box.

12. Notice the settings under Save Workbooks
    The two autorecovery options may be switched on, as indicated by checkmarks.

13. On a classroom computer, click **Cancel** to close the dialog box without changing the default save options.
    On a computer you own, you may place a checkmark next to Save AutoRecover Information Every and enter the desired number in the Minutes box. You may place a checkmark next to Keep the Last Autosaved Version If I Close Without Saving.

    Leave the workbook open for the next exercise.

Weekend Hours Worked - Microsoft Excel

1.8 Closing and Starting New Workbooks

Video Lesson   labyrinthelab.com/videos

The Close 📁 command is used to close an open workbook. When you close a workbook that has not been saved, Excel prompts you to save the changes. If you choose to save at the prompt and the workbook has previously been saved, Excel simply saves the changes and closes the workbook. If the workbook is new, Excel displays the Save As dialog box, allowing you to assign a name and file storage location to the workbook.

FROM THE KEYBOARD

Ctrl+N to open a new, blank workbook

The New command on the File menu displays Backstage view, where you may start a new, blank workbook. You can create a new workbook at any time because multiple workbooks may be open simultaneously.

Close the Workbook and Start a New Workbook

In this exercise, you will close the workbook that you have been working on throughout this lesson. Then you will open a new, blank workbook.

1. Choose **File→Close** 🗀.

2. Click the **Save** or **Yes** button if Excel asks you if you want to save the changes.
   Notice that no workbook appears in the Excel window. The Excel window always has this appearance when all workbooks have been closed.

3. Choose **File→New**.

4. Follow these steps to create a new, blank workbook:

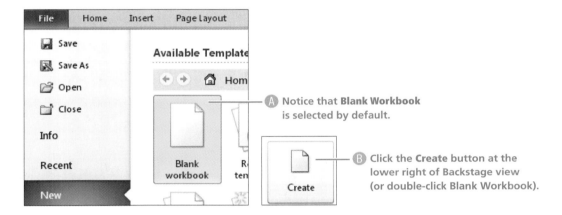

You will not enter any data into this workbook.

1.9 Exiting from Excel

Video Lesson   labyrinthelab.com/videos

You should exit Excel and other programs if you are certain you won't be using them for some time. This will free up memory for other programs. When you exit Excel, you will be prompted to save any workbooks that have unsaved edits. The Close command differs from the Exit command in that Close affects only the active workbook and leaves Excel open. Any other workbooks that are being used will remain open until you close them or exit Excel.

QUICK REFERENCE	CLOSING WORKBOOKS AND EXITING EXCEL
Task	**Procedure**
Close the active workbook	▪ Choose File→Close 🗀.
	▪ Respond if asked to save changes to the workbook.
Close all open workbooks and exit Excel	▪ Choose File→Exit ☒.
	▪ Respond if asked to save changes for any open workbooks.

Exit from Excel

In this exercise, you will exit from the Excel program.

1. Choose **File→Exit** ☒.

   Excel will close without prompting you to save the workbook because you have not entered any data into it.

1.10 Concepts Review

Concepts Review	labyrinthelab.com/excel10

To check your knowledge of the key concepts introduced in this lesson, complete the Concepts Review quiz by going to the URL listed above. If your classroom is using Labyrinth eLab, you may complete the Concepts Review quiz from within your eLab course.

Reinforce Your Skills

Create a Workbook

In this exercise, you will create a workbook. You will start Excel and then enter text and numbers that contain two decimal places.

Start Excel and Enter Text

1. Start Excel by selecting **All Programs→Microsoft Office→Microsoft Office Excel 2010** from the Start menu.
   Notice that a blank workbook with three worksheets is displayed when you open Excel.

2. Enter text in **rows 1 through 9** as shown in the following illustration.
   Use the [Tab] *and* [Enter] *keys as necessary to enter the data. Type the customer's name and address in cells B5, B6, and B7.*

	A	B	C	D	E
1	Order Tracking Sheet				
2					
3	Order No.	1552			
4					
5	Sold to:	Empire Dry Cleaning			
6		1833 Franklin Highway			
7		Huntington, WV 25716			
8					
9	Item	In Stock?	Quantity	Price	Discount

Enter Decimal and Negative Numbers

3. In **cells A9 through E14**, enter the data shown in the illustration at right.
   Type a decimal point (.) in the Price numbers and Discount numbers. Type a minus (–) sign before the Discount numbers.

	A	B	C	D	E
9	Item	In Stock?	Quantity	Price	Discount
10	A423	Y	2	63.95	-3.15
11	A321	Y	4	28.95	0
12	D928	N	16	5.85	-0.59
13	S251	N	8	3.09	-0.31
14	B444	Y	20	8.77	-0.88

Save the Workbook

4. Choose **Save** 💾 on the Quick Access toolbar.

5. **Type** the filename **rs-Order Tracking** and **navigate** to the Lesson 01 folder in your file storage location.

6. Click **Save** or **tap** [Enter].
   The workbook will be saved in the location that you specified. Leave the workbook open.

Explore the Excel Window and Save and Close Your Workbook

In this exercise, you will take a look at the features of the Excel window before saving the changes and closing your new workbook.

1. **Click** to display the Data tab of the Ribbon.
   Look at the types of commands available. Many of them will be covered in later lessons of this book.

2. Select the **View** tab of the Ribbon.

3. Click the **Minimize the Ribbon** ⌃ button at the upper-right corner of the window to hide the Ribbon.

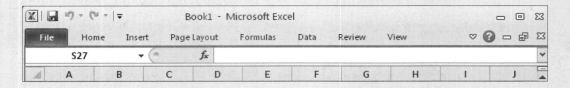

4. **Double-click** the Home tab to display the Ribbon once again.
   Notice that the Home tab is displayed because you chose it to redisplay the Ribbon.

5. Click **cell C5**, and then look at the **Formula Bar**.

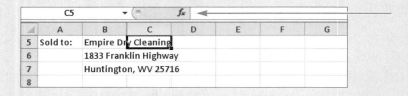

   There is nothing displayed because the entire entry is contained in cell B5 and is simply spilling over cell C5 because it is empty.

6. **Type** your name, and then click the **Enter** ✔ button.
   Your name will now appear in cell C5, and the customer name in cell B5 will be truncated.

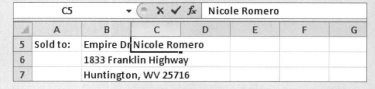

7. **Tap** ⌷Delete⌷.
   Your name will be deleted, and the customer name from B5 will once again spill over the cells to the right.

8. Select **cell A16** and **enter** your first and last names.

9. Use ⌷Ctrl⌷+⌷S⌷ to save the changes to the workbook.
   The workbook saves to your same file storage location as before.

10. Choose **File→Exit** to close Excel.

Apply Your Skills

Create a New Workbook

In this exercise, you will create a new worksheet and then save and close the workbook.

1. Start **Excel** by selecting **All Programs** from the Start menu.
   A new, blank workbook appears.

2. Create the **worksheet** shown in the following illustration and **type** your first and last names in **cell D1**.
   Proofread all data. You will not create formulas to calculate totals in this exercise.

	A	B	C	D	E
1	Green Clean Q1 Expenses			Student Name	
2					
3	Item		January	February	March
4	Building	Lease	3000	3000	3000
5		Utilities	1689	1572	1646
6		Phone	250	242	329
7		Insurance	8696	0	0
8		Total			
9					
10	Equipment		1211	506	4890
11					
12	Salaries	Mgmt	4500	4500	4500
13		Full time	20658	19777	21422
14		Part time	24656	25980	25316
15		Total			
16					
17	Supplies	Office	1963	2432	1784
18		Vehicle	872	944	903
19		Total			
20					
21	Other	Fuel			
22		Marketing	500	300	200
23		Uniforms	63	101	83
24		Misc	162	471	65
25		Total			

3. **Save** the workbook with the name **as-Q1 Expenses** in **your** Lesson 01 folder and then **exit** Excel.

Critical Thinking & Work-Readiness Skills

In the course of working through the following Microsoft Office-based Critical Thinking exercises, you will also be utilizing various work-readiness skills, some of which are listed next to each exercise. Go to labyrinthelab.com/workreadiness *to learn more about the work-readiness skills.*

1.1 Enter Missing Data into a Worksheet

WORK-READINESS SKILLS APPLIED

- Listening
- Reading
- Showing responsibility

Nicole's manager at Green Clean mentions the importance of the spreadsheet for daily reporting of timesheet hours for employees. Hearing this, Nicole realizes that doing a good job every day on this report will be appreciated. She decides from now on to double-check that she has transferred the numbers correctly before she shows it to her manager. Sure enough, she sees that Tan's Friday number should have been 4, and that Silva's Saturday number should have been 3. Open ct-Timesheet Hours (Lesson 01 folder), enter the corrections, and save the corrected workbook as **ct-Timesheet Hours Revised**.

1.2 Enter New Data into a Worksheet

WORK-READINESS SKILLS APPLIED

- Serving clients/customers
- Solving problems
- Showing responsibility

Nicole begins to understand that mileage for employees driving to jobs is a big concern. Trying to anticipate her manager's needs, she decides that a handy reminder of the mileage to each customer might be useful. Using Google Maps and MapQuest, she figures out the mileage from Green Clean headquarters to each of the locations. The distances are as follows: Alton Mall, 10 miles; Century Bank, 12.5 miles; and Newport Medical, 24 miles. She wants to get her manager's feedback before going any further with her idea. Open ct-Timesheet Hours Revised, if necessary, and insert these values in column B next to each facility. Do not be concerned that the column A entries do not display completely. Save the edited worksheet as **ct-Mileage** in your Lesson 01 folder. Close the workbook but do not exit Excel.

1.3 Use the Numeric Keypad

WORK-READINESS SKILLS APPLIED

- Solving problems
- Managing the self
- Selecting technology

Now that she has proven she can create accurate spreadsheets, Nicole is asked to put together additional spreadsheets. Nicole sees that streamlining the way she does data entry will help her handle her workload. She decides to practice using the numeric keypad. Create a new, blank workbook. Practice data entry, reading numbers from various exercises in this lesson and entering the data down a column of the blank worksheet using the numeric keypad. Practice until you feel comfortable. (There is no need to save your work.) Why should Nicole (and you) pay attention to speed as well as accuracy when creating spreadsheets? Type your answer in a Word document named **ct-Questions** saved to your Lesson 01 folder.

Editing, Viewing, and Printing Worksheets

LEARNING OBJECTIVES

After studying this lesson, you will be able to:

■ Use a variety of techniques to select, move, and copy cells and ranges
■ Clear cell contents, including formatting
■ Complete cell entries automatically
■ Work with various Excel views and the zoom feature
■ Print your worksheet and change workbook properties

In this lesson, you will expand on basic skills in Excel. You will learn various methods of editing worksheets: replacing and deleting entries, using Undo and Redo, working with AutoCorrect, and more. You will also learn about printing Excel worksheets and working with different views. When you have finished this lesson, you will have developed the skills necessary to produce carefully edited and proofed worksheets.

CASE STUDY

Creating a Basic List in Excel

Ken Hazell is the human resources manager of Green Clean, a janitorial product supplier and cleaning service contractor. He realizes that Excel can be used as a simple database to maintain lists of employees, product inventory, or other items. He and other managers use Excel's view options to work with data and preview how the worksheet will look when printed.

Green Clean				
Management and Support Roster				
Name	Phone	Position	Employment Date	On Call
Tommy Choi	619-555-3224	President		
Mary Wright	858-555-3098	VP, Sales and Marketing	5/22/2007	Monday
Derek Navarro	619-555-3309	VP, Operations	3/30/2009	Tuesday
Isabella Riso-Neff	858-555-0211	Risk Management Director	4/13/2009	Wednesday
Kenneth Hazell	619-555-3224	Human Resources Director	7/17/2006	Thursday
D'Andre Adams	760-555-3876	Facilities Services Manager	12/7/2005	Friday
Talos Bouras	858-555-1002	Sales Manager	5/10/2004	Saturday
Michael Chowdery	858-555-0021	Purchasing Manager	10/26/2009	Sunday
Ahn Tran	760-555-0728	Office Manager	6/26/2006	
Jenna Mann	951-555-0826	Administrative Assistant	3/15/2010	
Nicole Romero	858-555-4987	Payroll Assistant	5/25/2009	
Amy Wyatt	619-555-4016	Customer Service Rep	8/17/2009	

Ken will use this spreadsheet to organize the management and support employees' phone numbers, dates of employment, and the evening that each manager is on call in case of emergency.

Ken previews the worksheet in Page Layout view prior to printing it.

2.1 Opening Workbooks

Video Lesson labyrinthelab.com/videos

FROM THE KEYBOARD
Ctrl+O to open

The File→Open command displays the Open dialog box. The Open dialog box lets you navigate to any file storage location and open previously saved workbooks. Once a workbook is open, you can browse it, print it, and make editing changes. The organization and layout of the Open dialog box are similar to those of the Save As dialog box.

DEVELOP YOUR SKILLS 2.1.1
Open the Workbook

In this exercise, you will open a workbook that lists various employees.

1. Start **Excel**.

2. Click the **File** tab on the Ribbon and choose the **Open** command.
   The Open dialog box is displayed.

In future lessons, this command will be written, Choose File→Open.

3. **Navigate** to your file storage location (such as a USB flash drive).

4. **Double-click** the Lesson 02 folder to open it.

5. Select the Management Roster workbook and click **Open**.

You can also double-click a document in the Open dialog box to open it.

2.2 Editing Entries

Video Lesson labyrinthelab.com/videos

You can edit the active cell by clicking in the Formula Bar and making the desired changes. You can also double-click a cell and edit the contents directly there. This technique is known as in-cell editing.

Replacing Entries

Editing an entry is efficient if the entry is so long that retyping it would be time-consuming. Editing can also be helpful when working with complex formulas and other functions that are difficult to re-create. If the entry requires little typing, however, it is usually easier to simply retype it. If you retype an entry, the new entry will replace whatever is contained in the cell.

Deleting Characters

Use the Delete and Backspace keys to edit entries in the Formula Bar and within a cell. The Delete key removes the character to the right of the insertion point, while the Backspace key removes the character to the left of the insertion point.

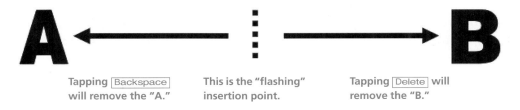

Tapping Backspace will remove the "A."

This is the "flashing" insertion point.

Tapping Delete will remove the "B."

DEVELOP YOUR SKILLS 2.2.1
Edit Entries

In this exercise, you will use the Formula Bar to revise the contents of cell A2. You will also edit cells B3 and B15 directly in the cells.

Edit in the Formula Bar

1. Click **cell A2** to select it.

2. Follow these steps to edit cell A2 using the Formula Bar:

Ⓐ Click in the **Formula Bar** just to the right of the word *List*.

Ⓑ Tap Backspace four times to remove the word *List*, and then type **Roster**.

Ⓒ Click the Enter button.

Replace an Entry

3. Click **cell D4**.

4. Type **Employment Date** and **tap** Enter.
   The entry Employment Date *replaces the entry* Starting Date. *Notice that the cell formatting (underlining the word) has been applied to the new entry as well. Also note that the new entry is cut off or truncated because the cell to the right contains an entry.*

Use In-Cell Editing

5. **Double-click** cell A8 (the cell with the name Isabella Riso).

6. Use the mouse or the → key to position the flashing **insertion point** to the right of the last name, Riso.

7. Type **–Neff**, and then **tap** Enter to complete the change.
   The entry should now read Isabella Riso-Neff.

8. Click the **Save** 🖫 button to update the changes.
   Clicking the Save button automatically saves changes to a workbook that has previously been saved.

2.3 Selecting Cells and Ranges

Video Lesson labyrinthelab.com/videos

FROM THE KEYBOARD
Ctrl+A to select all
Ctrl+Spacebar to select a column
Shift+Spacebar to select a row

When you want to change something in a worksheet—for instance, move, copy, delete, format, or print specific data—you must first select the cell(s). The most efficient way to select cells is with the mouse, though you can also use the keyboard method. You can select one or many cells. A group of contiguous (adjacent) cells is called a range. Entire columns or rows may be selected by clicking or dragging the column headings (such as A, B, C) or row headings (such as 1, 2, 3).

Excel Ranges

Each cell has a reference. For example, A1 refers to the first cell in a worksheet. Likewise, a range reference specifies the cells included within a range. The range reference includes the first and last cells in the range separated by a colon (:). For example, the range A4:E4 includes all cells between A4 and E4 inclusive. The following illustration highlights several ranges and their corresponding range references.

	A6	▼	*f*x	Mary Wright	
	A	**B**	**C**	**D**	**E**
1	Green Clean				
2	Management and Support Roster				
3					
4	Name	Phone	Position	Employment Date	On Call
5	Tommy Choi	619-555-3224	President		
6	Mary Wright	858-555-3098	VP, Sales and Marketing	5/22/2007	
7	Derek Navarro	619-555-3309	VP, Operations	3/30/2009	
8	Isabella Riso-Neff	858-555-0211	Risk Management Director	4/13/2009	
9	Kenneth Hazell	619-555-3224	Human Resources Director	7/17/2006	
10	D'Andre Adams	760-555-3876	Facilities Services Manager	12/7/2005	
11	Talos Bouras	858-555-1002	Sales Manager	5/10/2004	
12	Michael Chowdery	858-555-0021	Purchasing Manager	10/26/2009	
13	Ahn Tran	760-555-0728	Office Manager	6/26/2006	
14	Jenna Mann	951-555-0826	Administrative Assistant	3/15/2010	

Range A1:A2 — (rows 1–2)
Range A4:E4 — (row 4)
Range A6:D10 — (rows 6–10)

The selected ranges in the worksheet are shaded, as displayed above. In addition, the first cell in the last range selected, A6, shows no shading and has an outline around it. This cell display indicates that it is the active cell, which is displayed in the Name Box and Formula Bar.

The following Quick Reference table describes selection techniques in Excel.

QUICK REFERENCE	SELECTING CELLS AND RANGES
Techniques	**How to Do It**
Select a range	Drag the mouse pointer over the desired cells.
Select several ranges	Select a range, and then press Ctrl while selecting additional range(s).
Select an entire column	Click a column heading or press Ctrl+Spacebar.

Techniques	How to Do It
Select an entire row	Click a row heading or press ⎰Shift⎱+⎰Spacebar⎱.
Select multiple columns or rows	Drag the mouse pointer over the desired column or row headings.
Select an entire worksheet	Click the Select All button ⊿ at the top-left corner of the worksheet or press ⎰Ctrl⎱+⎰A⎱.
Select a range with ⎰Shift⎱	Position the highlight in the first cell you wish to select, press ⎰Shift⎱, and click the last cell in the range.
Extend or decrease a selection with ⎰Shift⎱	Press ⎰Shift⎱ while tapping an arrow key.

DEVELOP YOUR SKILLS 2.3.1
Practice Making Selections

In this exercise, you will practice selecting multiple ranges and entire rows and columns using the mouse. You will also use the ⎰Shift⎱ *and* ⎰Ctrl⎱ *keys to practice selecting cell ranges.*

Click and Drag to Select a Range

1. Position the **mouse pointer** ✚ over **cell A4**.

2. **Press** and **hold down** the left mouse button while dragging the mouse to the right until the **range A4:E4** is selected, and then **release** the mouse button.
   Notice that for each range that is selected, the corresponding row and column headings are displayed in orange.

3. **Click** once anywhere in the worksheet to deselect the cells.

Select Multiple Ranges

4. Follow these steps to select two ranges:

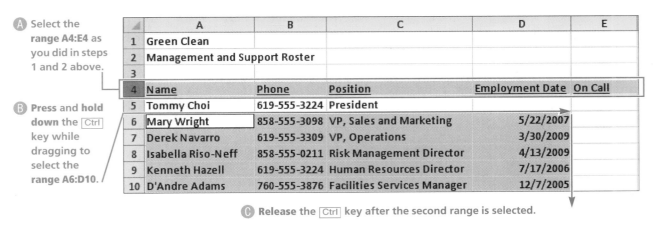

Ⓐ Select the range A4:E4 as you did in steps 1 and 2 above.

Ⓑ Press and hold down the ⎰Ctrl⎱ key while dragging to select the range A6:D10.

⊿	A	B	C	D	E
1	Green Clean				
2	Management and Support Roster				
3					
4	Name	Phone	Position	Employment Date	On Call
5	Tommy Choi	619-555-3224	President		
6	Mary Wright	858-555-3098	VP, Sales and Marketing	5/22/2007	
7	Derek Navarro	619-555-3309	VP, Operations	3/30/2009	
8	Isabella Riso-Neff	858-555-0211	Risk Management Director	4/13/2009	
9	Kenneth Hazell	619-555-3224	Human Resources Director	7/17/2006	
10	D'Andre Adams	760-555-3876	Facilities Services Manager	12/7/2005	

Ⓒ Release the ⎰Ctrl⎱ key after the second range is selected.

Both the A4:E4 and A6:D10 ranges are selected now. The ⎰Ctrl⎱ *key lets you select more than one range at the same time.*

5. **Press** and **hold down** the ⌈Ctrl⌉ key while you select another range, and then **release** the ⌈Ctrl⌉ key.

   You should now have three ranges selected.

6. Make sure you have **released** the ⌈Ctrl⌉ key, and then **click** once anywhere on the worksheet to deselect the ranges.

   The highlighting of the previous selections disappears.

Select Entire Rows and Columns

7. Follow these steps to select various rows and columns:

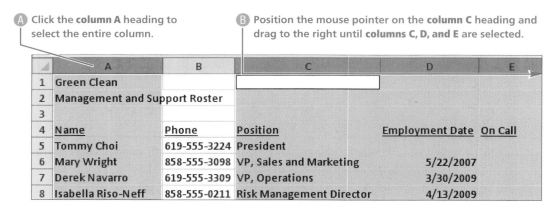

Ⓐ Click the **column A** heading to select the entire column.

Ⓑ Position the mouse pointer on the **column C** heading and drag to the right until **columns C, D, and E** are selected.

Column A will be deselected because you were not holding down the ⌈Ctrl⌉ key.

Ⓒ Click the **Select All** button to select the entire worksheet.

Ⓓ Click the **row 1** heading to select the entire row.

Ⓔ Drag the mouse pointer down over the headings from **row 6 to row 10** to select them.

Only rows 6–10 will be selected because you did not hold down ⌈Ctrl⌉.

Use Keyboard Techniques

8. Follow these steps to use keyboard techniques to select cells:

Ⓐ Click cell A4.

	A	B	C	D	E
4	Name	Phone	Position	Employment Date	On Call
5	Tommy Choi	619-555-3224	President		
6	Mary Wright	858-555-3098	VP, Sales and Marketing	5/22/2007	
7	Derek Navarro	619-555-3309	VP, Operations	3/30/2009	
8	Isabella Riso-Neff	858-555-0211	Risk Management Director	4/13/2009	
9	Kenneth Hazell	619-555-3224	Human Resources Director	7/17/2006	
10	D'Andre Adams	760-555-3876	Facilities Services Manager	12/7/2005	
11	Talos Bouras	858-555-1002	Sales Manager	5/10/2004	
12	Michael Chowdery	858-555-0021	Purchasing Manager	10/26/2009	
13	Ahn Tran	760-555-0728	Office Manager	6/26/2006	
14	Jenna Mann	951-555-0826	Administrative Assistant	3/15/2010	
15	Nicole Romero	858-555-4987	Payroll Assistant	5/25/2009	
16	Amy Wyatt	619-555-4016	Customer Service Rep	8/17/2009	

Ⓑ **Press** and **hold down** the ⎵Shift key and click **cell E16** to select the range **A4:E16**.

Ⓒ Click **cell A12**.

	A	B	C	D
12	Michael Chowdery	858-555-0021	Purchasing Manager	10/26/2009
13	Ahn Tran	760-555-0728	Office Manager	6/26/2006
14	Jenna Mann	951-555-0826	Administrative Assistant	3/15/2010
15	Nicole Romero	858-555-4987	Payroll Assistant	5/25/2009
16	Amy Wyatt	619-555-4016	Customer Service Rep	8/17/2009

Ⓓ **Press** and **hold down** the ⎵Shift key, and then **tap** →⎶ three times and ↓⎶ four times.

The range A12:D16 is selected. Notice that the ⎵Shift key techniques give you precise control when selecting. You should use the ⎵Shift key techniques if you find selecting with the mouse difficult or if you have a large range to select that is not entirely visible on your screen.

9. Take a few moments to practice selection techniques. See if you can select a specific portion of a worksheet.

2.4 Working with Cut, Copy, and Paste

Video Lesson   labyrinthelab.com/videos

FROM THE KEYBOARD
Ctrl+C to copy
Ctrl+X to cut
Ctrl+V to paste

The Cut, Copy, and Paste commands are available in all Office suite applications. With Cut, Copy, and Paste, you can move or copy cells within a worksheet, between worksheets, or between different Office applications. For example, you could use the Copy command to copy a range from one worksheet and the Paste command to paste the range into another worksheet. Cut, Copy, and Paste are most efficient for moving or copying cells a long distance within a worksheet or between worksheets. Cut, Copy, and Paste are easy to use if you remember the following guidelines:

- You must select cells before issuing a Cut or Copy command.
- You must position the highlight at the desired location before issuing the Paste command. The highlight's position is important because the range you paste will overwrite any cells in the paste area.

You need only to select the upper-left cell of the destination range before pasting a copied range. It is not necessary to select the entire destination range.

Marquee and Paste Options Button

A marquee (animated dashed line) surrounds the selected cell(s) after you choose the Cut or Copy command. The marquee disappears upon the next action you take after pasting.

The Paste Options 📋 button displays at the lower-right corner of the destination cell(s) after a paste action. Its drop-down list allows you to customize what will be pasted, such as only the cell contents or their formatting. The button disappears upon the next action you take. You will not work with paste options in this lesson.

Tap the Esc key to remove the marquee manually.

You can also right-click on a cell or range of cells in order to get a shortcut menu specific to the selection. The Cut, Copy, and Paste commands are available on this menu as well. There are many ways to issue commands; your job is to simply figure out which method works best for you!

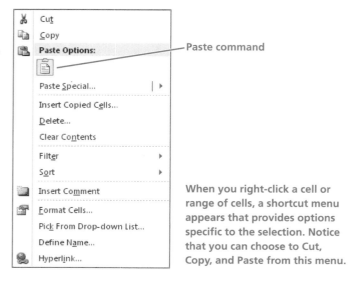

When you right-click a cell or range of cells, a shortcut menu appears that provides options specific to the selection. Notice that you can choose to Cut, Copy, and Paste from this menu.

The Office Clipboard

The Office Clipboard lets you collect items from any Office worksheet or program and paste them into any other Office document. For example, you can collect a paragraph from a Word document, data from an Excel worksheet, and a graphic from a PowerPoint slide and then paste them all into a new Word document. The Office Clipboard can also be used within a single application like Excel to collect several items and then paste them as desired. The Office Clipboard can hold up to 24 items.

The Office Clipboard containing a copied graphic and two text blocks

How It Works

You can place multiple items on the Office Clipboard using the standard Cut and Copy commands; however, the Office Clipboard task pane must first be displayed. It is displayed by clicking the launcher button in the Clipboard area of the Home tab. Once text or other objects are on the Clipboard, you may paste any item to one or more selected cells in a worksheet.

Moving and Copying Cells via Drag and Drop

Drag and Drop produces the same results as Cut, Copy, and Paste. However, Drag and Drop is usually more efficient if you are moving or copying entries a short distance within the same worksheet. If the original location and

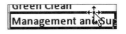

The mouse pointer changes to a four-pointed arrow as you point at the dark line surrounding the selected cell or range. Dragging the selection will move it to another location in the worksheet.

new destination are both visible in the current window, then it is usually easier to use Drag and Drop. With Drag and Drop, you select the cells you wish to move or copy, and then you point to the dark line around the selected range and drag the range to the desired destination. If you press the Ctrl key while dragging the selected area, the cells are copied to the destination. Drag and Drop does not place items on the Office Clipboard, however, so you will want to use either the Cut or the Copy command if you wish to work with the Office Clipboard.

Editing Cells via Right-Dragging

Right-dragging is a variation of the drag and drop technique. Many beginners have trouble using drag and drop because they have difficulty controlling the mouse. This difficulty is compounded if they are trying to copy entries using drag and drop. This is because copying requires the Ctrl key to be held while the selected range is dragged. With the right-drag method, the right mouse button is used when dragging. When the right mouse button is released at the desti-

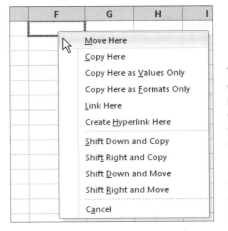

When you right-drag and drop, you will receive a pop-up menu at the destination so that you can choose whether to move or copy the data. You may cancel the action and then repeat the right-drag and drop if the indicated destination is not what you wanted.

nation, a pop-up menu appears. The pop-up menu gives you several options including Move, Copy, and Cancel. This approach provides more control because there is no need to use the Ctrl key when copying and you have the option of canceling the move or copy.

Command	Explanation	Procedure
Cut	The Cut command removes entries from selected cells and places them on the Office Clipboard.	■ Select what you wish to move. ■ Choose Home→Clipboard→Cut ✄ from the Ribbon, or press Ctrl+X.
Copy	The Copy command also places entries on the Office Clipboard, but it leaves a copy of the entries in the original cells.	■ Select what you wish to copy. ■ Choose Home→Clipboard→Copy 📋 from the Ribbon or press Ctrl+C.
Paste	The Paste command pastes entries from the Office Clipboard to worksheet cells beginning at the highlight location.	■ Click once where you wish the clipboard contents to be pasted. ■ Choose Home→Clipboard→ Paste from the Ribbon, or press Ctrl+V.

Move and Copy Selections

In this exercise, you will have the opportunity to use the Cut, Copy, and Paste commands as well as drag and drop to move and copy selections.

Copy and Paste

1. Click **cell A1** to select it.

2. Display the **Home** tab, locate the **Clipboard** command group, and click the **Copy** 📋 button on the Ribbon.
   A marquee will surround the selection that you have copied and placed on the clipboard.

3. Click **cell C2**.

4. Choose **Home→Clipboard→Paste** 📋 from the Ribbon to **paste** the selection in cell C2.
   The Paste command consists of two parts. Make certain to click the button in the upper part. If you accidentally click the drop-down arrow in the lower part of the command, you may still choose Paste from the list.

▲	A	B	C	D
1	Green Clean			
2	Management and Support Roster		Green Clean	
3				📋 (Ctrl) ▾

The contents of cell A1 will remain there as well as appear in cell C2 when you choose to copy the selection. Notice the marquee surrounding the cell that is being copied and the Paste Options button that appears to the lower right of the cell in which the selection was pasted.

Cut and Paste

5. **Right-click** cell C2.
When you right-click a cell, a shortcut menu appears with options specific to the cell, as well as the Mini toolbar.

6. Choose **Cut** from the shortcut menu.

7. **Right-click** cell E2 and choose **Paste** 📋 under Paste Options from the shortcut menu.

C	D	E
		Green Clean

Cell C2 will now be empty because the contents were moved to cell E2.

Drag and Drop

8. Follow these steps to move the contents of cell E2 via the drag-and-drop method:

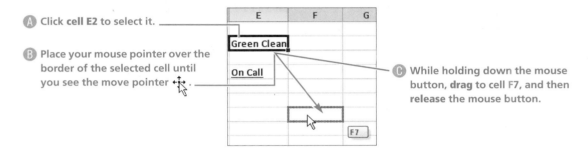

Ⓐ Click **cell E2** to select it.

Ⓑ Place your mouse pointer over the border of the selected cell until you see the move pointer ⊹.

Ⓒ While holding down the mouse button, **drag** to cell F7, and then **release** the mouse button.

When you drag a cell with this method, Excel shows what cell the selection will be dropped into by displaying it on a ScreenTip as well as placing a highlight around the cell.

Right-Drag a Selection

9. Select **cell E4**, and then place your mouse pointer over the border of the selected cell until you see the move pointer as shown at right.

10. Start **dragging** with the **right** (not the left) mouse button. Keep the right mouse button held down until told to release it in the next step.

11. Drag down to **cell F5**, and then **release** the right mouse button.
A pop-up menu appears, listing your choices for the right-drag.

12. Choose **Copy Here** from the pop-up menu.
The contents of cell E4 remain in the cell and are copied to the destination cell, F5. Do not save, but keep the workbook open. In the next exercise, you will undo some recent actions.

2.5 Using Undo and Redo

Video Lesson labyrinthelab.com/videos

Excel's Undo button lets you reverse actions that have occurred in Excel. You can reverse simple actions such as accidentally deleting a cell's content or more complex actions such as deleting an entire row. Most actions can be undone, but those that cannot include printing and saving workbooks. The Undo command can become your best friend when you have to undo an action that you are not sure how you issued. Don't you wish life had an undo button at times?

The Redo button reverses an Undo command. Use Redo when you undo an action but then decide to go through with that action after all. The Redo button will be visible on the Quick Access toolbar only after you have undone an action.

Undoing Multiple Actions

FROM THE KEYBOARD
Ctrl+Z to undo
Ctrl+Y to redo

Clicking the arrow on the Undo button displays a list of actions that can be undone. You can undo multiple actions by dragging the mouse over the desired actions. However, you must undo actions in the order in which they appear on the drop-down list. For example, you cannot skip the first and second items to undo only the third item.

When you click the arrow on the Undo button, you will see a list of previous actions with the most recent at the top.

Limitations to "Undoing"

In Excel, there are times when the Undo command will not work. If you click the File tab on the Ribbon and choose any command (such as saving a workbook), it cannot be undone. When an action cannot be undone, Excel will change the Undo ScreenTip to "Can't Undo."

QUICK REFERENCE	UNDOING AND REDOING ACTIONS
Task	**Procedure**
Undo the last action	▪ Click the Undo button on the Quick Access toolbar or tap Ctrl+Z.
Undo a series of actions	▪ Click the drop-down arrow on the Undo button to display a list of previous actions.
	▪ Choose the last command that you wish to have undone.
Redo an undone action	▪ Click the Redo button on the Quick Access toolbar.

Reverse Actions

In this exercise, you will delete the contents of a column and then use Undo to reverse the deletion. When you do, the original data will display in the column again. You will also use Redo to reverse an Undo command.

Delete the Column Contents

1. Click the **column A** heading to select the entire column.

2. **Tap** ⌞Delete⌟.
   All of the contents in column A have been deleted! There are many times that you will use Undo in order to reverse an action you did not wish to make.

Use Undo and Redo

3. Click **Undo** 🔄 to restore the entry.

4. Follow these steps to undo the last four commands from the previous section:

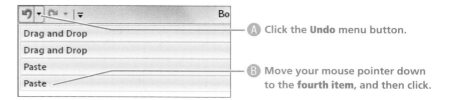

   Ⓐ Click the **Undo** menu button.

   Ⓑ Move your mouse pointer down to the **fourth item**, and then click.

   Excel undoes your last four commands.

5. Click the **Redo** 🔁 button four times to restore the four actions that you "undid."

6. Use ⌞Ctrl⌟+⌞S⌟ to save the changes, but don't close the workbook.
   You must hold down the ⌞Ctrl⌟ key first and then tap the ⌞S⌟ to issue the Save command.

2.6 Clearing Cell Contents and Formats

Video Lesson labyrinthelab.com/videos

FROM THE KEYBOARD
Delete to clear cell contents

In Excel, you can format cell content by changing the font style, size, and color. You can also add enhancements such as bold, italics, and underline. Cells with numeric data can be formatted as currency, dates, times, percents, and more. In this lesson, you will learn how to clear existing formatting.

Clicking the Clear ⟨Ø▾⟩ button displays a menu that lets you clear content, formats, and comments from cells. The submenu also contains a Clear All option that clears all of these items from the selected cell(s).

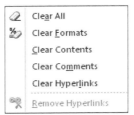

Clicking the Clear button in the Editing group of the Home ribbon will display a menu that shows all of the options for clearing cell contents.

Excel's Options for Clearing Cells

Clear Contents	Clearing the content has the same effect as tapping the Delete key. The cell contents are deleted, but any format applied to the cell remains and will be in effect when new data is entered in the cell.
Clear Formats	The clear Formats option removes all text and number formats, leaving unformatted entries in the cell(s).
Clear Comments	You can insert comments in cells to document your worksheet. The Clear Comments option also removes comments from the selected cells.
Clear Hyperlinks	Clearing a hyperlink leaves the entry in the cell but removes its link to a workbook object, a web address, or an external document.
Clear All	This command will clear everything listed above.

One of the most useful functions of Excel's Clear command is removing numeric value formats. Once a cell is formatted as a particular numeric format, such as a date or currency, Excel remembers that formatting even if the cell contents are deleted.

QUICK REFERENCE | CLEARING CELL CONTENTS AND FORMATTING

Task	Procedure
Clear the contents of a cell	▪ Select the cell or range that you wish to clear. ▪ Choose Home→Editing→Clear ⟨Ø▾⟩ from the Ribbon. ▪ Choose Clear Contents from the resulting menu.
Clear the formatting from a cell	▪ Select the cell or range that you wish to clear. ▪ Choose Home→Editing→Clear ⟨Ø▾⟩ from the Ribbon. ▪ Choose Clear Formats from the resulting menu.
Clear contents and formatting from a cell	▪ Select the cell or range that you wish to clear. ▪ Choose Home→Editing→Clear ⟨Ø▾⟩ from the Ribbon. ▪ Choose Clear All from the resulting menu.

Clear Cell Contents and Formatting

In this exercise, you will use the Clear command to delete cell contents and cell formats.

1. Click **cell F5**.

2. Choose **Home→Editing→Clear** $\boxed{\mathcal{Q}^{\star}}$ from the Ribbon and choose **Clear Formats**.
   The contents of the cell were underlined, a type of formatting. When you choose to clear only the formats, the contents will remain and only the formatting is removed. Notice that the contents are no longer underlined.

3. Click the **Undo** $\boxed{\text{⟲}}$ button on the Quick Access toolbar.

4. Ensure that **cell F5** is selected, click the **Clear** $\boxed{\mathcal{Q}^{\star}}$ button, and choose **Clear All**.

5. **Type** your name and **tap** $\boxed{\text{Enter}}$.
   Notice that the contents are no longer underlined in cell F5 because you cleared "all" (formatting and contents) from it.

6. Use $\boxed{\text{Ctrl}}+\boxed{\text{Z}}$ to undo the typing of your name.

7. Click **cell F7** and **tap** $\boxed{\text{Delete}}$.
   The entry Green Clean *is deleted. The* $\boxed{\text{Delete}}$ *key functions the same as if you had clicked the Clear button and chosen Clear Contents. Any formatting will remain in the cell.*

8. **Save** $\boxed{\text{🖫}}$ the workbook.

2.7 Using Auto Features

Video Lesson labyrinthelab.com/videos

Excel offers "auto" features that help you to work more efficiently. AutoFill allows you to quickly fill a range of cells. AutoComplete makes it easy to enter long entries by typing an acronym or a series of characters, which are "converted" to the desired entry. AutoCorrect can also assist in correcting commonly misspelled words.

Working with AutoFill

AutoFill allows you to quickly extend a series, copy data, or copy a formula into adjacent cells by selecting cells and dragging the fill handle. If the selected cell does not contain data that AutoFill recognizes as a series, the data will simply be copied into the adjacent cells. The fill handle is a small black square at the bottom-right corner of the selected cell or cell range. A black cross appears when you position the mouse pointer on the fill handle. You can drag the fill handle to fill adjacent cells to accomplish the following:

- **Copy an entry**—If the entry in the active cell is a number, a formula, or a text entry, the fill handle copies the entry to adjacent cells.

- **Expand a repeating series of numbers**—If you select two or more cells containing numbers, Excel assumes you want to expand a repeating series. For example, if you select two cells containing the numbers 5 and 10 and drag the fill handle, Excel will fill the adjacent cells with the numbers 15, 20, 25, etc.

- **AutoFill of date entries**—If the active cell contains any type of date entry, Excel will determine the increment of the date value and fill in the adjacent cells. For example, if the current cell contains the entry May and you drag the fill handle, AutoFill will insert the entries Jun, Jul, and Aug in the adjacent cells.

The following table and illustrations provide examples of series that AutoFill can extend.

Selected Cells	Extended Series
Mon	Tue, Wed, Thu
Monday	Tuesday, Wednesday, Thursday
Jan	Feb, Mar, Apr
January	February, March, April
Jan, Apr	Jul, Oct, Jan
1, 2	3, 4, 5, 6
100, 125	150, 175, 200
1/10/11	1/11/11, 1/12/11, 1/13/11
1/15/11, 2/15/11	3/15/11, 4/15/11, 5/15/11
1st Qtr	2nd Qtr, 3rd Qtr, 4th Qtr

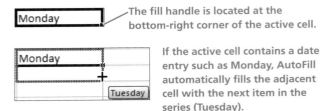

The fill handle is located at the bottom-right corner of the active cell.

If the active cell contains a date entry such as Monday, AutoFill automatically fills the adjacent cell with the next item in the series (Tuesday).

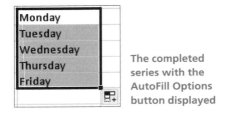

The completed series with the AutoFill Options button displayed

AutoComplete vs. AutoFill

The AutoComplete feature is useful when you want the same entry repeated more than once in a column. AutoFill allows you to select a cell and fill in entries either by completing a series or copying the source cell, whereas AutoComplete works within a cell as you type. If the first few characters you type match another entry in the column, then AutoComplete will offer to complete the entry for you. You accept the offer by tapping ⟦Tab⟧ or ⟦Enter⟧, or reject the offer by typing the remainder of the entry yourself.

| 16 | Amy Wyatt | 619-555-4016 | Customer Service Rep |
| 17 | Brian Simpson | 858-555-3718 | Customer Service Rep |

In this situation, a "c" was typed and the AutoComplete feature kicked into gear, suggesting that you may be interested in completing the entry as *Customer Service Rep* because you have already typed that entry earlier in the column. In order to accept *Customer Service Rep* as the entry, you would simply tap ⟦Tab⟧ to move to the next cell.

AutoComplete will complete the entry "case sensitive" to match capitalization from the existing column entry.

Use the AutoComplete and AutoFill Features

In this exercise, you will enter two new employees in the worksheet and use AutoComplete to aid in your entries. In addition, you will look at how to use AutoFill to complete a series of the days of the week.

Use AutoComplete

1. Click **cell A17** and type **Brian Simpson**, and then **tap** Tab to move to the next cell to the right.

2. Type **858-555-3718** and **tap** Tab.

3. Type **c** and notice that Excel suggests *Customer Service Rep* as the entry. **Tap** Tab to accept the suggestion and move to the next cell to the right.
   Notice that the entry will be capitalized just as it is in the cell above.

4. **Type** today's date, and then **tap** Enter.
   Notice that when you tap Enter, *the highlight moves to cell A18 where you can begin typing the next entry of the list.*

5. Type **Leisa Malimali** and **tap** Tab.

6. Type **619-555-4017** and **tap** Tab.

7. Type **S** in **cell C18**.
   Excel will suggest Sales Manager *from a previous row. In this case, Leisa is a sales assistant, so you will need to continue typing your entry. Make sure that you have typed a capital S as it will not pull from the previous entries.*

8. Continue typing **ales Assistant** and **tap** Tab.
   Excel will replace the AutoComplete suggestion with the entry that you type, Sales Assistant.

9. **Type** today's date and **tap** Enter.

Use AutoFill to Expand a Series

In this section of the exercise, you will fill in the column showing the manager responsible for being on emergency call each evening.

10. Click **cell E6**.

11. Type **Monday**, and then click the **Enter** ✔ button.
    Now that cell E6 contains Monday, Excel will recognize it as the beginning of the series, Tuesday, Wednesday, Thursday, and so forth. E6 will remain the active cell.

12. Follow these steps to fill the adjacent cells:

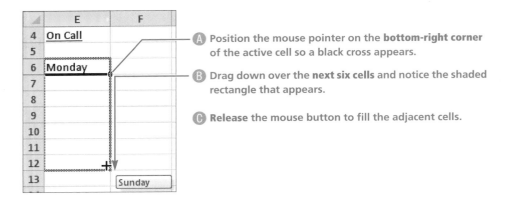

Ⓐ Position the mouse pointer on the **bottom-right corner** of the active cell so a black cross appears.

Ⓑ Drag down over the **next six cells** and notice the shaded rectangle that appears.

Ⓒ **Release** the mouse button to fill the adjacent cells.

Excel recognizes days of the week (Monday), quarters (1st Qtr, Quarter 1, First Quarter), months (January), and other date values as the beginning of a series. You can expand any of these series with the fill handle.

13. Click in the **Name Box** to the left of the Formula Bar, type **A1**, and **tap** Enter.

14. **Save** 🖫 the changes and leave the workbook **open**.

Auto Fill Options

Video Lesson   labyrinthelab.com/videos

The Auto Fill Options ⊞ button appears below your filled selection after you fill cells in a worksheet. A menu of fill options appears when you click the button.

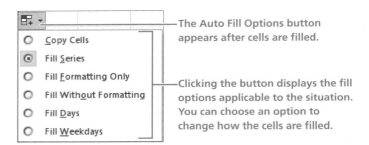

The Auto Fill Options button appears after cells are filled.

Clicking the button displays the fill options applicable to the situation. You can choose an option to change how the cells are filled.

If you choose Fill Without Formatting, you can fill cells without copying the formatting from the original cell. Fill Formatting Only copies the formatting but not the contents from the source cells.

Use Auto Fill Options

In this exercise, you will use Auto Fill Options to fill a data series without applying the source cell's formatting. You also will fill by applying only the formatting so that you may enter different data in cells.

1. Click the **Sheet2** tab at the bottom of the window.

2. With **cell A1** selected, **drag** the fill handle to **cell D1**.

   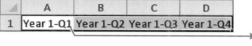

   The data series expands to Year 1 – Q4, and the bold and shaded formatting from cell A1 is applied to the other series cells.

3. Click the **Auto Fill Options** button at the lower-right corner of cell D1 and choose **Fill Without Formatting**.

   The formatting is removed from B1:D1.

4. **Deselect** the cells to view the actual formatting.

5. Select the **range A1:D1**.

6. **Drag** the fill handle in D1 down to **D7**.

7. Click the **Auto Fill Options** button and choose **Fill Formatting Only**.

   The contents are removed from A2:D7, but the formatting is still applied.

8. Enter numbers of your choice in **cells A2:D2**.
   Notice that the formatting matches that of A1:D1.

9. Select the **Sheet1** tab of the workbook.

10. **Save** the changes and leave the workbook **open**.

2.8 Exploring the Many Views of Excel

Video Lesson   labyrinthelab.com/videos

Changing the view in Excel does not change how the worksheet will print. For instance, if you change the zoom to 300%, the worksheet will appear much larger on the screen but will still print normally. There are other views in Excel that will aid you in working with your file and assist you in making changes to the final printed worksheet. This lesson will cover Page Layout view and Zoom. Remember that your Ribbon may appear differently, depending on the size of your Excel window. There is an additional view option, , Page Break Preview, that allows you to set where pages will break when printed.

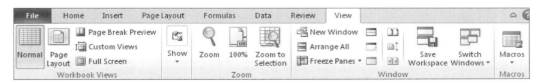

The View tab on the Ribbon provides options to view your workbook, show or hide screen items, control the zoom, and view multiple areas of the workbook at once.

Working in Page Layout View

Page Layout view allows you to see how your spreadsheet will appear when you print it, page by page. You may edit your worksheet in this view. You also can add headers and footers with text, page numbering, and other items that print at the top and bottom of every page. You may use either the View ribbon or the view buttons in the lower-right corner of the worksheet window to switch between the Normal and Page Layout views.

The view buttons displayed in the lower-right corner of the worksheet window

Zooming the View

The Zoom control lets you zoom in to get a close-up view of a worksheet and zoom out to see the full view. Zooming changes the size of the onscreen worksheet but has no effect on the printed worksheet. You can zoom from 10% to 400%.

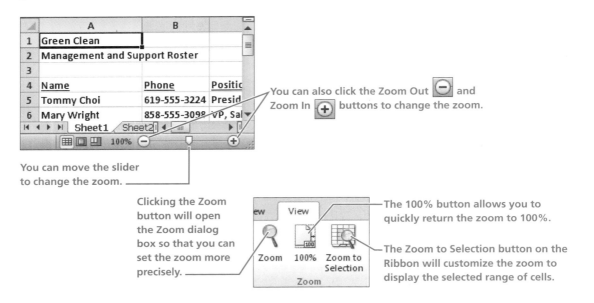

QUICK REFERENCE	WORKING WITH EXCEL'S VIEWS
Task	**Procedure**
Change the zoom of a worksheet	■ Click and drag the zoom slider at the bottom-right corner of the worksheet window.
Zoom by increments	■ Click the Zoom In and Zoom Out buttons on the View toolbar.
Zoom in to a selection	■ Select the range you wish to zoom in on. ■ Choose View→Zoom→Zoom to Selection from the Ribbon.
View a worksheet in Page Layout view	■ Choose View→Workbook Views→Page Layout from the Ribbon. *or* ■ Choose the Page Layout view button to the left of the zoom slider in the lower-right corner of the worksheet window.

Change Views and Use the Zoom Control

In this exercise, you will practice using commands to change the zoom and switch between Page Layout and Normal views.

Change the Zoom

1. Follow these steps to adjust the zoom percentage:

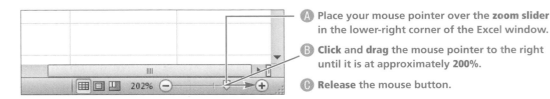

Ⓐ Place your mouse pointer over the **zoom slider** in the lower-right corner of the Excel window.

Ⓑ **Click** and **drag** the mouse pointer to the right until it is at approximately **200%**.

Ⓒ **Release** the mouse button.

2. Click the **Zoom Out** ⊖ button several times until the zoom displays **100%**.

3. Drag to select the **range A1:C18**.

4. Choose **View→Zoom→Zoom to Selection** 🔍 from the Ribbon.

5. Choose **View→Zoom→100%** from the Ribbon.

Switch Between Page Layout and Normal Views

6. Choose **View→Workbook Views→Page Layout View** 📄 from the Ribbon.
   This view displays the worksheet as if printed on paper so that you may check that it fits on one page before printing.

7. Choose **View→Workbook Views→Normal View** ▦ from the Ribbon.

8. Click the **Page Layout** ▣ button on the toolbar at the left of the zoom slider in the lower-right corner of the worksheet window.
   The view buttons allow you to quickly toggle between views. The workbook may be printed from either Page Layout or Normal view.

Check That Data Fit on One Page

9. **Scroll down** to view the bottom of the page and then **scroll up** to the top of the page.

10. Scroll to the **right**.
    The grayed areas will not print. They indicate which rows and columns would extend to additional printed pages if data were in them. Notice that all data in range A1:E18 do fit on one page.

11. **Scroll back** to the left so that columns A–E are in view

Edit in Page Layout View

12. **Delete** the contents of **cell A1**.
    You may edit the worksheet in Page Layout view just as you would in Normal view.

13. **Undo** ↶ the change.

14. **Save** 💾 the workbook.
    The current workbook view is saved and would reappear the next time the workbook is opened. Leave the workbook open for the next exercise.

2.9 Printing Worksheets

Video Lesson labyrinthelab.com/videos

Excel gives you several ways to print your work. The method you choose depends on what you want to print. When you display the Print tab on the File menu, Backstage view displays a column of print options. The Print dialog box, familiar to users of previous Excel versions, has been eliminated. You may print specified pages, a selected range, or all data in the entire workbook. Additional choices include printing multiple copies and collating document pages in sets.

The Quick Print button can be added to the Quick Access toolbar. When clicked, it will print one copy of the entire worksheet. For large workbooks in which you frequently want to print only a certain selection, you can print a selection or set a print area. Before printing, you can preview in Backstage view or Page Layout view to see what is going to be printed. Additional page setup options such as changing the print orientation, printing column headings on every page, setting the print area, and many others are accessible from Backstage view or the Page Layout ribbon.

The light gridlines displayed around cells in Normal and Page Layout views do not print.

Print Preview

You have learned to use Page Layout view to preview the worksheet prior to printing. This view lets you see exactly how a worksheet will look when printed. Previewing can save time, paper, and wear and tear on your printer. It is especially useful when printing large worksheets and those with charts and intricate formatting. It is always wise to preview a large or complex worksheet before sending it to the printer.

In previous Excel versions, users also could display a separate Print Preview screen. Now, to save you time when you are ready to print, the Print tab of Backstage view displays a preview along with print options. The preview displays the overall look of the page that will be printed. You will usually need to zoom in to read any text. Scroll bars allow you to navigate to various areas of the zoomed-in page. The print preview is a very valuable tool for looking at how your worksheet will look when printed, but you are not able to edit your worksheet when you are in print preview mode (you will want to use Page Layout view for this purpose).

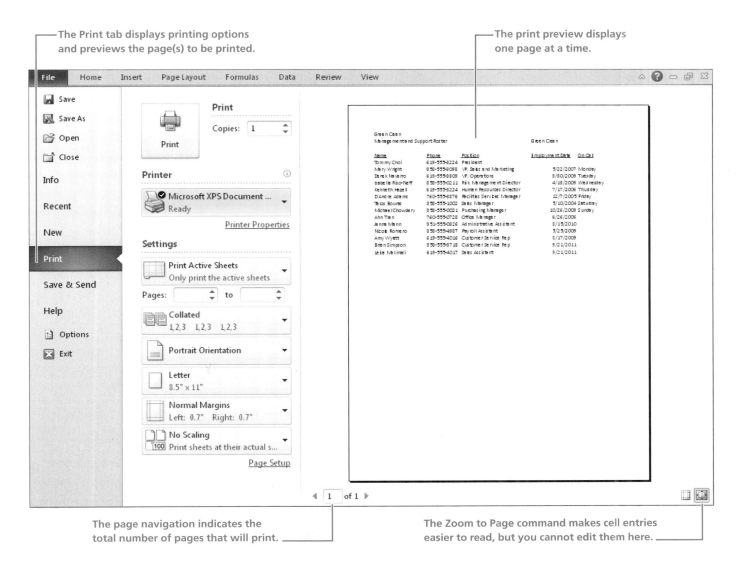

The Print tab displays printing options and previews the page(s) to be printed.

The print preview displays one page at a time.

The page navigation indicates the total number of pages that will print.

The Zoom to Page command makes cell entries easier to read, but you cannot edit them here.

Print the Worksheet

You can customize your Quick Access toolbar to include the Quick Print button, which sends the entire worksheet to the current printer using whatever print options are currently in effect. You must use the Print command on the File menu if you want to change printers, adjust the number of copies to be printed, or set other printing options such as printing only selected cells. The following illustration explains the most important options available in the Print tab of Backstage view.

Sends the document to
the printer using the
print options in effect

Prints one or multiple copies

Changes printers

Contains preferences for the
selected printer model

Controls what is printed—
the selected worksheet(s),
only a selected range, or
the entire workbook

Prints collated or
uncollated document sets

Limits printing to specified
document pages

The options on the Print tab
in Backstage view

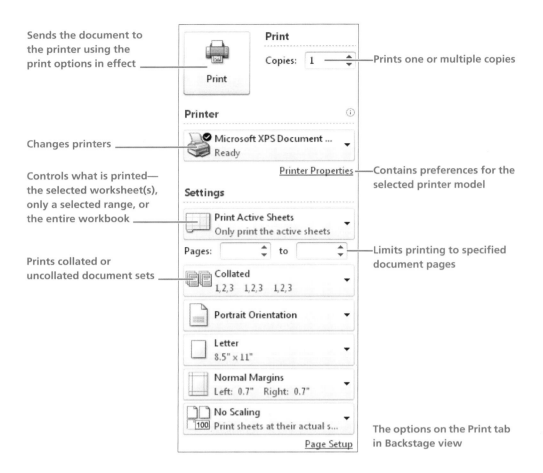

Printing Selections

FROM THE KEYBOARD

Ctrl + P to print

Many times you will want to print only a range of cells. You can do this by selecting the
desired cells, choosing the Print command, choosing to print the selection, and clicking Print.
You may also use this technique to print nonadjacent selections within a worksheet.
Nonadjacent selections print on separate pages.

To print a selection, you must select the cell range before issuing the Print command.

QUICK REFERENCE	PRINTING IN EXCEL
Task	**Procedure**
Preview how a worksheet will appear when printed	■ Choose File→Print or display Page Layout view.
Print a worksheet using default settings	■ Add the Quick Print 🖨 button on the Quick Access toolbar, if necessary. ■ Click the Quick Print 🖨 button on the Quick Access toolbar.

Task	Procedure
Open the Print tab in Backstage view to make changes to printing options before printing	▪ Choose File→Print.
Close the Print tab of Backstage view without printing	▪ Tap the ⎡Esc⎤ key or choose any tab from the Ribbon.
Print a selection	▪ Highlight the selection you wish to print. ▪ Choose File→Print. ▪ Under Settings, choose Print Selection from the Print What list. ▪ Click Print.

DEVELOP YOUR SKILLS 2.9.1
Preview and Print a Worksheet

In this exercise, you will preview the worksheet you have been working on in the Print tab of Backstage view and send it to the printer.

Preview How Your Worksheet Will Print

1. Choose **File→Print**.
   The File tab of Backstage view displays, and a preview of page 1 displays at the right of the window. Notice that the page navigation option at the bottom-left corner of the preview indicates that you are viewing page 1 of 1 page total in the document.

2. Click the **Zoom to Page** 🖳 button at the lower-right corner of the preview to zoom in on your worksheet.

3. Use the **scroll bars** to view the zoomed-in view.

4. Click the **Zoom to Page** 🖳 button again to zoom out.

Print Your Worksheet

5. Look at the options available at the left of the File tab of Backstage view, and then click **Print** at the top-left corner of the options to print the worksheet.

6. **Tap** ⎡Ctrl⎤+⎡S⎤ to save the changes and leave the workbook open.

2.10 Editing Workbook Properties

Video Lesson labyrinthelab.com/videos

Certain information about a workbook is saved along with the workbook contents. You can view these file properties while a workbook is open in Excel. The Windows operating system also displays document properties for a selected file.

Standard Properties

The Info tab of Backstage view displays a group of standard properties associated with Microsoft Office files. The file size, creation date, date last modified, and author name properties are included automatically. The default author name is the User Name set in Microsoft Office, although you may change the author name if you wish. You may enter a title, subject, categories, and comments about the workbook. Any tags, or keywords, that you enter may help users search for the document in a folder, drive, or the entire computer. For example, a roster of management employees could be tagged as *management, employee,* and *contact.*

You may add properties, such as tags to identify and organize workbooks, in the Info tab of Backstage view.

Advanced Properties

In Backstage view, you can use the Show All Properties link to display an expanded properties list. These additional properties include Comments, project Status, and Manager. You can access two other views by displaying the Properties menu in Backstage view. The menu choices include a

The Properties menu in the Info tab of Backstage view gives access to advanced and custom properties.

basic Document Properties panel that displays above the active worksheet and a Properties dialog box where you may create additional properties on its Custom tab. Custom properties do not display in Backstage view. If you know how to use a computer programming language such as Visual Basic for Applications (VBA), you can create code using custom properties to perform additional tasks in workbooks.

Task	Procedure
Set the username	▪ Choose File→Options. ▪ Enter the desired name in the User Name box in the General options window.
Edit standard properties	▪ Choose File→Info. ▪ Add or change the desired properties at the right of Backstage view, or choose Properties menu ▼→Show Document Panel to work with properties while viewing the active worksheet.
Expand the Properties list	▪ Choose File→Info from the Ribbon. ▪ Choose Properties menu ▼→Show All Properties.
Edit standard, advanced, and custom properties	▪ Choose File→Info. ▪ Choose Properties menu ▼→Advanced Properties. ▪ Click the appropriate tab in the Properties dialog box and edit the desired items.

DEVELOP YOUR SKILLS 2.10.1
Edit Workbook Properties

In this exercise, you will verify the Microsoft Office user name, display document properties in various ways, and enter several properties.

Verify the User Name

1. Choose **File→Options** 🗒.
   The General options category already should be selected in the categories at the left.

2. Read the existing User Name at the bottom of the options window. (Your User Name will differ from the illustration.)
   This is the user name set for all Microsoft Office documents. Do not change it unless your instructor directs you to do so.

Personalize your copy of Microsoft Office

User name: | Ken Hazell

3. Click **Cancel** to exit Excel Options.

Enter Standard Properties

4. Follow these steps to enter tags, a category, and an additional author for the workbook file:

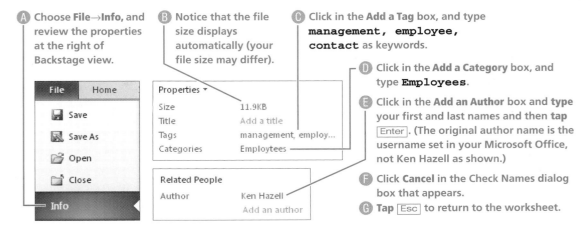

Ⓐ Choose **File→Info,** and review the properties at the right of Backstage view.

Ⓑ Notice that the file size displays automatically (your file size may differ).

Ⓒ Click in the **Add a Tag** box, and type `management, employee, contact` as keywords.

Ⓓ Click in the **Add a Category** box, and type `Employees`.

Ⓔ Click in the **Add an Author** box and **type** your first and last names and then **tap** Enter. (The original author name is the username set in your Microsoft Office, not Ken Hazell as shown.)

Ⓕ Click **Cancel** in the Check Names dialog box that appears.

Ⓖ Tap Esc to return to the worksheet.

Expand the Properties

5. Click the **File** tab, and then click **Info**, if necessary.
   The Info tab should be displayed in Backstage view.

6. Choose **Show All Properties** at the bottom-right of Backstage view. (**Scroll down** to locate the command, if necessary.)

7. **Scroll** the expanded list of properties, which include Comments, Status, and Manager.

Explore Advanced and Custom Properties

8. Choose **Properties** above the properties list and choose **Show Document Panel**.
   After a few moments, the panel displays above the active worksheet with the properties you entered. You can edit properties in the panel, if you prefer.

9. Click **Document Properties** in the upper-left corner of the panel and choose **Advanced Properties**.

The Management Roster Properties dialog box displays.

10. **Click** each tab in the dialog box to view the workbook details available, ending with the Custom tab displayed.

A custom property may be selected from the list or a name entered to create a new property. After the property's type and value are specified, the Add button is enabled. Remember that custom properties will not display in Backstage view.

11. Click **Cancel** to exit the dialog box without saving any changes.

12. Close the **Document Properties** panel.

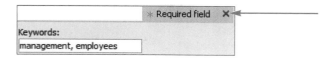

13. **Save** 🖫 the changes and **close** ⊠ the workbook.

2.11 Concepts Review

Concepts Review   labyrinthelab.com/excel10

To check your knowledge of the key concepts introduced in this lesson, complete the Concepts Review quiz by going to the URL listed above. If your classroom is using Labyrinth eLab, you may complete the Concepts Review quiz from within your eLab course.

Reinforce Your Skills

Edit a Worksheet

In this exercise, you will edit a worksheet. This exercise demonstrates that sometimes it is easier to replace entries, whereas at other times it is easier to edit them.

Replace Several Entries

1. Start **Excel** and choose **File→Open** 📁 from the Ribbon.

2. **Navigate** to the Lesson 02 folder in your file storage location and **open** rs-Customers.

3. Select **cell B4**.

4. Type **Ralph** and **tap** ⌷Enter⌷.
   Notice that it is easy to replace the entry because the name Ralph is easy to type.

5. **Replace** the name *Calvin* in **cell B6** with the name **Stephen**.

Edit Using the Formula Bar

6. Select **cell D4**.

7. Click in the **Formula Bar** just in front of the telephone prefix *333*.

8. **Tap** ⌷Delete⌷ three times to remove the prefix.

9. Type **222** and **complete** ✔ the entry.

10. **Change** the area code in cell D8 from *814* to **914**.
    In these entries, it was easier to edit than to retype entire phone numbers.

Use In-Cell and "Your Choice" Editing

11. **Double-click** cell E4.

12. Use ⌷→⌷ or ⌷←⌷ to position the **insertion point** in front of the word *Lane*.

13. **Tap** ⌷Delete⌷ four times to remove the word *Lane*.

14. Type **Reservoir** and complete the entry.

15. Edit the next five addresses using either the Formula Bar or in-cell editing. The required changes appear bold in the following table.

Cell	Make These Changes
E5	2900 **Carleton** Drive, San Mateo, CA 94401
E6	**2300** Palm Drive, Miami, FL 33147
E7	888 Wilson Street, **Concord**, CA 94565
E8	320 Main Street, **Pittsburgh**, PA 17951
E9	**5120** 132nd Street, Los Angeles, CA **90045**

16. **Save** the workbook.
    Leave the workbook open as you will use it for Reinforce Your Skills 2.2

Use AutoComplete and AutoFill

In this exercise, you will add data to the worksheet you created in the previous exercise by using AutoComplete and AutoFill. You also will use Auto Fill Options to restrict a fill action.

Before You Begin: You must have completed Reinforce Your Skills 2.1 and the rs-Customers workbook should be open.

Use AutoComplete

1. Select **cell B10**, and type **ja**.

   Notice that AutoComplete does not suggest an entry when you only type a "j" as there are two "j" entries in the column.

2. **Tap** Tab to accept the suggested entry of Jack.

3. Using the following figure, complete the customer's information, using **AutoComplete** in column F.

	A	B	C	D	E	F
9		Judy	Alioto	(213) 222-3344	132nd Street, Los Angeles, CA 95544	West
10		Jack	LaRue	(360) 444-0489	359 Peninsula Avenue, Port Angeles, WA 98363	West

Use AutoFill to Extend a Series

4. Select **cell A4**.

   Before using AutoFill, you must first select the cell that you will be using as the basis for the fill information.

5. Place your mouse pointer over the **fill handle** at the bottom-right corner of the selected cell, **drag** down through cell A10, and then **release** the mouse button when the ScreenTip shows C-07.

	A	B
3	Customer #	Firstna
4	C-01	Burt
5		Willie
6		Calvin
7		Susan
8		Jack
9		Judy
10		Jack
11		C-07
12		

	A
3	Customer #
4	C-01
5	C-02
6	C-03
7	C-04
8	C-05
9	C-06
10	C-07

Notice that Excel recognizes C-01 as the beginning of a series (C-02, C-03, C-04, ...).

Enter Additional Customers

6. Enter the following three customers, in rows 11–13, into the list, using **AutoFill** and **AutoComplete** when possible.

	A	B	C	D	E	F
10	C-07	Jack	LaRue	(360) 444-0489	359 Peninsula Avenue, Port Angeles, WA 983	West
11	C-08	Edgar	Martinez	(206) 111-1111	11 Mariners Way Seattle, WA 98101	West
12	C-09	Trevor	Hoffman	(619) 555-1111	51 Camino de Padres, San Diego, CA 92101	West
13	C-10	Derek	Jeffries	(212) 222-5555	2 York Avenue, New York, NY 10002	East

Use an Auto Fill Option

7. Select **cell A3**.
You will apply its bold and blue text formatting to the other column labels.

8. **Drag** the fill handle in cell A3 to the right through cell F3, and then **release** the mouse button.

3	Customer #	Firstname	Lastname	Phone	Address	Region

The cells are filled with Customer # because both the contents and formatting are copied by default.

9. Click the **Auto Fill Options** button at the lower-right corner of cell F3 and choose **Fill Formatting Only** from the list.
The contents of range B3:F3 return to their former entries and only the formatting is applied.

10. **Deselect** the cells by clicking on any other cell.

11. Use [Ctrl]+[S] to **save** your workbook. Leave the workbook open for the next exercise.

REINFORCE YOUR SKILLS 2.3
Move and Copy Cell Contents

In this exercise, you will use the workbook from Reinforce Your Skills 2.2 and move and copy the contents of cells.

Before You Begin: You must have completed Reinforce Your Skills 2.1 and Reinforce Your Skills 2.2, and the rs-Customers workbook should be open.

Use Keyboard Shortcuts

1. Select **cell E1**.

2. Choose **Home→Clipboard→Cut** from the Ribbon.

3. Select **cell A1**, and choose **Home→Clipboard→Paste** from the Ribbon.

4. Select the range **A11:F11**, and **copy** the range using the keyboard command [Ctrl]+[C].

5. Select **cell A14**, and paste the range using [Ctrl]+[V].
This approach can come in handy if you have a new entry that is very similar to an existing one!

6. Use [Ctrl]+[Z] to **undo** the Paste command.

Copy Using the Context Menu

7. Select **cell D6**.

8. Taking care to avoid the fill handle, **point** at the dark line surrounding the cell, press the **right** mouse button, and **drag** down to cell D7. *The pop-up, or context, menu appears when you release the mouse button.*

9. Choose **Copy Here** from the shortcut menu. *The phone number from cell D6 is copied to cell D7.*

10. Edit the last four digits of the phone number in cell D7 to **3535**.

11. Use ⌈Ctrl⌉+⌈Home⌉ to return to cell A1.

12. **Close** ⊠ the workbook, choosing to **save** your workbook.

REINFORCE YOUR SKILLS 2.4

Preview a Worksheet, Print, and Edit a Workbook Property

In this exercise, you will use the workbook from Reinforce Your Skills 2.3 to preview and then print a selection from the workbook. You will view workbook properties and edit one of them.

Before You Begin: You must have completed Reinforce Your Skills 2.1, 2.2, and 2.3, and the rs-Customers workbook should be open.

Preview in Page Layout View

1. Click the **Page Layout** ▣ button on the toolbar at the left of the zoom slider in the lower-right corner of the worksheet window.

2. Look at the Status Bar at the bottom-left corner of the **Page Layout** window to verify that the worksheet fits on one page. *The Status Bar should indicate Page: 1 of 1.*

3. Check the overall look of data on the page. *Some text in the Address column is truncated (cut off). Normally you would correct any problem discovered during the preview, but you may leave the text as is in this lesson.*

Cancel a Print

4. Choose **File→Print**. *A preview displays at the right of the Print tab in Backstage view.*

5. Take a moment to look at the print options but **do not** change them.

6. **Tap** the ⌈Esc⌉ key to cancel the print and return to Page Layout view.

Print a Selection

7. Click the **Normal view** ▦ button on the toolbar at the left of the zoom slider in the lower-right corner of the worksheet window.
   You will print just the last names and phone numbers in the next steps. You could have selected the range in Page Layout view also.

8. Select the **range C3:D13**.

9. Use ⌈Ctrl⌉+⌈P⌉ to display the Print tab of Backstage view.

10. Follow these steps to print the selected range:

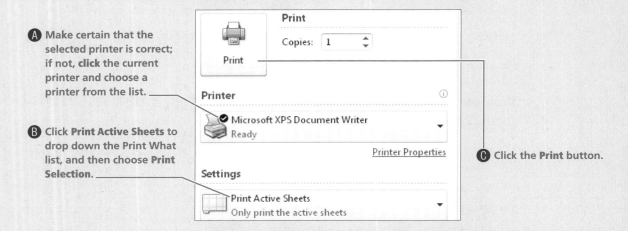

Ⓐ Make certain that the selected printer is correct; if not, **click** the current printer and choose a printer from the list.

Ⓑ Click **Print Active Sheets** to drop down the Print What list, and then choose **Print Selection**.

Ⓒ Click the **Print** button.

Only the selected range prints. Excel displays a page break (dashed line) to the right of column F in Normal view to indicate the edge of page 1.

11. **Scroll down** to view the page break at the bottom of the page (after row 52, depending on your printer).
    These page breaks disappear from Normal view when the workbook is closed, but Page Layout view always shows you the page break locations.

12. Use ⌈Ctrl⌉+⌈Home⌉ to go to cell A1.

Edit a Workbook Property

13. Choose **File→Info** to display Backstage view.

14. Enter the keywords `customers, contacts` in the Tags box under Properties at the right of Backstage view.

15. Click the **File** tab to exit Backstage view.

16. **Save** 🖫 the changes and **close** the workbook.

Apply Your Skills

Edit a Worksheet, Use Page Layout View, and Edit a Workbook Property

In this exercise, you will edit a worksheet in both Normal and Page Layout views. You will also use AutoFill to extend a series.

1. **Open** the workbook named as-Bonuses from the Lesson 02 folder in your file storage location.

2. Edit the title in **cell A1** to read **Site Safety Bonuses**.

3. **AutoFill** the months February through June in **cells C3:G3**.

4. **Edit** the label in **cell A3** to **Employee Name**.

5. **Change** the name Garcia, H. in **cell A5** to **Wilson, T**.

6. View the worksheet in **Page Layout view**.

7. While in Page Layout view, **edit** the label in **cell A8** to read **Grand Total** and **complete** the entry.

8. **AutoFill** just the contents without the formatting from the range **F4:F7** to **G4:G7**. *The values in range G4:G7 should appear black when you are done.*

9. Change the entry in **cell G4** to **300**.

10. Change the **Author** workbook property from the existing user name to your first and last names.

11. **Save** the changes and **close** the workbook.

Select, Move, and Copy in a Worksheet

In this exercise, you will practice selecting various ranges and cells in order to move and copy them.

1. **Open** the workbook named as-Carpet Products from the Lesson 02 folder in your file storage location.

2. Select **A6:D19**; try using the Shift technique.

3. Place your **mouse pointer** over the edge of the selection until you see the move pointer, and then **click** and **drag up** until the top left of the selection is in row 3.
   The selection will now be contained in the range A3:D16.

4. Select **B3:D3** and issue the **Cut** command.

5. Click **cell B4** and issue the **Paste** command.

6. **Copy** the contents of **B4:D4** into **B12:D12**.

7. **Save** the workbook and leave it **open** for the next exercise.

	A	B	C	D
1	Green Clean			
2	Carpet Products			
3				
4	CARPET CLEANING SOLUTIONS	Type	Size	Price
5	EarthWise Carpet Cleaner	Concentrate	64 ounces	$17.50
6	EarthWise Carpet Cleaner		32 ounces	$9.85
7	EarthWise Carpet Cleaner	Spray	16 ounces	$4.50
8	GBS All Purpose Carpet	Liquid	120 ounces	$11.95
9	GBS Dry Powder Cleaner	Powder	16 ounces	$4.25
10	Taz Carpet and Upholstery	Liquid	Gallon	$7.95
11				
12	CARPET STAIN REMOVERS	Type	Size	Price
13	EarthWise Carpet Stain Remover	Concentrate	64 ounces	$9.95
14	EarthWise Carpet Stain Remover	Concentrate	32 ounces	$5.50
15	EarthWise Carpet Stain Remover	Spray	16 ounces	$4.65
16	Carpet Bright Stain Eliminator	Spray	32 ounces	$7.35

Work with Undo, Clear, and AutoComplete

In this exercise, you will work with the workbook from Apply Your Skills 2.2 to clear formatting, undo commands, and use AutoComplete.

Before You Begin: You must have completed Apply Your Skills 2.1 and 2.2, and the as-Carpet Products workbook should be open.

1. Select **column D** by clicking the column header.

2. Choose **Home→Editing→Clear→Clear Formats** from the Ribbon.
   Notice that the numbers remain in column D, but they are no longer formatted as currency.

3. Click the **Undo** button on the Quick Access toolbar to bring back the cleared formatting.

4. Click **cell B6** and type **c**, observing the AutoComplete option that appears.

5. **Tap** Enter to accept the AutoComplete suggestion.

6. Select the **range A10:D10** and **tap** Delete to clear the contents of the cells.

7. Choose **File→Print**.

8. Check the print preview in the **Print** tab of Backstage view to make certain that the worksheet will print on one page.

9. **Print** the worksheet.

10. **Save** the changes to the workbook and **exit** from Excel.

	A	B	C	D
1	Green Clean			
2	Carpet Products			
3				
4	CARPET CLEANING SOLUTIONS	Type	Size	Price
5	EarthWise Carpet Cleaner	Concentrate	64 ounces	$17.50
6	EarthWise Carpet Cleaner	Concentrate	32 ounces	$9.85
7	EarthWise Carpet Cleaner	Spray	16 ounces	$4.50
8	GBS All Purpose Carpet	Liquid	120 ounces	$11.95
9	GBS Dry Powder Cleaner	Powder	16 ounces	$4.25
10				
11				
12	CARPET STAIN REMOVERS	Type	Size	Price
13	EarthWise Carpet Stain Remover	Concentrate	64 ounces	$9.95
14	EarthWise Carpet Stain Remover	Concentrate	32 ounces	$5.50
15	EarthWise Carpet Stain Remover	Spray	16 ounces	$4.65
16	Carpet Bright Stain Eliminator	Spray	32 ounces	$7.35

Critical Thinking & Work-Readiness Skills

In the course of working through the following Microsoft Office-based Critical Thinking exercises, you will also be utilizing various work-readiness skills, some of which are listed next to each exercise. Go to labyrinthelab.com/ workreadiness to learn more about the work-readiness skills.

2.1 Edit and Replace Entries

WORK-READINESS SKILLS APPLIED

- Making decisions
- Showing responsibility
- Knowing how to learn

Ken asks Jenna Mann to update the birthday list for Green Clean employees. Jenna finds the current birthday list in a Microsoft Excel file. She decides to contact each employee personally, as an excuse to introduce herself, as well as to verify the dates. Open ct-Birthdays (Lesson 02 folder) and make these edits: change Mary Wright's birthday to March 2; delete all information for Michael Tsang and Joe Smith; change Mary Jones to **Amy Wyatt** and her birthday of June 26; and add Alan Sedgwick and his birthday of September 25 at the end of the list. Save the file as **ct-Birthday Update**. If working in a group, discuss why a company might want to recognize birthdays. If working alone, type your answer in a Word document named **ct-Questions** saved to your Lesson 02 folder.

2.2 Edit and Print a Workbook

WORK-READINESS SKILLS APPLIED

- Acquiring and using information
- Exercising leadership
- Interpreting and communicating information

Ken decides to add a column to Jenna's birthday worksheet for monthly highlights (a job completed, a customer compliment, etc.) at the November employee meeting. Open ct-Birthday Update, if necessary. Add a column labeled **Highlight** and add the following:

Mary Wright – Congratulations on deal with Hall Properties; Amy Wyatt – Congratulations on recent marriage; Jenna Mann – Thanks for updating birthday list; Talos Bouras – Happy birthday!; Michael Chowdery – Welcome, will report to Derek.

Proofread your work and correct as necessary. Print preview the birthday list with the new column. Print the document. Save the file as **ct-Birthday Highlights** in your Lesson 02 folder.

2.3 Rearrange Data and use Auto Features

WORK-READINESS SKILLS APPLIED

- Organizing and maintaining information
- Seeing things in the mind's eye
- Showing responsibility

Ken wants an employee roster. Also, every employee has a quarterly "green" project to complete and Ken would like to track these. Open ct-Birthdays Highlights, if necessary. Select just the employee names and copy them to the Clipboard. Open ct-Employee Roster (Lesson 13 folder), and paste the names into column B. Select the names Kenneth Hazell through Alan Sedgwick, and move the names up one cell to eliminate the blank cell. Label column A as **Empoyee #**. Create a unique number for each employee in the Employee # column, starting with EN-001. Then, assign each employee randomly to one of the following: **Light Bulb Replacement**, **Product Improvement**, **Commute Reduction**. Save file as **ct-Employee Roster and Project** in your Lesson 02 folder and close all files.

Working with Formulas and Functions

LESSON OUTLINE

LEARNING OBJECTIVES

After studying this lesson, you will be able to:

- Create formulas to calculate values, utilizing the proper syntax and order of operations
- Employ a variety of methods to use the IF logical function and statistical functions that determine the sum, average, count, maximum, and minimum of a range of numbers
- Use relative, absolute, and mixed cell references in formulas
- Modify and copy formulas
- Display the formulas contained within cells rather than the resulting values

The magic of the Excel spreadsheet lies in its ability to crunch numbers and make sense of data. The heart of this magic lies in the formulas and functions that are used for this number crunching. In this lesson, you will be introduced to creating and modifying basic formulas and functions in Excel. You will learn how to reference cells in formulas as well as how to use another automated feature of Excel, AutoSum. With an IF function, you may flag a cell with a text label, display a value, or perform a calculation when specific criteria are satisfied.

CASE STUDY

Creating a Spreadsheet with Formulas

Green Clean earns revenue by selling janitorial products and contracts for cleaning services. Talos Bouras is a sales manager. He wants to set up a workbook with two worksheets, one to track commissions and the other to report how the projected profit would change based on costs and an increase or decrease in sales. He will create the necessary formulas for the workbook calculations.

	A	B	C	D	E
1	Sales Department				
2		Projected Net Profit			
3		Base	2%	5%	-5%
4	Product Sales	$ 53,200	54,264	55,860	50,540
5	Contracts	241,000	245,820	258,111	245,205
6	Total Revenue	$ 294,200	$ 300,084	$ 313,971	$ 295,745
7					
8	Fixed Operating Cost	101,400	101,400	101,400	101,400
9	Marketing Expense	15,000	15,000	15,000	15,000
10	Commissions	27,824	28,380	29,721	28,058
11	Total Costs	$ 144,224	$ 144,780	$ 146,121	$ 144,458
12					
13	Gross Profit	$ 149,976	$ 155,304	$ 167,850	$ 151,287
14	Net Profit	$ 138,353	$ 143,267	$ 154,841	$ 139,562
15	Gross Profit vs. Revenue	51.0%	51.8%	53.5%	51.2%
16					
17	Contracts	482			
18	Average Contract	500	Marketing	15,000	
19	Product Commission Rate	7%	Fixed Cost	101,400	
20	Contract Commission Rate	10%	Tax Rate	7.75%	

The Profit Projection worksheet reports the effect of various sales projections and costs on net profit. When Talos changes the numbers in rows 17–20, the formulas recalculate the results in rows 4–15 automatically.

	A	B	C	D	E	F	G
1	Sales Department						
2		First Quarter Commissions					
3							
4	Sales Team Member	January	February	March	Qtr 1 Total	Sales	Met Goal?
5	Talos Bouras	250	486	415	1151	28775	
6	Leisa Malimali	74	88	101	263	6575	
7	Brian Simpson	389	303	422	1114	27850	
8	Amy Wyatt	346	381	502	1229	30725	Yes
9	Monthly Total	1059	1258	1440	3757		
10							
11	Average	264.75	314.5	360	939.25		
12	Maximum	389	486	502	1229		
13	Minimum	74	88	101	263		
14	Count	4	4	4	4		
15	Goal					30000	

The Qtr 1 Commissions worksheet sums the monthly totals for all team members and each team member's quarterly sales. Formulas also calculate the monthly average, maximum, minimum, and item count. The IF function returns a message if the sales goal is met or leaves the cell blank if not met.

3.1 Working with Formulas and Functions

Video Lesson labyrinthelab.com/videos

A formula is simply a math problem done in Excel. You can add, subtract, multiply, divide, and group numbers and cell contents in order to make your data work for you. A function is a prewritten formula that helps to simplify complex procedures, both for numbers and for text. For instance, a function can be used to sum a group of numbers, to determine the payment amount on a loan, and to convert a number to text.

Using AutoSum to Create a SUM Formula

FROM THE KEYBOARD

Alt + = for Autosum

The power of Excel becomes apparent when you begin using formulas and functions. The most common type of calculation is summing a column or row of numbers. In fact, this type of calculation is so common that Excel provides the AutoSum feature specifically for this purpose.

The **Σ** button on the Home tab, also known as Sum, automatically sums a column or row of numbers. When you click AutoSum, Excel starts the formula for you by entering =SUM() and proposes a range of adjacent cells within parentheses. Excel will first look upward for a range to sum, and if a range is not found there, it will next look left. You can accept the proposed range or drag in the worksheet to select a different range. You can see the formula, such as =SUM(B5:B8), in the Formula Bar as you edit cell contents. Then, the calculation result displays in the cell after you complete the entry. Empty cells in the sum range are ignored in the calculation.

If your Excel window is smaller, the button may be displayed like this: **Σ ▾**.

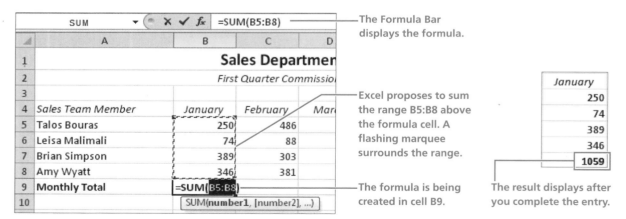

The Formula Bar displays the formula.

Excel proposes to sum the range B5:B8 above the formula cell. A flashing marquee surrounds the range.

The formula is being created in cell B9.

The result displays after you complete the entry.

AVERAGE, COUNT, COUNTA, MAX, and MIN Functions

The AutoSum button does not stop at simply summing a group of numbers. The following statistical functions are also available on the AutoSum drop-down list: average, count numbers, maximum, and minimum.

An additional Count command equal to the COUNTA function in formulas is available on the Status Bar. The following table describes these functions. The COUNTA function counts all nonblank cells in the specified range. At times, you will want use COUNTA to count all entries, whether or not they contain numbers. You could use the Count Numbers command, equal to the COUNT function, when it is important to identify any non-number cells as possible errors.

AutoSum and/or Status Bar Function	How Function Appears in Formula	Description
Sum	SUM	Adds the values in the cells indicated in the formula
Average	AVERAGE	Averages the values in the cells indicated in the formula by dividing the sum total by the number of values
Count Numbers or Numerical Count	COUNT	Counts the number of values in the cells indicated in the formula; cells containing text and blank cells are ignored
Count	COUNTA	Counts the number of nonblank cells in the cells indicated in the formula; cells containing text are included; empty cells are ignored
Max or Maximum	MAX	Returns the maximum (highest) value in the cells indicated in the formula
Min or Minimum	MIN	Returns the minimum (lowest) value in the cells indicated in the formula

Once you have entered a formula in a cell, you can use AutoFill to copy it to adjacent cells.

Status Bar Functions and Customization

The Status Bar, which is displayed at the bottom of the Excel window, allows you to view information about a range of numbers without actually inserting a function formula in the worksheet. You can customize the Status Bar to display the following functions: Average, Count, Numerical Count, Minimum, Maximum, and Sum. To customize the Status Bar, right-click anywhere on it and click to add or remove features. Other than functions, you can also customize additional features of the Status Bar, such as Zoom, Signatures, Overtype Mode, and Macro Recording.

The range B5:B8 is selected in the worksheet.

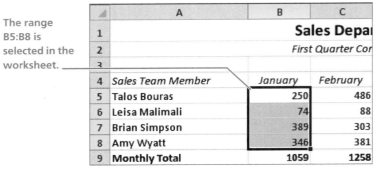

By default, Excel displays in the Status Bar the average, count of values, and sum of the selected range.

Right-clicking the Status Bar displays a menu from which you can add items to or delete them from the Status Bar.

QUICK REFERENCE	USING AUTOSUM AND THE STATUS BAR FUNCTIONS
Task	**Procedure**
AutoSum a range of cells	▪ Click in the cell where you want the sum to appear. ▪ Choose Home→Editing→AutoSum **Σ** from the Ribbon. ▪ If the proposed range is correct, tap ⌊Enter⌋ or click the AutoSum button to complete the function. ▪ If the proposed range is incorrect, click and drag to select the correct range before tapping ⌊Enter⌋.
AutoSum across columns or down rows	▪ Select the cell range in the row below or column to the right of the data where you want the sums to appear. ▪ Choose Home→Editing→AutoSum **Σ** from the Ribbon.
Use Status Bar functions	▪ Right-click the Status Bar and add or remove the desired functions, if necessary. ▪ Drag to select the range of cells to which you wish to apply the function. ▪ Look at the Status Bar at the bottom of your Excel window to view the average, count of values, and sum of the selected range.

Use AutoSum and Status Bar Functions

In this exercise, you will use AutoSum to calculate the monthly commission total for the sales team as well as the quarterly total for each sales team member. You will also explore the functions on the Status Bar.

Open an Excel File

1. Start **Excel**.

2. **Open** the Commissions workbook from the Lesson 03 folder in your file storage location.
   Take a look at the workbook. There are two tabs at the bottom of the window: Qtr 1 Commissions and Profit Projection. You will first work with the commissions worksheet to calculate monthly and quarterly commission totals. You also will find the average, maximum, minimum, and count of numbers for each month.

Use AutoSum

3. With the Qtr 1 Commissions worksheet displayed, select **cell B9**.

4. Choose **Home→Editing→Sum** Σ from the Ribbon.
   Excel displays a marquee (marching ants) around the part of the spreadsheet where it thinks the formula should be applied. You can change this selection as necessary.

5. Follow these steps to complete the Sum formula.

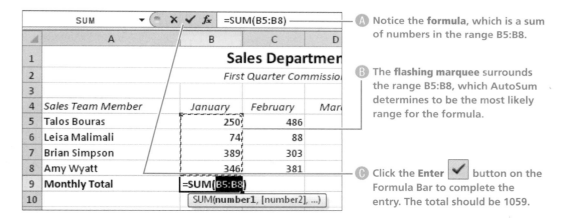

(A) Notice the **formula**, which is a sum of numbers in the range B5:B8.

(B) The **flashing marquee** surrounds the range B5:B8, which AutoSum determines to be the most likely range for the formula.

(C) Click the **Enter** ✔ button on the Formula Bar to complete the entry. The total should be 1059.

Override the Range AutoSum Proposes

6. Select **cell E7** and choose **Home→Editing→Sum** Σ from the Ribbon. *Notice that, as there are no values above cell E7, Excel looked to the left to find a range to sum, B7:D7. Now, assume that you wanted only cells B7:C7 to be summed.*

7. Follow these steps to override the proposed range:

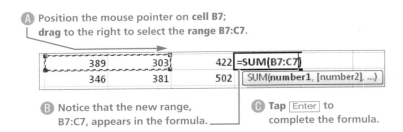

Ⓐ Position the mouse pointer on **cell B7;** drag to the right to select the **range B7:C7.**

Ⓑ Notice that the new range, B7:C7, appears in the formula.

Ⓒ Tap Enter to complete the formula.

8. **Undo** ↰ the formula.

Use AutoFill to Extend a Formula

You can use AutoFill to extend a formula just as you would use it to extend a series of days in the week.

9. Follow these steps to AutoFill the formula in cell B9 into the cells to its right:

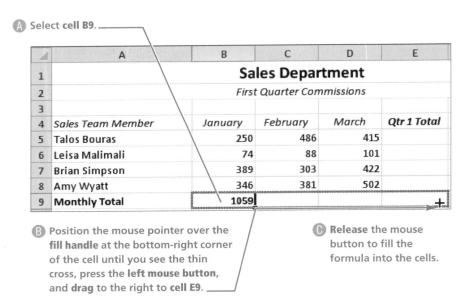

Ⓐ Select **cell B9.**

⊿	A	B	C	D	E
1		**Sales Department**			
2		*First Quarter Commissions*			
3					
4	*Sales Team Member*	*January*	*February*	*March*	**Qtr 1 Total**
5	Talos Bouras	250	486	415	
6	Leisa Malimali	74	88	101	
7	Brian Simpson	389	303	422	
8	Amy Wyatt	346	381	502	
9	Monthly Total	1059			+

Ⓑ Position the mouse pointer over the **fill handle** at the bottom-right corner of the cell until you see the thin cross, press the **left mouse button,** and **drag** to the right to **cell E9.**

Ⓒ **Release** the mouse button to fill the formula into the cells.

Cell E9 displays 0 because the cells above it are empty. You can create formulas that include empty cells and then enter data later.

Calculate the Quarterly Totals

10. Select the **range E5:E8**.

11. Choose **Home→Editing→Sum** $\boxed{\Sigma}$ from the Ribbon.
    Excel created a formula in each cell of the selected range without requiring you to complete the formulas.

Qtr 1 Total
1151
263
1114
1229
3757

12. **Delete** the formulas in **range B9:E9** and **range E5:E8**.
    The data are returned to their original state. Next you will create all formulas at once by selecting the data and the empty cells to the right and below the data.

Sum Columns and Rows Simultaneously

13. Select the **range B5:E9** and click **Sum** $\boxed{\Sigma}$.
    The formula results appear in B9:D9 and E5:E9. This procedure is the most efficient to use when the data are arranged in this way.

Explore Statistical Functions with AutoSum

14. Select **cell B11**.

15. On the Home ribbon in the Editing group, click the **drop-down arrow** at the right of the **AutoSum** button.

     $\boxed{\Sigma \text{ AutoSum } \blacktriangledown}$

16. Choose **Average** from the drop-down menu.
    Excel proposes the range B5:B10, which is incorrect.

17. Select the correct **range B5:B8** and **tap** $\boxed{\text{Enter}}$ to complete the entry.
    The result should equal 264.75.

18. Select **cell B12**.

19. Choose **Home→Editing** $\boxed{\Sigma \text{ AutoSum } \blacktriangledown}$ **menu** ▾→**Max** from the Ribbon.
    Max means Maximum.

20. Select the correct **range B5:B8** and **tap** $\boxed{\text{Enter}}$ to display the highest value in the range you chose.

21. Select **cell B13** and choose **Home→Editing→AutoSum menu** ▾→**Min** from the Ribbon.
    Min means Minimum, or the lowest value.

22. Correct the range to **B5:B8** and then click **Enter** $\boxed{✔}$ on the Formula Bar to complete the entry.

23. Select **cell B14** and choose **Home→Editing** $\boxed{\Sigma \text{ AutoSum } \blacktriangledown}$ **menu** ▾ from the Ribbon.

24. Choose **Count Numbers** from the menu, correct the range to **B5:B8**, and click **Enter** on the Formula Bar to complete the entry.

Notice that the function COUNT is used in the formula. This function counts all cells in the range that contain a number. You can use this function to check that all cells have a number.

25. Select **cell B6** and **delete** the contents.

The formula recalculates the count as 3 and recalculates the average because one cell in the range is now blank.

26. **Undo** the deletion.

Use Status Bar Functions

27. Select the **range B5:B8**.

28. Look at the Status Bar in the lower-right corner of the window to see the **sum value** displayed.

29. **Save** the workbook and keep it **open** for the next exercise.

	=COUNT(B5:B8	
	B	**C**
	January	*February*
	250	486
	74	88
	389	303
	346	381
	1059	1258
	264.75	314.5
	389	486
	74	88
	=COUNT(B5:B8	
	COUNT(**value1**, [value2], ...)	

Average: 264.75	Count: 4	Sum: 1059

3.2 Creating Formulas

Video Lesson   labyrinthelab.com/videos

You have already learned how to compute totals with AutoSum. AutoSum provides a convenient method for summing a range of numbers. However, you will need to use many other types of formulas in Excel. In fact, many worksheets, such as financial models, require hundreds or even thousands of complex formulas.

Beginning Character in Formulas

As you saw in the AutoSum discussion in the previous section, functions begin with an equals (=) sign. If you are typing a formula in a cell, it is recommended that you also begin it with an equals (=) sign, even though you can begin it with a plus (+) or a minus (−) sign. It is best to adopt one method in order to create consistency.

Cell and Range References

Formulas derive their power from the use of cell and range references. For example, in the previous exercise, you used AutoSum to insert the formula =SUM(B5:B8) in cell B9. Because the range reference (B5:B8) was used in the formula, you were able to copy the formula across the row using the fill handle. There are two important benefits to using references in formulas.

■ When references are used, formulas can be copied to other cells.

■ Because a reference refers to a cell or a range of cells, the formula results are automatically recalculated when the data is changed in the referenced cell(s).

Do not type results of calculations directly into cells. Always use formulas.

The Language of Excel Formulas

Formulas can include the standard arithmetic operators shown in the following table. You can also use spaces within formulas to improve their appearance and readability. Notice that each formula in the table begins with an equals (=) sign. Also, keep in mind that each formula is entered into the same cell that displays the resulting calculation.

QUICK REFERENCE	USING ARITHMETIC OPERATORS IN FORMULAS	
Operator	**Example**	**Comments**
+ (addition)	=B7+B11	Adds the values in B7 and B11
− (subtraction)	=B7−B11	Subtracts the value in B11 from the value in B7
* (multiplication)	=B7*B11	Multiplies the values in B7 and B11
/ (division)	=B7/B11	Divides the value in B7 by the value in B11
^ (exponentiation)	=B7^3	Raises the value in B7 to the third power (B7*B7*B7)
% (percent)	=B7*10%	Multiplies the value in B7 by 10% (0.10)
( ) (grouping)	=B7/(C4−C2)	Subtracts the value in C2 from the value in C4 and then divides B7 by the subtraction result

When typing a cell reference in a formula, you can simply type the column letter in lowercase and Excel will capitalize it for you.

"Please Excuse My Dear Aunt Sally"

Excel formulas follow the algebraic hierarchy. This means that the formula completes operations in a specific order. You can memorize this hierarchy with the mnemonic "Please Excuse My Dear Aunt Sally":

Please	Parentheses (grouping symbols)
Excuse	Exponents
My	Multiplication
Dear	Division
Aunt	Addition
Sally	Subtraction

To control the order of operations, you can use parentheses to cause Excel to add or subtract before multiplying or dividing. Take a look at the following examples to see how the order of operations works with and without parentheses and how the resulting value will be different.

=53+ 7*5	= 53+35 = 88	Multiplication then addition
=(53+7)*5	= (60)*5 = 300	Parentheses then multiplication

Excel includes two additional items in the order of operations between parentheses and exponents. At the beginning of a formula, a minus (−) sign is interpreted as a negative. You may need to use parentheses around an operation that includes a negative number to ensure a correct answer. A percent sign is also considered as an operator.

=−4*2	= −8	Negative number multiplied by positive number
=2+50%+3^2	= 2.5+9 = 11.5	Percent then exponent

Use the Keyboard to Create Formulas

In this exercise, you will use the keyboard to enter formulas into the spreadsheet.

1. Click the **Profit Projection** sheet tab at the bottom of the Excel window.

   | ◄ ◄ ► ►| | Qtr 1 Commissions | Profit Projection ◄

2. Select **cell B5** and view its formula in the Formula Bar.
   This formula multiplies the number of contracts (B17) by the average contract revenue (B18).

3. Select **cell B6** and use **AutoSum** to sum the sales in the **range B4:B5**.

4. Select **cell B11** and **sum** the costs in the **range B8:B10**.
   The total costs result is not correct, but you will enter data in cells B9 and B10 in the next exercise.

5. Select **cell B13**, the Gross Profit for the Base column.

6. Type **=B6−B11** in the cell, and then **tap** ⌷Enter⌷ to complete the formula.
   In order to calculate the gross profit, you need to subtract the total costs (B11) from total revenue (B6).

7. Select **cell B15**, Gross Profit vs. Revenue.

8. Type **=b13/b6** in the cell, and then **tap** ⌷Enter⌷ to complete the formula.
   Formulas are not case sensitive. Notice that regardless of whether you type the cell references as upper- or lowercase, the formula will work properly. In this worksheet, the cell has been formatted to display a percentage for you.

9. **Save** 🖫 the workbook and keep it **open** for the next exercise.

3.3 Using Cell References in Formulas

Video Lesson	labyrinthelab.com/videos

A cell reference identifies which cell or range of cells contains the values to use in a formula. Cell references are one of three types: relative, absolute, or mixed. All formulas use the relative cell reference unless you specifically instruct Excel to use another type. You used relative cell references in the formulas you created in the last exercise. As this lesson continues, you will learn about the other two types of cell references.

Relative Cell References

A relative cell reference means the cell is *relative* to the cell that contains the formula. For example, when you create a formula in cell C3 to calculate A3 minus B3 (=A3–B3), Excel finds that the first value is two cells to the left of the formula. The second value is one cell to the left of the formula.

When you copy a formula, the cell references update automatically and refer to new cells relative to the new formula cell. For example, if you copied the formula mentioned in the previous paragraph down to cell C4, the new formula would be A4 minus B4 (=A4–B4). The first and second values are still relative to the same number of cells to the left of the formula cell.

	A	B	C	D	E
11	Total Costs	=SUM(B8:B10)	=SUM(C8:C10)	=SUM(D8:D10)	=SUM(E8:E10)
12					
13	Gross Profit	=B6-B11	=C6-C11	=D6-D11	=E6-E11

Notice that when a formula utilizing relative cell references in column B is copied through to column E, the cells referenced in the copied formulas will refer to cells relative to where they are pasted.

Point Mode

One potential danger that can occur when typing formulas is accidentally typing the incorrect cell reference. This is easy to do, especially if the worksheet is complex. Point mode can help you avoid this problem. With point mode, you can insert a cell reference in a formula by clicking the desired cell as you are typing the formula. Likewise, you can insert a range reference in a formula by dragging over the desired cells. You will use point mode in the next exercise.

Absolute Cell References

You have been using relative references thus far in this course. Relative references are convenient because they update automatically when formulas are moved or copied. In some situations, you may not want references updated when a formula is moved or copied. You must use absolute or mixed references in these situations. Absolute references always refer to the same cell, regardless of which cell the formula is moved or copied to. You can refer to cells on other worksheets or in other workbooks as well.

Creating Absolute References

You create absolute references by placing dollar signs in front of the column and row components of the reference, for example, $C$1. You can type the dollar signs as you enter a formula or add them later by editing the formula. The following illustration shows an example of how absolute references are used in formulas.

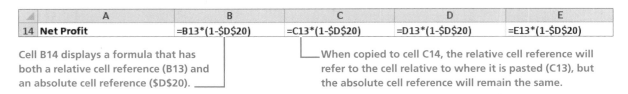

	A	B	C	D	E
14	Net Profit	=B13*(1-$D$20)	=C13*(1-$D$20)	=D13*(1-$D$20)	=E13*(1-$D$20)

Cell B14 displays a formula that has both a relative cell reference (B13) and an absolute cell reference ($D$20).

When copied to cell C14, the relative cell reference will refer to the cell relative to where it is pasted (C13), but the absolute cell reference will remain the same.

Mixed References

You can mix relative and absolute references within a reference. For example, the reference $C1 is a combination of an absolute reference to column C and a relative reference to row 1. Mixed references are useful when copying many types of formulas.

Using the F4 Function Key

You make a reference absolute or mixed by typing dollar signs while entering the reference. You can also use the F4 function key to insert the dollar signs. You may do so right after typing the cell reference or by clicking for an insertion point in the cell reference in the Formula Bar. The first time you tap F4, dollar signs are placed in front of both the column and row components of the reference. If you tap F4 again, the dollar sign is removed from the column component, thus creating a mixed reference. If you tap F4 a third time, a dollar sign is placed in front of just the column component and removed from the row component. One more tap of F4 will return you to a relative cell reference. The following table indicates what happens to a cell reference when its formula is copied and pasted to the next column or row.

Cell Reference	Type	Copy-and-Paste Action	Result When Pasted
B6	Relative	One column to the right	C6
B6	Relative	One row down	B7
$B$6	Absolute	One column to the right	$B$6
$B$6	Absolute	One row down	$B$6
$B6	Mixed	One column to the right	$B6
$B6	Mixed	One row down	$B7
B$6	Mixed	One column to the right	C$6
B$6	Mixed	One row down	B$6

What-If Analysis

Another great advantage to using cell references in formulas is that it allows you to perform what-if analyses. A what-if analysis is as simple as changing the value in a cell that is referenced in a formula and observing the overall change in the data. You can perform these simple analyses at any time by replacing the value(s) in referenced cells. The Undo command can come in very handy when performing a what-if analysis as it provides a quick way to return the worksheet to the original values. If you wish to perform an extensive what-if analysis and not worry about losing your original data, you may wish to save your workbook under a different name as a "practice" file.

DEVELOP YOUR SKILLS 3.3.1

Create Formulas Using Cell References

In this exercise, you will use absolute cell references to create formulas that can be copied to other cells.

Enter a Formula Using Point Mode

1. Select **cell B9** and type **=** to begin a formula.

2. Select **cell D18** and **tap** the F4 function key.

If you have a keyboard that uses the function keys for other purposes, you may have to tap the F Lock key to be able to utilize F4 for absolute or mixed references in Excel.

Tapping F4 will make the D18 cell reference an absolute by adding the $ symbol to both the column and row references. Take a look at the Formula Bar and you will see $D$18. A formula can consist of just one cell reference. In this case, you want the marketing expense always to reflect the value in cell D18.

3. **Tap** Enter to complete the formula.

Calculate the Commissions Using Order of Operations

You will enter a more complex formula to calculate the total commissions for product sales and contract sales. You want Excel to perform calculations in the following order. First, multiply product sales (B4) by their commission rate (B19). Second, multiply contract sales (B5) by their commission rate (B20). Last, add the two products together.

4. Select **cell B10** and type **=** to begin a formula.

5. Select **cell B4** and type *****.

6. Select **cell B19** and **tap** F4.

7. Type **+** to continue the formula.

8. Select **cell B5** and type *****.

9. Select **cell B20** and **tap** F4.

10. Click the **Enter** ✔ button to complete the formula.
    The result should equal 27,824. You have used point mode to create a formula containing both relative and absolute cell references. Notice how the formula appears in the Formula Bar: =B4 * $B$19 + B5 * $B$20. No matter where you copy and paste this formula, the formula always will reference the commission rates in cells B19 and B20.

Calculate the Net Profit Using Parentheses

You will create the formula =B13 * (1 - $D$20) to calculate the net profit. The gross profit in cell B13 will be multiplied by a factor that takes into account a tax on profits. The calculation in parentheses means "100% minus 7.75%," or 92.25%. The gross profit in cell B13 then will be multiplied by 92.25%.

11. Select **cell B14** and type **=** to begin a formula.

12. Select **cell B13** and type ***(1–** to continue the formula.

13. Select **cell D20** and **tap** F4.

14. Type **)** and **tap** Enter to complete the formula.
    The result should be $138,353.

Project a Sales Increase

You will create the formula =$B$4 * (1 + C$3) to project a 2 percent increase over the base product sales. The sales in cell B4 will be multiplied by (100% + 2%), or 102%. Notice that, when the formula is copied across the row later, the absolute reference will always refer to $B$4 as the base sales. The percentage of increase or decrease will change from C$3 to D$3 or E$3, the corresponding percentage over each column.

15. Select **cell C4** and type **=** to begin a formula.

16. Select **cell B4** and **tap** F4.

17. Type ***(1+** to continue the formula.

18. Select **cell C3** and **tap** F4 two times to create the C$3 mixed cell reference.

19. Type **)** and **tap** Enter to complete the formula.
    The result should equal 54,264.

20. Select **cell C5**.

21. Repeat the above procedure to project a **2 percent increase** for base contract sales.
    The result should equal 245,820.

22. **Save** 💾 the changes.

23. Compare your worksheet formulas and their results with the following illustrations.

	A	B	C	D	E
1		**Sales Department**			
2		*Projected Net Profit*			
3		*Base*	*2%*	*5%*	*-5%*
4	Product Sales	$ 53,200	$ 54,264		
5	Contracts	$ 241,000	$ 245,820		
6	Total Revenue	$ 294,200	$ 300,084	$ -	$ -
7					
8	Fixed Operating Cost	$ 101,400			
9	Marketing Expense	$ 15,000			
10	Commissions	$ 27,824			
11	Total Costs	$ 144,224			
12					
13	Gross Profit	$ 149,976			
14	Net Profit	$ 138,353			
15	Gross Profit vs. Revenue	$ 1			
16					
17	Contracts	$ 482			
18	Average Contract	$ 500	Marketing	$ 15,000	
19	Product Commission Rate	7%	Fixed Cost	$ 101,400	
20	Contract Commission Rate	10%	Tax Rate	7.75%	

	A	B	C	D	E
1		**Sales Department**			
2		*Projected Net Profit*			
3		*Base*	*0.02*	*0.05*	*-0.05*
4	Product Sales	53200	=$B$4*(1+C$3)		
5	Contracts	241000	=B5*(1+C$3)		
6	Total Revenue	=SUM(B4:B5)	=SUM(C4:C5)	=SUM(D4:D5)	=SUM(E4:E5)
7					
8	Fixed Operating Cost	=D19			
9	Marketing Expense	=$D$18			
10	Commissions	=B4*$B$19+B5*$B$20			
11	Total Costs	=SUM(B8:B10)			
12					
13	Gross Profit	=B6-B11			
14	Net Profit	=B13*(1-$D$20)			
15	Gross Profit vs. Revenue	=B13/B6			

Video Lesson   labyrinthelab.com/videos

You can modify and copy formulas in much the same way that you edit and copy cells.

Modifying Formulas

You can edit a formula either in the Formula Bar or by double-clicking the formula cell to complete an in-cell edit. If you select a cell and enter a new formula, it replaces the previous contents of the cell.

When you select a formula to edit it, you will see colored lines around all of the cells that are referenced by the formula. This feature can help you to visually determine whether the formula is correct.

	SUM	▼ X ✓ *fx*	=B13*(1-$D$20)	
	A	B	C	D
13	Gross Profit	$ 149,976		
14	Net Profit	=B13*(1-$D$20)		
15	Gross Profit vs. Revenue	51.0%		
16				
17	Contracts	$ 482		
18	Average Contract	$ 500	Marketing	$ 15,000
19	Product Commission Rate	7%	Fixed Cost	$ 101,400
20	Contract Commission Rate	10%	Tax Rate	7.75%

The formula in B14 is selected for editing (as indicated by the insertion point in the cell). Excel graphically displays the cells that are being referenced by the formula, B13 and D20.

Circular References

You may inadvertently use a circular reference when creating or editing a formula. A circular reference occurs when the formula refers to its own cell or to another formula that refers to that cell. For example, a formula in cell C6 is =B6*C6. Excel cannot complete the calculation because cell C6 is the formula cell, not a reference to a value. When Excel displays a Circular Reference Warning message, you may either click OK to read the circular reference help topic or click Cancel to close the warning. Either option allows the circular reference to remain in the formula until you correct the formula.

You must correct the formula manually after you close Help or the Circular Reference Warning message.

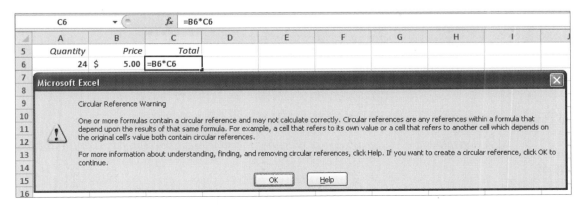

Copying Formulas

You can use either the Copy and Paste commands with formulas or AutoFill in order to copy them to new cells. You can copy formulas to one cell at a time or to a range of cells using either method.

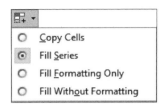

If you use Auto Fill, the Auto Fill Options button will appear once you have released the mouse button. Clicking this button will allow you to customize your fill. The Fill Series option displays in the list if you AutoFill a value but does not display for a formula.

You can change what was copied in the cells through AutoFill by clicking the Auto Fill Options button and choosing a different option.

DEVELOP YOUR SKILLS 3.4.1

Modify and Copy Formulas

In this exercise, you will use techniques to modify and copy formulas in order to complete your profit projection.

Modify Formulas and Correct a Circular Reference

1. Select **cell B8**, and then follow these steps to edit the formula in the Formula Bar:

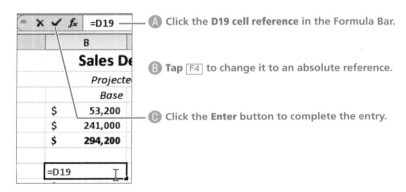

(A) Click the **D19 cell reference** in the Formula Bar.

(B) Tap F4 to change it to an absolute reference.

(C) Click the **Enter** button to complete the entry.

2. **Double-click** cell C6 to begin an in-cell edit.
Notice that the cell references are displayed in color in the formula and on the worksheet.

3. Follow these steps to complete an in-cell edit:

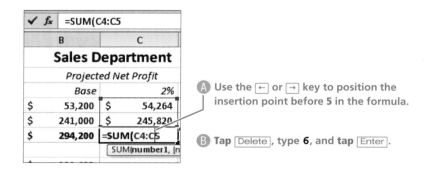

(A) Use the ← or → key to position the insertion point before **5** in the formula.

(B) Tap Delete, type **6**, and tap Enter.

Excel displays a Circular Reference Warning message because you referred to C6, the formula cell itself.

4. Choose **OK** in the Circular Reference Warning message.

5. **Undo** ↰ the change.

Use Copy and Paste Commands to Copy a Formula

6. Select **cell B14** and then use ⌨Ctrl+⌨C to **copy** the formula.

7. Select **cell C14** and then use ⌨Ctrl+⌨V to **paste** the formula in the new cell.
This method works great if you need to copy a formula to just one cell. You can use these commands to copy a formula to a range of cells as well.

8. Select the **range D14:E14** and then use ⌨Ctrl+⌨V.
The formula that you copied in step 6 is now pasted to the range of cells selected.

9. **Tap** ⌨Esc to cancel the marquee around cell B14.

10. Select **cell D14** and look at the formula in the Formula Bar.

D14	▾	*fx*	=D13*(1-$D$20)	
◢	A	B	C	D
13	Gross Profit	$ 149,976		
14	Net Profit	$ 138,353	$ -	$ ⊹ -

Notice that the relative cell reference now indicates cell D13, whereas the absolute cell reference is still looking to cell D20.

Use AutoFill to Copy Formulas

11. Follow these steps to copy the formula from cell C4 to the range D4:E4.

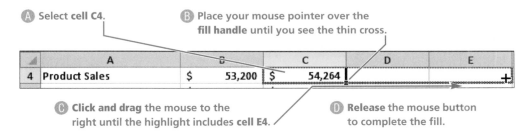

Ⓐ Select **cell C4**.   Ⓑ Place your mouse pointer over the **fill handle** until you see the thin cross.

◢	A	B	C	D	E
4	Product Sales	$ 53,200	$ 54,264		⊞

Ⓒ **Click and drag** the mouse to the right until the highlight includes **cell E4**.   Ⓓ **Release** the mouse button to complete the fill.

12. Use **AutoFill** to copy the formula from **cell C5** to the **range D5:E5**.
Next, you will use AutoFill to copy formulas from B8:B15 all the way through C8:E15.

13. Select the **range B8:B15**.

14. Place your mouse pointer over the **fill handle** at the bottom right of the selected range.

15. When you see the thin cross ✚, **drag** to the **right** until the highlight includes the cells in **column E** and then release the mouse.

⬓	A	B	C	D	E
8	Fixed Operating Cost	$ 101,400	$ 101,400	$ 101,400	$ 101,400
9	Marketing Expense	$ 15,000	$ 15,000	$ 15,000	$ 15,000
10	Commissions	$ 27,824	$ 28,380	$ 29,215	$ 26,433
11	**Total Costs**	$ 144,224	$ 144,780	$ 145,615	$ 142,833
12					
13	Gross Profit	$ 149,976	$ 155,304	$ 163,295	$ 136,657
14	Net Profit	$ 138,353	$ 143,267	$ 150,639	$ 126,066
15	Gross Profit vs. Revenue	51.0%	51.8%	52.9%	48.9%
16					

16. **Deselect** the filled range.
Make it a habit to deselect highlighted cells after performing an action. This step will help avoid unintended changes to cell contents.

17. **Save** 💾 the changes and leave the workbook **open**.

3.5 Displaying and Printing Formulas

Video Lesson   labyrinthelab.com/videos

FROM THE KEYBOARD

Ctrl+` to show formulas

Excel normally displays the results of formulas in worksheet cells. However, you may need to display the actual formulas from time to time. Displaying formulas, especially in complex financial worksheets, can help you understand how a worksheet functions, enabling you to "debug" the worksheet and locate potential problems.

To display formulas, you will use the Show Formulas command on the Formulas tab of the Ribbon. You can edit a formula in this view, but you will need to show values again to see the result. To view the values once again, choose Show Formulas again.

While formulas are displayed, Excel automatically widens columns to show more of the cell contents. You can print the formula display as you would any other worksheet. You may wish to switch to landscape orientation, which prints the worksheet across the wide edge of the paper.

Depending on your monitor size, the buttons may appear as only icons, without the text descriptors, or as large buttons.

B	C	D
Sales Department		
Projected Net Profit		
Base	0.02	0.05
53200	=$B$4*(1+C$3)	=$B$4*(1+D$3)
=B17*B18	=$B$5*(1+C$3)	=$B$5*(1+D$3)
=SUM(B4:B5)	=SUM(C4:C5)	=SUM(D4:D5)
=$D$19	=$D$19	=$D$19
15000	15000	15000
=B4*$B$19+B5*$B$20	=C4*$B$19+C5*$B$20	=D4*$B$19+D5*$B$20
=SUM(B8:B10)	=SUM(C8:C10)	=SUM(D8:D10)
=B6-B11	=C6-C11	=D6-D11
=B13*(1-$D$20)	=C13*(1-$D$20)	=D13*(1-$D$20)
=B13/B6	=C13/C6	=D13/D6

When you choose to show formulas, you will see the formulas in the cells rather than the values as before. If a cell does not contain a formula, the contents will be visible in this view.

QUICK REFERENCE   VIEWING AND PRINTING FORMULAS

Task	Procedure
Display or hide the formulas in a workbook	■ Choose Formulas→Formula Auditing→Show Formulas from the Ribbon.
Change paper orientation to print across the wide edge	■ Choose Page Layout→Page Setup→Orientation→Landscape from the Ribbon.
Print displayed formulas	■ Choose File→Print.
	■ Choose any desired options in the Print tab and click Print.

DEVELOP YOUR SKILLS 3.5.1
Display Formulas in a Worksheet

In this exercise, you will display the formulas in the profit projection worksheet to see how it is constructed and to be able to troubleshoot any potentially inaccurate formulas.

1. Choose **Formulas→Formula Auditing→Show Formulas** from the Ribbon.
   Take a look at the worksheet. You can use this feature to examine your formulas more closely.

2. Choose **Formulas→Formula Auditing→Show Formulas** from the Ribbon.
   The values will be displayed once again.

3.6 Using Formula AutoComplete

Video Lesson   labyrinthelab.com/videos

Excel includes a feature that assists you in creating and editing formulas. Formula AutoComplete will jump into action once you have typed an equals (=) sign and the beginning letters of a function in a cell. It works by displaying a list of functions beginning with the typed letters below the active cell.

Functions Defined

A function is a predefined formula that performs calculations or returns a desired result. Excel has more than 400 built-in functions. You construct functions using a set of basic rules known as syntax. Fortunately, most functions use the same or similar syntax. This syntax also applies to the MIN, MAX, AVERAGE, COUNT, and COUNTA functions.

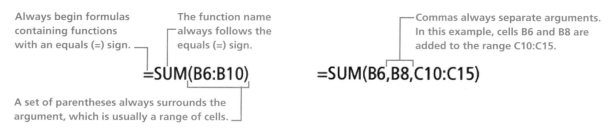

Always begin formulas containing functions with an equals (=) sign.

The function name always follows the equals (=) sign.

Commas always separate arguments. In this example, cells B6 and B8 are added to the range C10:C15.

=SUM(B6:B10)   =SUM(B6,B8,C10:C15)

A set of parentheses always surrounds the argument, which is usually a range of cells.

QUICK REFERENCE	USING FORMULA AUTOCOMPLETE TO ENTER A FORMULA INTO A CELL
Task	**Procedure**
Use Formula AutoComplete	▪ Type an equals (=) sign and begin typing the desired formula.
	▪ Double-click the formula once you see it in the list.
	▪ Select the range to which you wish to apply the formula.
	▪ Type a closed parenthesis,), to finish the formula.
	▪ Complete the entry.

DEVELOP YOUR SKILLS 3.6.1
Use Formula AutoComplete

In this exercise, you will have an opportunity to use the Formula AutoComplete feature to create a formula.

1. Display the **Qtr 1 Commissions** worksheet by clicking the sheet tab.

2. Select **cell C11**.

3. Type **=ave** and observe the list that results.

=AVE							
ƒ AVEDEV							
ƒ AVERAGE	Returns the average (arithmetic mean) of its arguments, which can be numbers or names, arrays, or references that contain numbers						
ƒ AVERAGEA							
ƒ AVERAGEIF							
ƒ AVERAGEIFS							

When you use Formula AutoComplete, Excel will show you a list of functions that begin with the letters you type in. If you click on a function in the list, a ScreenTip will describe the function.

4. **Double-click** AVERAGE in the list.
Excel will fill in the function name for you. It will be up to you to select the range next.

5. Drag to select **cells C5:C8** as the range for the formula.

You do not include total rows or columns when completing most functions.

6. **Tap** ⌷Enter⌷ to complete the function.
Notice that Excel added the parenthesis at the end of the formula for you. The result should be 314.5.

7. Select **cell C11** and use the fill handle to **copy** the function to the **range D11:E11**.

	A	B	C	D	E
11	Average	264.75	314.5	360	939.25
12	Maximum	389			

You now have the average commission for each month and the entire quarter.

8. **Save** 💾 the changes and leave the workbook **open**.

3.7 Using Insert Function

Video Lesson labyrinthelab.com/videos

The Insert Function f_x button displays the Insert Function dialog box. This dialog box provides access to all of Excel's built-in functions. It allows you to locate a function by typing a description or searching by category. When you locate the desired function and click OK, Excel displays the Function Arguments box. The Function Arguments box helps you enter arguments in functions. The Insert Function box and the Function Arguments box are shown in the following illustrations.

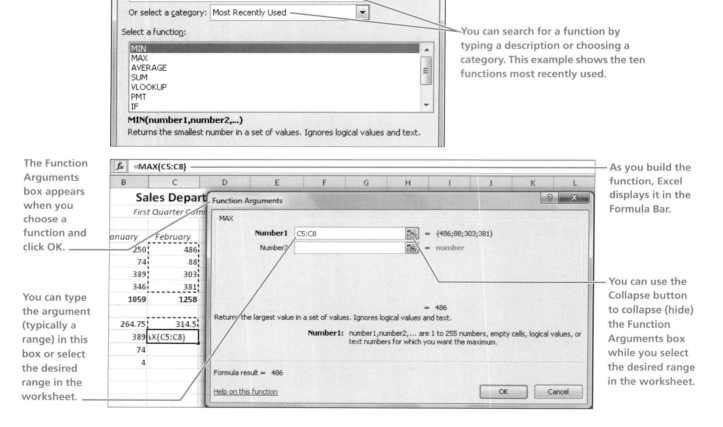

You can search for a function by typing a description or choosing a category. This example shows the ten functions most recently used.

The Function Arguments box appears when you choose a function and click OK.

You can type the argument (typically a range) in this box or select the desired range in the worksheet.

As you build the function, Excel displays it in the Formula Bar.

You can use the Collapse button to collapse (hide) the Function Arguments box while you select the desired range in the worksheet.

The Function Arguments dialog box can be moved by dragging its title bar to view the desired range on the worksheet.

Task	Procedure
Create a function using the Insert Function command	■ Select the cell(s) in which you wish to enter a function. ■ Click the Insert Function f_x button on the Formula Bar. ■ Choose the desired function and click OK. ■ Select the range to which you wish to apply the function. ■ Click OK.

DEVELOP YOUR SKILLS 3.7.1

Use Insert Function

In this exercise, you will complete the commissions worksheet by using the Insert Function command to create both the maximum and minimum functions.

1. Select **cell C12**.

2. Follow these steps to create the Maximum function:

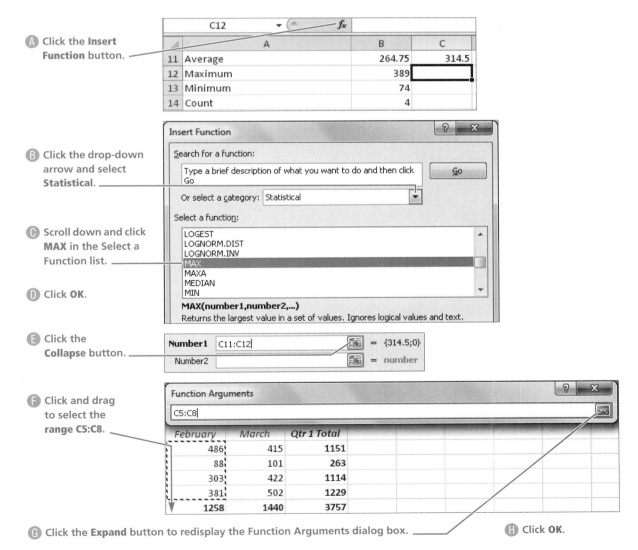

A Click the **Insert Function** button.

B Click the drop-down arrow and select **Statistical**.

C Scroll down and click **MAX** in the Select a Function list.

D Click **OK**.

E Click the **Collapse** button.

F Click and drag to select the range **C5:C8**.

G Click the **Expand** button to redisplay the Function Arguments dialog box.

H Click **OK**.

3. Using the procedure from **step 2**, create the **Minimum** function in **cell C13**.

4. Create the **Count** function in **cell C14**.

5. Select the **range C12:C14** and **copy** the formulas to the **range D12:E14**.

⊿	A	B	C	D	E
11	Average	264.75	314.5	360	939.25
12	Maximum	389	486	502	1377
13	Minimum	74	88	101	263
14	Count	4	4	4	12

6. **Save** 🖫 the changes and leave the workbook **open**.

3.8 Creating Formulas with the IF Function

Video Lesson   labyrinthelab.com/videos

Excel's IF function displays a value or message based on a logical test you design. Depending on the result of the logical test, the IF function displays whatever you choose for a true or false result. For example, you may check to see whether the purchase amount is greater than $200. If true, a discount is calculated; if false, the text *No discount* is displayed.

IF Function Syntax

NOTE

If you type the IF formula directly in its cell, you must add quotation (") marks around text arguments. If you use the Insert Function command, Excel will add the quotation marks for you.

The generic parts of the IF function are shown in the following table.

Function	Syntax	
IF	IF(logical_test, value_if_true, value_if_false)	

The following table outlines the arguments of the IF function.

Argument	Description
logical_test	The condition being checked using a comparison operator, such as =, >, <, >=, <=, or <> (not equal to)
value_if_true	The value, text in quotation (") marks, or calculation returned if the logical test result is found to be true
value_if_false	The value, text in quotation (") marks, or calculation returned if the logical test result is found to be false

How the IF Function Works

The formula =IF(C6>=200,C6*D6,0) is used as an example to explain the function result. Excel performs the logical test to determine whether the value in C6 is greater than or equal to 200. A value of 200 or more would evaluate as true. Any of the following would evaluate as false: the value 50, a blank cell, or text entered in cell C6. If the logical test proves true, the calculation C6*D6 is performed and the result displays in the formula cell. If the calculation proves false, the value 0 (zero) displays instead.

You may specify various actions to be performed for the value_if_true and value_if_false arguments. You may display a text message or leave the cell blank. You may create complex calculations and even use other functions in arguments within an IF function, called nesting. Two examples that display text are shown in the following table.

Formula	Action If True	Action If False
IF(F3>150000, "Over Budget", "Within Budget")	The text *Over Budget* displays	The text *Within Budget* displays
IF(D6<=30,"","Late")	The cell displays blank	The text *Late* displays

If you type "" (quotation marks without a space between) as the value_if_true or value_if_false argument, Excel leaves the cell blank.

Use the IF Function

In this exercise, you will use the IF function to display a text message when a salesperson achieves at least $30,000 in quarterly sales.

Create an IF Formula to Display a Message

1. Click the **Qtr 1 Commissions** sheet tab at the bottom of the Excel window if the sheet is not already displayed.

2. **Enter** the column heading **Sales** in cell F4 and **Met Goal?** in cell G4.

3. Enter values in the **range F5:F8** as shown at right.

4. Enter **Goal** in **cell A15** and **30000** in **cell F15**.
   You will create a formula that compares the value in the Sales cell with the goal of $30,000. If sales are equal or greater, the message Yes *displays. Otherwise, the cell displays* No.

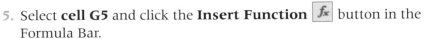

	F	G
4	Sales	Met Goal?
5	28775	
6	6575	
7	27850	
8	30725	

5. Select **cell G5** and click the **Insert Function** f_x button in the Formula Bar.

6. Follow these steps to find the IF function:

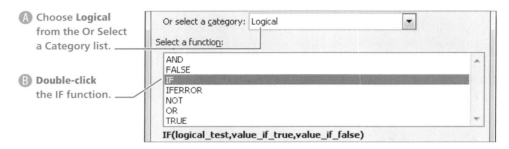

Ⓐ Choose **Logical** from the Or Select a Category list.

Ⓑ **Double-click** the IF function.

The Function Arguments dialog box appears for the IF function.

7. If necessary, move the Function Arguments dialog box out of the way by **dragging** its title bar until you can see column G.

8. Follow these steps to specify the IF function arguments:

Ⓐ Select **cell F5** in the worksheet, use ⎡Shift⎤+⎡>⎤ to type >, and then type = (greater than or equal to).

Ⓑ Select **cell F15** (the $30,000 goal amount) and **tap** ⎡F4⎤ to convert the cell to an absolute cell reference. (The reference must be absolute because the copied formula always should refer to this cell.)

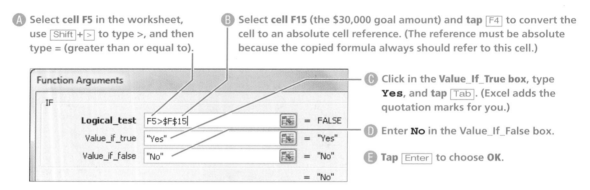

Ⓒ Click in the **Value_If_True box**, type **Yes**, and tap ⎡Tab⎤. (Excel adds the quotation marks for you.)

Ⓓ Enter **No** in the Value_If_False box.

Ⓔ Tap ⎡Enter⎤ to choose OK.

9. Review the completed formula in the Formula Bar.
   The formula is =IF(F5>=$F$15,"Yes","No"). The message No appears in cell G5 because Talos Bouras' sales are not at least $30,000, the value in cell F15. The value_if_false argument applies.

10. Use **AutoFill** to copy the formula in **cell G5** down to the **range G6:G8**.
    The cell for Amy Wyatt displays Yes as specified by your value_if_true argument. The cells for all other salespeople display No.

Edit the IF Function

Now you will edit the value_if_false argument to "" to display no message.

11. Select **cell G5**.

12. In the Formula Bar, **click** between the quotation (") mark and the N, and **tap** ⎡Delete⎤ twice to delete *No*.

13. Click **Enter** ☑ in the Formula Bar to complete the formula.
    Now cell G5 does not display any message because the value_if_false argument contains no text.

14. Use **AutoFill** to copy the formula in **cell G5** down to the **range G6:G8**.

Notice that the cells that previously displayed No in column G now display no message, as shown in the illustration below. The salespeople who met goal are easier to identify.

	A	B	C	D	E	F	G
4	Sales Team Member	January	February	March	Qtr 1 Total	Sales	Met Goal?
5	Talos Bouras	250	486	415	1151	28775	
6	Leisa Malimali	74	88	101	263	6575	
7	Brian Simpson	389	303	422	1114	27850	
8	Amy Wyatt	346	381	502	1229	30725	Yes
9	Monthly Total	1059	1258	1440	3757		
10							
11	Average	264.75	314.5	360	939.25		
12	Maximum	389	486	502	1377		
13	Minimum	74	88	101	263		
14	Count	4	4	4	12		
15	Goal					30000	

15. **Save** 💾 the changes and **close** the workbook.

3.9 Concepts Review

Concepts Review   labyrinthelab.com/excel10

To check your knowledge of the key concepts introduced in this lesson, complete the Concepts Review quiz by going to the URL listed above. If your classroom is using Labyrinth eLab, you may complete the Concepts Review quiz from within your eLab course.

Reinforce Your Skills

Use the AutoSum Function

In this exercise, you will use AutoSum to compute totals.

1. **Open** the rs-Benefit Plan workbook from the Lesson 03 folder in your file storage location.

2. Select **cell C10**, and then choose **Home→Editing→Sum** Σ from the Ribbon.
   Notice that Excel proposes the formula =SUM(C8:C9). Excel proposes this incorrect formula because there are empty cells in the range you are to sum.

3. **Drag** the mouse pointer over the **range C5:C9**.
   The flashing marquee will surround the range C5:C9.

4. **Complete** the entry.
   The total should equal 650.

5. Use the techniques described in the preceding steps to compute the **totals** in **cells E10, G10,** and **I10**.

6. **Save** the changes to your workbook and **close** it.

Amount	Con
100	
350	
200	
=SUM(C5:C9)	

Create Simple Formulas

In this exercise, you will create formulas using the keyboard as well as the point-and-click method.

1. **Open** the rs-Orders and Returns workbook from the Lesson 03 folder in your file storage location.

2. Select **cell B18**.

3. Type **=**.

4. Select **cell B4** and and type **+**.

5. Select **cell B9** and type **+**.

6. Select **cell B14** and **tap** Enter.

7. Use **AutoFill** to copy the formula to **cells C18** and **D18**.

8. Using the techniques described in the preceding steps, create a formula in **cell B19** that **totals** the exchanges from all three sales categories.

9. Create another formula in **cell B20** that **totals** the returns from all three sales categories.

10. Use **AutoFill** to copy the formulas into the appropriate cells.

11. Take a few minutes to examine the formulas in the Formula Bar.

12. **Save** the changes and **close** the workbook.

Use Formula AutoComplete, AutoFill, and Display Formulas

In this exercise, you will calculate averages by using the Formula AutoComplete feature. You will also display formulas and preview them in Page Layout View. You will explore the Landscape and Portrait print settings.

Use AutoComplete

1. **Open** the rs-Service Contracts workbook from the Lesson 03 folder in your file storage location.

2. Select **cell A10** and **edit** the label to read **Green Clean Service Contracts - Prior Year**.

3. Select **cell B2** and use **AutoFill** to copy the series Qtr 2, Qtr 3, and Qtr 4 into the **range C2:E2**.

4. Select **cell B8**.

5. Begin **typing** the formula **=aver**, and then **tap** Tab to choose **AVERAGE** as the function.

6. Drag to select **B3:B6**, and then **tap** Enter.
   The result should equal 33.

7. Use the **fill handle** to copy the formula across **row 8**.

8. Select **cell B17**.

9. Use **Formula AutoComplete** to average the **range B12:B15**.
   The result should equal 23.5. Remember that, you can type the function name and arguments in lowercase and Excel will convert them to uppercase.

10. Use the **fill handle** to copy the formula across **row 17**.

11. Select **cell B20**.

12. Use **point mode** to enter the formula =B7-B16, and **complete** the entry.
    The result should equal 38.

13. Use the **fill handle** to copy the formula across **row 20**.

Display Formulas and Preview in Page Layout View

14. Use Ctrl + ` to display the worksheet formulas.
    The grave accent ` *key is above the* Tab *key.*

15. Choose **View→Workbook Views→Page Layout** 🗋 from the Ribbon.

16. Take a few minutes to look at the way the data and formulas display.
    Notice that Excel widened the columns so that most of the cell contents display. In this view, the worksheet fits on two pages.

17. Choose **Page Layout→Page Setup→Orientation→Landscape** from the Ribbon.
    Landscape orientation prints across the wide edge of the paper, which is useful for printing the formula view. Now the formulas fit on one page.

18. Choose **Page Layout→Page Setup→Orientation→Portrait** from the Ribbon.
    Portrait orientation prints across the narrow edge of the paper, which is acceptable for printing this worksheet while formulas are hidden.

19. Click the **Normal View** button in the view toolbar at the bottom-right corner of the window.

20. Use ⎡Ctrl⎤+⎡ ⎤ to **hide** the formulas.

21. **Save** 🖫 the changes and **close** the workbook.

Use Absolute References and Perform a What-If Analysis

In this exercise, you will create a worksheet that calculates commissions as total sales multiplied by the commission rate. You will change the commission rate to see the impact this change has on the total sales. You will use an absolute reference when referencing the commission rate.

1. Start a **new** workbook, and set up the worksheet shown to the right. **Type** all numbers as shown.

	A	B	C
1	January Commission Report		
2			
3	Commission Rate		5%
4			
5		Sales	Commission
6	Bouras	44000	
7	Malimali	17000	
8	Simpson	41000	
9	Wyatt	36000	

2. Select **cell C6**, and **enter** the formula **=B6*$C$3** in the cell.
   The result should be 2200. Cell C3 needs an absolute reference because you will copy the formula down the column and because the new formulas must also reference C3.

3. Use the **fill handle** to copy the formula down the column to **cells C7 through C9**.

4. Select **cell C3**, and change the percentage to **3%**.
   By this time, you should see the benefit of setting up values first (such as the commission rate) and referencing them in formulas. This step allows you to perform what-if analyses. In most cases, you will need absolute references when referencing variables in this manner. Absolute references are necessary whenever you copy a formula that references a variable in a fixed location.

	A	B	C
1	January Commission Report		
2			
3	Commission Rate		3%
4			
5		Sales	Commission
6	Bouras	44000	1320
7	Malimali	17000	510
8	Simpson	41000	1230
9	Wyatt	36000	1080

5. **Save** 🖫 as **rs-January Commissions** in the Lesson 03 folder and continue with the next exercise.

Use COUNT and COUNTA Functions

In this exercise, you will create formulas using the COUNT and COUNTA functions.

Before You Begin: You must have completed Reinforce Your Skills 3.4 and the rs-January Commissions workbook should be open.

1. Type **Count** in **cell A11**.

2. Type **CountA** in **cell A12**.

3. Select **cell B11** and begin **typing** the formula **=cou**.

4. Read the description of the COUNT function in the list that appears.
   The COUNT function counts the cells containing numbers in the specified range.

5. **Tap** Tab to select **COUNT** in the list.

6. Drag to select **B5:B9** and **tap** Enter.
   The result should equal 4. The label in cell B5 is ignored.

7. Select **cell B12** and repeat the above procedure, this time selecting the **COUNTA** function.
   The result should equal 5, including the label in cell B5. The COUNTA function counts all nonblank cells in the specified range.

8. Select **cell B7** and **delete** the contents.
   The result is one less for both the COUNT and COUNTA formulas. Any blank cells are ignored.

9. Leaving **cell B7** as blank, **save** 💾 the changes, and **close** the workbook.

◢	A	B	C
1	January Commission Report		
2			
3	Commission Rate		3%
4			
5		Sales	Commission
6	Bouras	44000	1320
7	Malimali		0
8	Simpson	41000	1230
9	Wyatt	36000	1080
10			
11	Count	3	
12	CountA	4	

Use the IF Function

In this exercise, you will use the IF function to display a message if a project is going over budget as compared to the budget objective.

Add Budget Data to the Worksheet

1. **Open** the rs-Website Budget workbook from the Lesson 03 folder.

2. Enter **Budget Objective** in **cell A7** and **20000** in **cell B7**.

Create an IF Function

3. Select **cell C6** and click the **Insert Function** button in the Formula Bar.

4. Select the **IF** function from the Most Recently Used or Logical category and click **OK**. *The Function Arguments dialog box displays.*

5. For the Logical Test entry, select **cell B7** in the worksheet, and use Shift + > for the greater-than symbol.

6. Select **cell B6** and **tap** Tab to complete the entry.

7. Type **Within Budget** in the Value If True box and **tap** Tab.

8. Type **Exceeds Budget** in the Value If False box and **tap** Enter. *The result displays as* Within Budget.

9. **Change** the value in cell B7 from $20,000 to 15000. *Now the IF function result displays* Exceeds Budget.

10. **Save** the changes and **close** the workbook.

Apply Your Skills

APPLY YOUR SKILLS 3.1
Create Simple Formulas

In this exercise, you will develop a worksheet with simple formulas.

1. **Open** the as-Credit Lines workbook from the Lesson 03 folder in your file storage location.

2. Follow these guidelines to create the following worksheet:

   ■ **Enter** all remaining text and number entries.

   ■ Use **formulas** in **columns D** and **F** to calculate subtotals and new balances. Calculate each **subtotal** as the previous balance plus new charges. Calculate each **new balance** as the subtotal minus the payment amount.

   ■ Use **AutoSum** to calculate totals for the **range B10:F10**.

	A	B	C	D	E	F
1	Green Clean - Credit Lines					
2						
3	Customer	Previous Balance	New Charges	Subtotal	Payment Amount	New Balance
4	Abel Printing Inc.	104	50		154	
5	Charley's Restaurant	230	85		315	
6	Hightower Electric	58	116		0	
7	Mendez Foods	423	320		423	
8	Ota Beverage Supply	140	65		0	
9	Sara Yang, CPA	97	43		100	
10	Total Credit					

3. Issue the command to display the **formulas**.
   Notice that the column widths are automatically increased to accommodate the width of the formulas. This will cause the worksheet to print on two pages.

4. Display **Page Layout** view to preview how formulas will print; **print** the formulas.

5. **Hide** the formulas and then display **Normal view**.

6. **Save** 🖫 the changes and **close** the workbook.

Use AutoSum, MIN, and MAX

In this exercise, you will create a new worksheet that includes text and numbers. You will enter formulas and functions. Finally, you will save, print, and close the workbook.

1. Follow these guidelines to create the worksheet shown:

   - **Enter** the text and numbers as shown in the following illustration.

   - Use the **generic formulas** shown below to calculate the interest charge in column E and the new balance in column F. Use **parentheses** in the Interest Charge formula to change the order of the calculation. You want Excel to subtract the payments from the beginning balance and then multiply the result by 1.5%. **Don't type** the words *Beginning Balance, Charges*, etc., in the formulas; use the appropriate cell references. Use **Auto-Fill** to extend the formulas from **row 4 through row 9**.

   Interest Charge = 1.5% * (Beginning Balance – Payments)

   New Balance = Beginning Balance + Charges – Payments + Interest Charge

   - Use **AutoSum** to calculate the totals in **row 10**.

   - Use the **MAX** and **MIN** functions to calculate the highest and lowest numbers in **rows 11** and **12**.

	A	B	C	D	E	F
1	Green Clean - Accounts Receivable					
2						
3	Customer	Beg. Bal.	Charges	Payments	Interest	New Balance
4	R202	2000	2300	1000		
5	R314	2450	100	2450		
6	R572	5400	2190	3000		
7	W016	3450	500	1450		
8	W215	100	3400	100		
9	W264	1600	600	0		
10	Totals					
11	Highest					
12	Lowest					

2. Display the formulas in **Page Layout** view.

3. Change to **Landscape** orientation; **print** the formulas.
   The formulas will print on one page.

4. **Hide** the formulas and then display **Normal view**.

5. **Save** 🖫 with the name **as-Accounts Receivable** in the Lesson 03 folder and **close** the workbook.

Use Absolute References

In this exercise, you will create formulas using absolute references.

1. **Open** the as-Jan Price Change workbook from the Lesson 03 folder.

2. Follow these guidelines to complete the following worksheet:
   - **Enter** the text entries as shown. Enter the numbers in **column B** and the percentage in **cell B3**.
   - Use the **generic formula** shown below to calculate the discounted price in **cell C6**. Use an **absolute reference** when referring to the discount rate in **cell B3**. Remember that you are calculating the discounted price, so your formula must subtract the discount rate in **cell B3** from 1.

     Discounted Price = Original Price * (1 – Discount Rate)

   - **Copy** the formula in **cell C6** down the column.

     Cell C6 was formatted for you so it displays the price with two decimal places.

3. Change the percentage in **cell B3** to **10%**, and watch the worksheet recalculate.

4. Change the percentage in **cell B3** back to **15%**, and watch the worksheet recalculate.

5. **Print** the worksheet.

6. **Display** the formulas; **print** the formulas.
   The formulas will print on one page.

7. **Hide** the formulas and then make certain Normal view is displayed.

8. **Save** 💾 the changes and **close** the workbook.

	A	B	C
1	January Price Changes		
2			
3	January Discount Rate	15%	
4			
5		Original Price	Discounted Price
6	Bamboo Ware Plates	3.65	
7	Biograde Garbage Bags, 25	1.89	
8	Biograde Garbage Bags, 50	3.69	
9	Biograde Garbage Bags, 100	6.89	
10	Green Earth Scrub Pads	2.25	
11	Reusable Cloths, 2 dozen	2.49	
12	Reusable Cloths, 4 dozen	4.69	

Create a Financial Report

In this exercise, you will create a worksheet by entering data, creating formulas, and using absolute references. You will also save, print a section of, and close the workbook.

1. **Open** the as-Projected Net Profit workbook from the Lesson 03 folder.

2. Use these guidelines to create the financial report at right:

   - **Type** the headings, labels, and numbers as shown in the illustration to the right. Use **AutoFill** whenever possible to copy cells or complete a series (for example, with the Q1, Q2, Q3, and Q4 headings).

   - Use a **formula** to calculate the employee costs in **cell B6**. The formula should calculate the revenue in **cell B4** multiplied by the percentage in **cell B15**. Use a **mixed reference** to refer to the revenue in **cell B4** and an **absolute reference** to refer to the cost percentage in **cell B15**.

⊿	A	B	C	D	E
1	Projected Net Profit				
2					
3		Q1	Q2	Q3	Q4
4	Revenue	345000	390000	480000	500000
5					
6	Employee Costs				
7	Capital Expenditures				
8	Manufacturing				
9	Marketing & Sales				
10	Total Costs				
11					
12	Gross Profit				
13	Net Profit				
14					
15	Employee Costs	18%			
16	Capital Expenditures	22%			
17	Manufacturing	17%			
18	Marketing & Sales	16%			
19	Tax Rate	40%			

   Use **formulas** to calculate the other costs in the **range B7:B9**. Each formula should multiply the revenue in **row 4** by the related cost percentage in **rows 16–18**.

   - Use **AutoSum** to calculate the total cost in **cell B10**.

   - Calculate the **gross profit** in **cell B12** as **Revenue – Total Costs**.

   - Calculate the **net profit** in **cell B13** as **Gross Profit * (1 – Tax Rate)**. Once again, use an **absolute reference** when referring to the tax rate in **cell B19**.

   - Copy the cost and profit formulas from Q1 across the rows to Q2, Q3, and Q4. You must use the correct cell references in formulas to get the correct results for this exercise.

3. Perform a **what-if analysis** on your worksheet by changing the employee costs percentage in **row 15** to **25%**. Make certain that the report recalculates correctly when the value is changed.

4. Display the formulas in **Page Layout** view.

5. Change to **Landscape** orientation; **print** the formulas.
   The formulas will print on one page.

6. **Hide** the formulas and then display **Normal view**.

7. Select the **range A3:E13** and **print** just that area.

8. **Save** 🖫 the changes and **close** the workbook.

Use the SUM, AVERAGE, and IF Functions

In this exercise, you will create an IF function to indicate whether a department met the safety goal each month. You will create formulas to total the safety incidents in a six-month period and calculate the average number of incidents per month.

1. **Open** the as-Safety Goal workbook from the Lesson 03 folder.

2. Enter **January** in **cell A6**; **AutoFill** down **column A** to display the months January through June.

3. Enter the data in the **range B5:B11** and **cells C5**, **A12**, and **A14**, referring to the illustration at the end of this exercise.

4. **Sum** the total safety incidents for January through June in **cell B12**.

5. Use the **IF** function to create a formula in **cell C6** that indicates whether the department met its goal of no safety incidents during the month. Display **Met Goal** if the incidents are equal to zero (0). Display **Not Met** if the incidents are more than 0.

6. **Copy** the formula down the column for the months **February through June**.

7. Use the **AVERAGE** function to create a formula in **cell B14** that finds the average number of safety incidents per month during January through June.

8. **Display** and **print** the worksheet formulas.

9. **Save** 💾 the changes and **close** the workbook.

◢	A	B	C
1	Green Clean		
2	Safety Scores		
3	Operations Department		
4	January-June		
5		Incidents	Goal Met?
6	January	0	Met Goal
7	February	3	Not Met
8	March	1	Not Met
9	April	2	Not Met
10	May	0	Met Goal
11	June	0	Met Goal
12	Total	6	
13			
14	Average Incidents	1	

Critical Thinking & Work-Readiness Skills

In the course of working through the following Microsoft Office-based Critical Thinking exercises, you will also be utilizing various work-readiness skills, some of which are listed next to each exercise. Go to labyrinthelab.com/workreadiness to learn more about the work-readiness skills.

3.1 Calculate Totals

WORK-READINESS SKILLS APPLIED

- Reasoning
- Evaluating information
- Using computers to process information

Sales manager Talos Bouras needs to analyze his customer base so he knows where his best chances for new sales contacts will be. Open ct-Customer Base (Lesson 03 folder). Calculate the number of projects and total billings for each company type listed in column A. Save your changes as **ct-Customer Base Totals** in the Lesson 03 folder. Which company type has the largest billings? Which customer type has the largest billing per company? If working in a group, discuss these questions. If working alone, type your answers in a Word document named **ct-Questions** saved to your Lesson 03 folder.

3.2 Create Formulas to Calculate Averages

WORK-READINESS SKILLS APPLIED

- Reasoning
- Using arithmetic/mathematics
- Thinking creatively

Talos Bouras also wants to know the average number of projects and average billings per company type. He is thinking of adding a new type of customer—health care—to his base, but first he wants to be sure that the new customer type will perform at least as well as his current average customer type. Open ct-Customer Base Totals, if necessary, and calculate these averages. Do not be concerned about formatting the formula results. Save the file in your Lesson 03 folder as **ct-Customer Base Averages**. If Talos wants the average of total billings per customer to rise over time, what categories of customers should he pursue and which should he deemphasize? Why would knowing his average number of projects and billings help him make decisions in the future? If working in a group, discuss these questions. If working alone, type your answers in a Word document named **ct-Questions2** saved to your Lesson 03 folder.

3.3 Use Absolute Cell References

WORK-READINESS SKILLS APPLIED

- Reasoning
- Thinking creatively
- Using arithmetic/mathematics

Green Clean is raising prices across the board by 4.5 percent in the new year. Open ct-Customer Base Averages, if necessary. Use an absolute reference to calculate the new amount of billings for each company if increased by 4.5 percent. (Hint: Calculate total billings plus 4.5 percent of total billings.) In another column, calculate each company type if the billings are increased to 7.5 percent. Save the file as **ct-Customer Base Projections**. What factors go into deciding to raise prices and commit to a 7.5 percent target increase in billings? If working in a group, discuss this question. If working alone, type your answer in a Word document named **ct-Questions3** saved to your Lesson 03 folder.

Formatting the Contents of Cells

In this lesson, you will learn how to use several of Excel's formatting features to enhance your worksheets. You will also learn powerful tools and techniques such as AutoFormat and the Format Painter. Moreover, you will learn to use Excel's Conditional Formatting tool, which may be used to format values that fall within an acceptable range, thus drawing attention to those values. By the end of this lesson, you will have developed the skills necessary to produce professional-looking worksheets.

LESSON OUTLINE

LEARNING OBJECTIVES

After studying this lesson, you will be able to:

- Format worksheets using a variety of methods and apply workbook themes
- Control text to align and fit within cells
- Format cells with borders, fill colors, and cell styles
- Work with date functions and create custom number formats
- Apply conditional formatting to flag positive and negative trends

Student Resources   labyrinthelab.com/excel10

CASE STUDY

Formatting with Excel

Tommy Choi is the president of Green Clean, a janitorial product supplier and cleaning service contractor. The company's accountant drafted an income statement, which Tommy will use to compare revenues and expenses for each quarter of the year. He will use many of Excel's formatting features to make the spreadsheet easier to read and understand. Tommy especially wants the text to align better and the numbers to clearly indicate dollar and percent amounts. He will create a workbook theme so that uniform formatting may be applied to Green Clean's other worksheets.

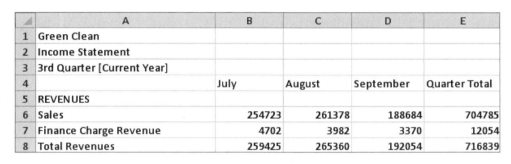

	A	B	C	D	E
1	Green Clean				
2	Income Statement				
3	3rd Quarter [Current Year]				
4		July	August	September	Quarter Total
5	REVENUES				
6	Sales	254723	261378	188684	704785
7	Finance Charge Revenue	4702	3982	3370	12054
8	Total Revenues	259425	265360	192054	716839

	A	B	C	D	E
1			Green Clean		
2			Income Statement		
3			3rd Quarter [Current Year]		
4		July	August	September	Quarter Total
5	REVENUES				
6	Sales	$ 254,723	$ 261,378	$ 188,684	$ 704,785
7	Finance Charge Revenue	4,702	3,982	3,370	12,054
8	Total Revenues	$ 259,425	$ 265,360	192054	$ 716,839

The top figure represents the Revenues portion of the Income Statement before you work your formatting magic. The bottom figure shows how the worksheet will appear at the end of the lesson.

4.1 Formatting Worksheets

Video Lesson labyrinthelab.com/videos

Formatting deals with changing how the data in your worksheet looks, not with changing the data itself. In Excel and other Microsoft Office programs, you can format text by changing the font, font size, and font color. You can also apply various font enhancements, including bold, italic, and underline. To format cells, select the desired cell(s) and apply formats using buttons on the Home tab of the Ribbon, by using the Format Cells dialog box, or by using the Mini toolbar that appears when you right-click a cell or select text.

Formatting Entries with the Ribbon

The Font group on the Home tab of the Ribbon provides you with many popular formatting commands.

The Font group on the Home tab of the Ribbon makes finding formatting options easy.

Using the Mini Toolbar

The Mini toolbar, a feature common to several applications in the Office Suite, will appear when text is selected. It will appear transparent until you move the mouse pointer over it. If you right-click a cell, the Mini toolbar will appear nontransparent, ready to use. The Mini toolbar will allow you to format the selected text without needing the Home tab of the Ribbon to be displayed. This feature can be extremely convenient when you are primarily working with another tab of the Ribbon.

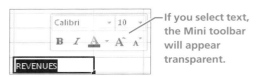 If you select text, the Mini toolbar will appear transparent.

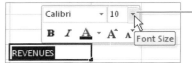 Once the mouse pointer is placed over the Mini toolbar or you right-click a cell, the Mini toolbar will appear "solid."

The Mini toolbar will appear when text is selected, such as when "REVENUES" is selected above.

Live Preview

FROM THE KEYBOARD
Ctrl+B for bold
Ctrl+I for italicize
Ctrl+U for underline

In Office, you can preview how many formatting changes will look before actually issuing the command. Where this feature is available, you will see how the selected area will look when you place your mouse pointer over the formatting option.

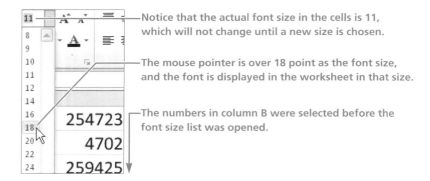

Notice that the actual font size in the cells is 11, which will not change until a new size is chosen.

The mouse pointer is over 18 point as the font size, and the font is displayed in the worksheet in that size.

The numbers in column B were selected before the font size list was opened.

Format Cells with the Ribbon and Mini Toolbar

In this exercise, you will begin to format the worksheet by using both the Ribbon and the Mini toolbar.

Open an Excel File

1. Start **Excel**.

2. **Open** the Income Statement workbook from the Lesson 04 folder in your file storage location.
   You will see a worksheet displayed that contains all of the data and formulas but that is very much in need of some "beautification!" We will begin by changing the font size of the entire worksheet.

Use the Ribbon to Format

In this section, you will first select the entire worksheet. This means that any formatting that is applied will affect every cell in the whole worksheet.

3. Follow these steps to change the font size of the entire worksheet:

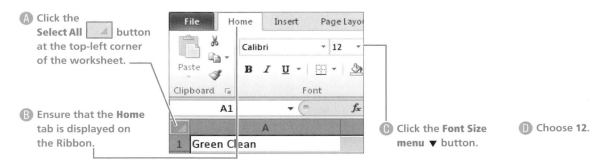

Ⓐ Click the **Select All** button at the top-left corner of the worksheet.

Ⓑ Ensure that the **Home** tab is displayed on the Ribbon.

Ⓒ Click the **Font Size menu ▼** button.

Ⓓ Choose **12**.

Notice that as you move the mouse pointer over the font size list, Excel will allow you to preview how the worksheet would appear if each font size were selected.

Use the Mini Toolbar to Format

4. Select **cell A5**.

5. **Double-click** the word *REVENUES* in **cell A5** two times.
   The first time you double-click, the cell will be available for editing; the second time, REVENUES will be selected and a translucent Mini toolbar will appear above the selection.

6. **Move** the mouse pointer over the **Mini toolbar**.
   When you move your mouse pointer over the transparent Mini toolbar, it will become visible and you can choose an option.

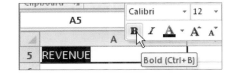

7. Click the **Bold B** button.

8. **Right-click** cell A10.
   Right-clicking a cell will also display the Mini toolbar.

9. Click the **Bold B** button on the Mini toolbar.

10. Use ⌈Ctrl⌋+⌈S⌋ to **save** the changes to the workbook and then continue with the next exercise.

4.2 Using Excel's Alignment and Indent Features

Video Lesson   labyrinthelab.com/videos

Excel allows you to alter how the text is aligned within cells. In addition to the standard left, center, and right horizontal alignments, you can indent the contents within a cell from either edge.

Aligning Entries

The Align Text Left ▤, Center ▦, and Align Text Right ▥ buttons on the Home tab of the Ribbon let you align entries within cells. By default, text entries are left aligned and number entries are right aligned. To change alignment, select the cell(s) and click the desired alignment button.

Indenting Cell Entries

The Increase Indent ▦ button and Decrease Indent ▦ button in the Alignment group on the Home tab of the Ribbon let you offset entries from the edges of cells. If a cell entry is left aligned, it will indent from the left edge, and if it is right aligned, it will indent from the right edge. Indenting is useful for conveying the hierarchy of entries. The following illustration shows indented cells.

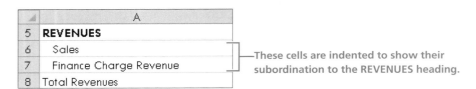

These cells are indented to show their subordination to the REVENUES heading.

QUICK REFERENCE	WORKING WITH ALIGNMENTS AND INDENTS
Task	**Procedure**
Change the alignment in cells	▪ Select the cells in which you wish to change the alignment. ▪ Click the appropriate button in the Alignment group on the Home tab of the Ribbon.
Indent a cell or range of cells	▪ Select the cells that you wish to indent. ▪ Click the appropriate button in the Alignment group on the Home tab of the Ribbon.

Work with Alignment and Indent

In this exercise, you will set the alignment in cells as well as indent entries.

Change the Alignment in Cells

1. Select the **range B4:E4**.

2. Choose **Home→Alignment→Align Text Right** ⬛ from the Ribbon.

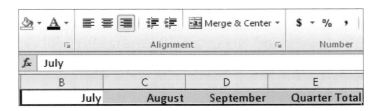

Indent Cell Entries

3. Follow these steps to indent entries in a range of cells:

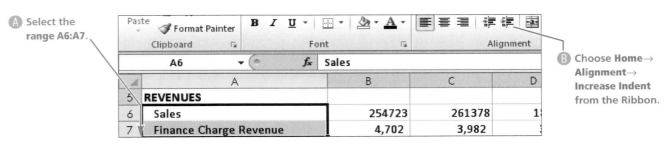

A Select the range A6:A7.

B Choose **Home→ Alignment→ Increase Indent** from the Ribbon.

4. Select the **range A11:A22**, taking care not to include **cell A23** in the selection.

5. Choose **Home→Alignment→Increase Indent** ⬛ from the Ribbon.
Now the types of revenue and expenses have been "set off" from the left edge of the cell.

6. **Save** ⬛ the changes to the workbook.

Video Lesson   labyrinthelab.com/videos

The Alignment group on the Home tab of the Ribbon provides options that allow you to merge cells and wrap lengthy text within a cell entry. You can insert a line break to place text on separate lines in a cell.

Merging and Splitting Cells

Excel's merge cells options allow you to combine cells. Merged cells behave as one large cell, and you can merge cells both vertically and horizontally. The merged cell takes on the name of the top left cell in the merged range. For example, if you merge cells A1:E1, the resulting merged cell will be named A1.

Merge & Center Command

The Merge & Center button merges selected cells and changes the alignment of the merged cell to center. This technique is often used to center a heading across columns. The Merge & Center command can format cells on only one row at a time. You would need to repeat the command for each heading on separate rows. You split a merged and centered cell by clicking the Merge & Center button again.

Cells A1:E1 selected and ready to be merged

The merged and centered cell A1 that results

Merging Cells

The Merge & Center menu contains additional merging options. The menu is accessed by clicking the ▼ arrow on the Merge & Center button.

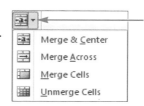

The Merge Across command merges cells without centering the contents. You may select cells in multiple rows and merge across each row with one command, as shown in the following illustration.

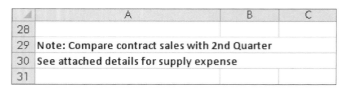

The range A29:C30 was selected and then the cells in each row were merged across the row. The gridline between cells A29 and A30 indicates that their contents are in separate rows.

The Merge Across command can be used to merge multiple headings across their rows in one step, after which they may be center aligned.

The Merge Cells command allows you to merge cells both across rows and down columns. In general, you should avoid merging any cells unless they are titles or headings at the top of the worksheet. Merged cells can restrict your ability to work with individual rows and columns. Also, some data will be lost if you merge multiple cells containing data.

Splitting Cells

Merged cells may be split again by clicking the Merge & Center button on the Ribbon or by choosing Unmerge Cells from the Merge & Center menu.

Wrapping Text

The Wrap Text option forces text to wrap within a cell as it would in a word-processing document. This is a good option to use when text is truncated (cut off) by the cell entry to the right and widening the column is not practical. The row height increases to accommodate the additional lines of wrapped text.

28		
29	Note: Compare contract sales with 2nd Quarter	
30		

The height of row 29 has increased to display all of the text wrapped in one cell.

Entering a Line Break

You can force text to display on the next line of a cell by inserting a line break. This feature is particularly useful for dividing a column heading to maintain a narrow column width, as shown in the illustration below.

FROM THE KEYBOARD

Alt + Enter to insert a line break

September	Quarter Total
$ 188,684	$ 704,785

A line break may be erased by moving the insertion point to the end of the line and tapping Delete. You may need to insert a space between words after removing the line break.

Shrinking Text to Fit Within a Cell

There may be times when changing the width of a column or wrapping text is not appropriate, yet you still want all of the text within the cell to be displayed. The Shrink to Fit option allows you to reduce the text size of the cell entry to whatever fits the existing cell width. Shrink to Fit is not available on the Ribbon but rather is in the Alignment tab of the Format Cells dialog box.

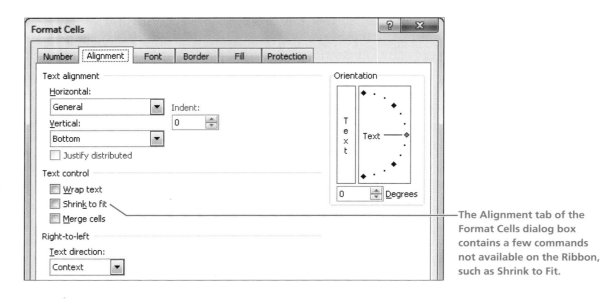

The Alignment tab of the Format Cells dialog box contains a few commands not available on the Ribbon, such as Shrink to Fit.

QUICK REFERENCE	MERGING CELLS AND WRAPPING TEXT
Task	**Procedure**
Merge and center a range of cells on one row	▪ Select the cells you wish to merge together. ▪ Choose Home →Alignment→Merge & Center 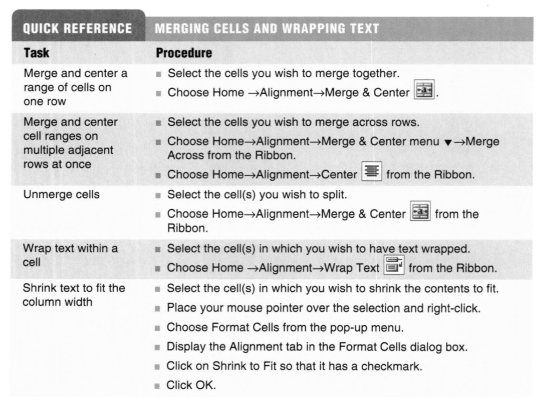.
Merge and center cell ranges on multiple adjacent rows at once	▪ Select the cells you wish to merge across rows. ▪ Choose Home→Alignment→Merge & Center menu ▼→Merge Across from the Ribbon. ▪ Choose Home→Alignment→Center ☰ from the Ribbon.
Unmerge cells	▪ Select the cell(s) you wish to split. ▪ Choose Home→Alignment→Merge & Center ☰ from the Ribbon.
Wrap text within a cell	▪ Select the cell(s) in which you wish to have text wrapped. ▪ Choose Home →Alignment→Wrap Text ☰ from the Ribbon.
Shrink text to fit the column width	▪ Select the cell(s) in which you wish to shrink the contents to fit. ▪ Place your mouse pointer over the selection and right-click. ▪ Choose Format Cells from the pop-up menu. ▪ Display the Alignment tab in the Format Cells dialog box. ▪ Click on Shrink to Fit so that it has a checkmark. ▪ Click OK.

Control Text in Cells

In this exercise, you will have the opportunity to merge and center cells as well as wrap text within a cell.

Merge and Center a Range of Cells

1. Select the **range A1:E1**.

2. Choose **Home→Alignment→Merge & Center**  from the Ribbon.
The entry from cell A1 is now centered over columns A through E.

3. Select **cell C1**.
Notice that A1 is displayed in the Name Box. While cell C1 is merged with A1, B1, D1, and E1, it essentially no longer exists!

Merge and Center on Multiple Adjacent Rows

4. Select the **range A2:E3**.

5. Choose **Home→Alignment→Merge & Center menu ▾→Merge Across** from the Ribbon.

6. Choose **Home→Alignment→Center ≣** from the Ribbon.
You may find this method more efficient than selecting and merging cells one row at a time.

Wrap Text within a Cell

7. Select **cell A29**.

8. Choose **Home→Alignment→Wrap Text** from the Ribbon.

9. Follow these steps to manually enter a line break in a cell:

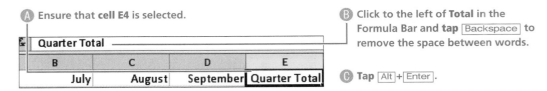

Ⓐ Ensure that **cell E4** is selected.

Ⓑ Click to the left of **Total** in the Formula Bar and **tap** Backspace to remove the space between words.

Ⓒ **Tap** Alt + Enter .

10. **Tap** Enter to complete the entry.
Excel applies wrapped text formatting to the cell and applies the line break where you tapped Alt + Enter .

11. **Save** the changes to the workbook.

4.4 Formatting Numbers

Video Lesson   labyrinthelab.com/videos

Excel lets you format numbers in a variety of ways. Number formats change the way numbers are displayed, though they do not change the actual numbers. Once a number formatting has been applied to a cell, it remains with the cell—even if the contents are deleted. The following table describes the most common number formats.

Number Format	Description
General	Numbers are formatted with the General format by default. This format does not apply any special formats to the numbers.
Comma Style	The Comma Style format inserts a comma after every third digit in the number. This format also inserts a decimal point and two decimal places, which can be removed if desired.
Currency	The Currency format is the same as the Comma Style format, except that it adds a dollar ($) sign in front of the number.
Accounting	The Accounting format is the same as Currency format, except that the dollar sign is placed at the left edge of the cell.
Percent Style	The Percent Style, also known as Percentage, inserts a percent (%) sign to the right of the number. The percentage is calculated by multiplying the number by 100.

If you begin an entry with a dollar sign, the Currency format will automatically be applied.

The following table provides several examples of formatted numbers.

Number Entered	Format	How the Number Is Displayed
5347.82	General	5347.82
5347.82	Comma with 0 decimal places	5,348
5347.82	Comma with 2 decimal places	5,347.82
5347.82	Currency with 0 decimal places	$5,347
5347.82	Currency with 2 decimal places	$5,347.82
.5347	Percentage with 0 decimal places	53%
.5347	Percentage with 2 decimal places	53.47%

Using the Number Command Group

The Number command group on the Home tab of the Ribbon allows you to format your numbers in a variety of ways, with the most common styles displayed as buttons. The top area of the group displays the number formatting of the selected cell(s). Clicking the menu button to the right of the current number formatting displays a menu of additional number format choices.

If you click the dialog box launcher button in the Number group, the Format Cells dialog box will appear with the Number tab displayed.

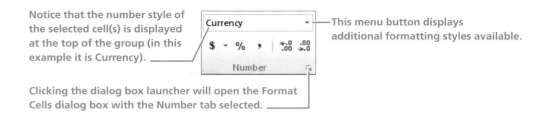

Notice that the number style of the selected cell(s) is displayed at the top of the group (in this example it is Currency).

This menu button displays additional formatting styles available.

Clicking the dialog box launcher will open the Format Cells dialog box with the Number tab selected.

Using Accounting and Currency Styles

There are two number styles that apply currency symbols (such as dollar signs) to numbers. You will notice a difference in where the dollar sign is placed based on the style you select. If you choose the Accounting style, currency symbols will appear fixed at the left of the cells. The Currency style, on the other hand, will display the currency symbol in front of the number in the cell.

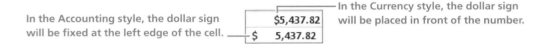

In the Accounting style, the dollar sign will be fixed at the left edge of the cell.

In the Currency style, the dollar sign will be placed in front of the number.

Applying the Percent Style

The Percent Style, also named Percentage in Excel, adds a percent sign (%) after the number. Depending on when you format the cell, you will enter a whole number or a decimal number. To achieve the correct result in the cell entry, follow one of the two procedures explained below.

- Select the cells that you wish to format as Percent Style and apply the formatting. If you format the cells first, you can type 25 and it will be formatted as 25%.

- Type the value in the cell first, and then apply the Percent Style formatting. If you type in the value first, you will need to type it in as a decimal. For instance, you will need to type in .25 in order for it to format properly as 25%. If you type in 25 and then apply Percent Style formatting, it will appear as 2500%.

How Numbers Display in Cells

You have seen that text entered in a cell spills over onto the empty cells to its right when the text cannot fit within its cell width. Numbers, on the other hand, do not spill over. Formula results that contain decimal numbers will display as many decimal places as can fit in the cell (see the illustration below).

| 27 | Net Income to Total Revenues | 0.271361665 | 0.311508894 | -0.038452727 | 0.203218575 |

Formula results will display as many decimal places as possible in the cell.

At times, a number combined with its formatting cannot fit within the cell width. For example, the number 254723 displays in a cell. After being formatted as Currency, the number should display as $254,423.00 but now cannot fit. Instead, you will see number signs (###) displayed across the cell width. There is no need to worry because the number is not lost; it just cannot display. The number display can be restored by increasing the column width. Other possible solutions include decreasing the decimal places and reducing the font size.

	A	B	C	D	E
6	Sales	###########	###########	###########	###########

The number signs (###) indicate numbers that cannot display within the cell width.

Adjusting Decimal Places

Most preset number formats, such as Comma Style, display two decimal places by default. You can adjust the number of decimal places displayed in the cell by using the Increase Decimal and Decrease Decimal buttons on the Ribbon. For example, clicking the Decrease Decimal button twice changes the number display from two to no decimal places in the selected cell(s). The number display is rounded up when necessary. For example, 525.83 would display as 526 when formatted with no decimal places, and 82.33 would display as 82. The actual number in the cell, however, is not changed and remains accurate when used in calculations.

Displaying Negative Numbers

Negative number displays can be either preceded by a minus sign or surrounded by parentheses. You can also display negative numbers in red. The Currency option and Number option in the Format Cells dialog box let you choose the format for negative numbers.

The negative number format you choose affects the alignment of numbers in the cells. If the format displays negative numbers in parentheses, a small space equal to the width of a closing parenthesis appears on the right edge of cells containing positive numbers. Excel does this so the decimal points are aligned in columns containing both positive and negative numbers.

16	Insurance	8696	0	9534	18230
17	Rent	8000	8000	9000	25000
18	Supplies	1263	2458	-22	3699
19	Telephone	300	300	300	900
20	Utilities	1689	1782	1824	5295
21	Vehicle Expenses	17823	18622	26781	63226
22	Wages	125622	124300	124015	373937
23	Total Expenses	189027	182698	199439	571164
24					
25	Net Income (Loss)	70398	82662	-7385	145675

When the numbers are formatted as General style, the negative numbers will be displayed with a minus sign in front of them.

16	Insurance	8,696.00	0.00	9,534.00	18,230.00
17	Rent	8,000.00	8,000.00	9,000.00	25,000.00
18	Supplies	1,263.00	2,458.00	(22.00)	3,699.00
19	Telephone	300.00	300.00	300.00	900.00
20	Utilities	1,689.00	1,782.00	1,824.00	5,295.00
21	Vehicle Expenses	17,823.00	18,622.00	26,781.00	63,226.00
22	Wages	125,622.00	124,300.00	124,015.00	373,937.00
23	Total Expenses	189,027.00	182,698.00	199,439.00	571,164.00
24					
25	Net Income (Loss)	70,398.00	82,662.00	(7,385.00)	145,675.00

When you choose the Comma Style format, you can accept the default negative number format with parentheses or change it to display a minus sign in the Format Cells dialog box. If you choose to format negative numbers with parentheses, the positive numbers will be set a bit further from the right edge of the cell in order for the decimal points to be aligned. Notice also that the cell containing the number 0 is displayed with a hyphen (-).

Format Numbers

In this exercise, you will apply various number formatting options to the worksheet.

Use the Accounting and Currency Styles

1. Follow these steps to apply the Accounting format to a range of cells:

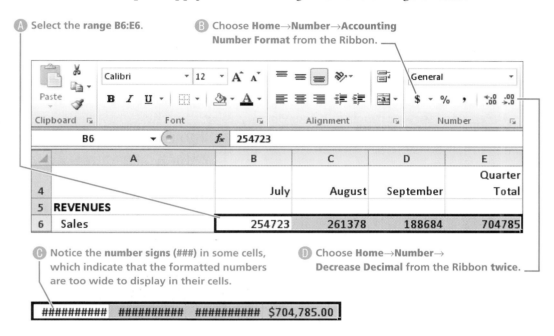

Ⓐ Select the **range B6:E6**.

Ⓑ Choose **Home→Number→Accounting Number Format** from the Ribbon.

Ⓒ Notice the **number signs (###)** in some cells, which indicate that the formatted numbers are too wide to display in their cells.

Ⓓ Choose **Home→Number→ Decrease Decimal** from the Ribbon **twice**.

Notice that the Accounting format displays the dollar sign as fixed at the left edge of the cells. "Custom" is displayed as the number format on the Ribbon because you changed the number of decimal places of the Accounting format.

2. Select the **range B7:E7**.

3. Choose **Home→Number→Comma Style** 🔘 from the Ribbon.

4. Choose **Home→ Number→Decrease Decimal** 🔘 from the Ribbon twice.

5. Select the **range B8:E8, hold down** Ctrl, and select the **range B11:E11**.
   Remember that by using Ctrl, *you can select multiple ranges to which you can apply formatting.*

6. Choose **Home→Accounting Number Format** 🔘 from the Ribbon.

7. Choose **Home→Decrease Decimal** 🔘 from the Ribbon twice.

8. **Repeat** the above steps to apply **Accounting Number Format** with **no decimals** to the **ranges A23:E23** and **A25:E25**.

Use Comma Style

9. Select the **range B12:E22**.

10. Apply **Comma Style formatting** with **no decimals** to the selection.
    Notice that the 0 entry in cell C16 now displays as a hyphen (–) with Comma Style formatting applied.

11. Select the **range B27:E27**.

12. Choose **Home→Number→Percent Style** 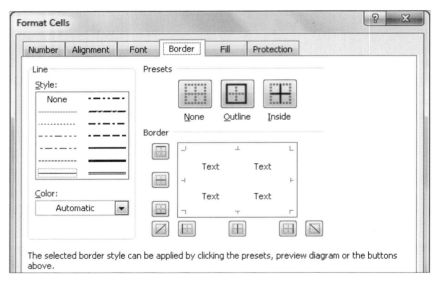 from the Ribbon.

13. Choose **Home→Number→Increase Decimal** from the Ribbon.
    The percentages are formatted with one decimal place.

14. **Save** the changes to the workbook.

4.5 Using the Format Cells Dialog Box

Video Lesson labyrinthelab.com/videos

The Format Cells dialog box contains six tabs that allow you to format different aspects of your worksheet: Number, Alignment, Font, Border, Fill, and Protection. Some options in this dialog box are not available on the Ribbon. Therefore, using the dialog box may be more convenient when you are setting complex formatting.

The Border tab of the Format Cells dialog box allows you to set the borders for the selected cells. In this example, the preview in the Border section shows that a line will appear around the entire selection as well as between each row that is selected.

4.6 Applying Borders and Fills to Cells

Borders are lines around the cell edges that print as well as display in the worksheet. Do not confuse these with the nonprinting gridlines that display in Normal view. Fills are background shading and pattern effects that fill entire cells. You can apply borders and fills using options on the Ribbon or in the Format Cells dialog box. Borders and fills should provide consistency, call attention to important details, and make the worksheet easier to understand. Keep in mind that "less is more" when applying colors and other formatting.

Applying Borders

The Borders button on the Home tab of the Ribbon lets you add borders to cell edges. When you click the Borders menu ▼ button, a list of options appears. You can apply one of these border Quick Styles to all selected cells by choosing it from the list. You can also choose More Borders from the bottom of the list to display the Borders tab of the Format Cells dialog box.

The image displayed on the Borders button on the Ribbon will change based on the last border applied. This feature makes it easy to apply the same border formatting throughout the workbook.

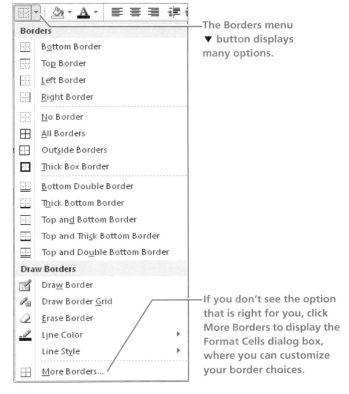

The Borders menu ▼ button displays many options.

If you don't see the option that is right for you, click More Borders to display the Format Cells dialog box, where you can customize your border choices.

Applying Fill Colors and Patterns

The Fill Color button on the Home tab of the Ribbon lets you fill the background of selected cells with color. When you click the Fill Color menu button, a palette of colors appears. You can apply a color to all selected cells by choosing it from the palette. The fill color is independent of the font color used to format text and numbers. The Format Cells dialog box has a Fill tab that lets you apply fill colors and a variety of patterns and effects.

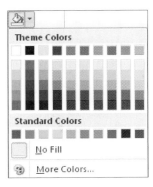

This palette of colors results when you click the Fill Color menu ▼ button. The color you choose will fill the cell but will not affect the color of the font.

Printing a test version of a worksheet allows you to see how your color choices will print, especially important for grayscale printers.

Format with the Format Cells Dialog Box

In this exercise, you will apply borders and fill coloring to the worksheet.

Apply Borders to a Selection

1. Select the **range A1:E27**.
   When you choose A1, you will actually be choosing the entire merged cell that spans across column E.

2. Choose **Home→Font→Borders menu ▼→More Borders** from the Ribbon.

3. Follow these steps to apply the border formatting:

Ⓐ Click the line style **third** from the bottom in the right column.

Ⓑ Click the **Outline** option.

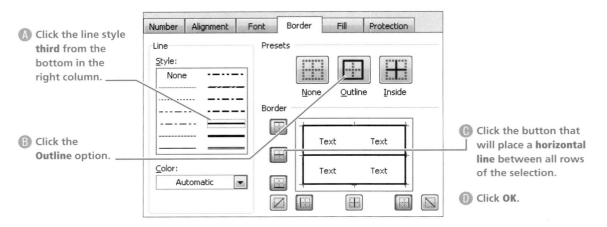

Ⓒ Click the button that will place a **horizontal line** between all rows of the selection.

Ⓓ Click **OK**.

Notice that the Borders button now displays the icon ⊞, which represents the More Borders option on the Borders menu. It will always display the last option selected from the Borders menu.

4. Use ⌈Ctrl⌉+⌈Z⌉ to undo the borders.

5. Select the **range B7:E7, hold down** the ⌈Ctrl⌉ key, and select the **range B22:E22**. Then **release** the ⌈Ctrl⌉ key.

6. Click the **Borders menu ▼** button.

7. Choose the **Bottom Border** option to place a border along the bottom of the selected cells.
   A border will appear along the bottom of both of the selected ranges. The Borders button will now display the Bottom Border icon.

8. Select the **range B25:E25**.

9. Click the **Borders menu ▼ button** and choose **Top and Double Bottom Border**.

Apply Fill Color to a Range

10. Select the **range A5:E5, hold down** the Ctrl key, and select **A10:E10**. Then **release** the Ctrl key.

11. Follow these steps to apply a fill color to the selected ranges:

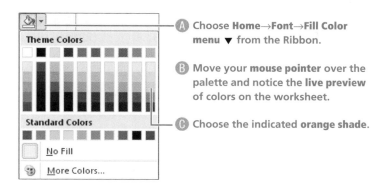

(A) Choose **Home→Font→Fill Color menu ▼** from the Ribbon.

(B) Move your **mouse pointer** over the palette and notice the **live preview** of colors on the worksheet.

(C) Choose the indicated **orange shade**.

12. **Click away** from the selection to view the color in the selected ranges.
    Notice that the cells are now orange, but the text has remained black.

13. **Save** 💾 the changes to the workbook.

4.7 Working with Format Painter and Quick Styles

Video Lesson   labyrinthelab.com/videos

Excel has two features, shared with several other Office Suite applications, that allow you to apply formatting quickly to cells. The Format Painter applies formatting from existing worksheet cells. You already have worked with Quick Styles when applying predefined borders. Now you will apply predefined formats as cell styles.

The Format Painter Tool

There may be times when you want to copy the formatting from one cell to another without copying the contents. The Format Painter lets you copy text formats and number formats from one cell to another. This tool can be extremely helpful if you have a cell to which many formatting options have been applied and you do not wish to apply each option individually to another cell or range of cells.

Applying Quick Styles to Cells

You can apply Excel's built-in cell styles, also called Quick Styles, or create your own styles for a uniform worksheet design. A cell style's formatting may include the font, number format, borders, and fill.

New cell styles that you create appear in the Custom section of the styles list. They are based on the workbook theme, so the colors change automatically to match any new theme that is applied. Among the built-in styles, only the Themed Cell Styles change colors. Any styles that you create or edit apply only to the currently open workbook. The Merge Styles command in the styles list allows you to import styles created in a different workbook into a currently open workbook.

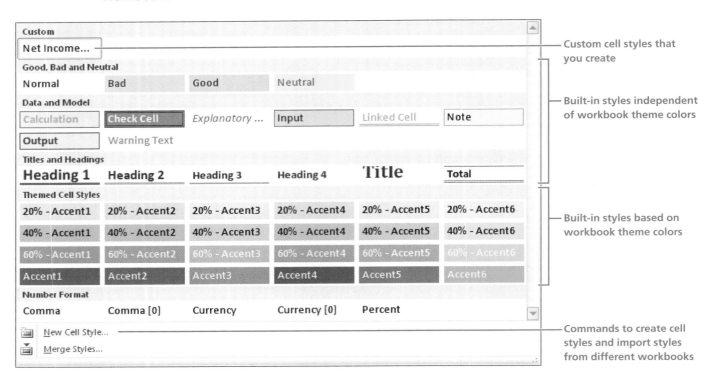

Custom cell styles that you create

Built-in styles independent of workbook theme colors

Built-in styles based on workbook theme colors

Commands to create cell styles and import styles from different workbooks

QUICK REFERENCE	WORKING WITH FORMAT PAINTER AND CELL STYLES
Task	**Procedure**
Copy formats to one other cell or range	■ Click the cell that has the format(s) you wish to copy.
	■ Choose Home →Clipboard→Format Painter ![icon] from the Ribbon.
	■ Select the cell or range to which you wish to copy the format(s).
Copy formats to multiple locations	■ Click the cell that has the format(s) you wish to copy.
	■ Double-click the Home →Clipboard→Format Painter ![icon] button.
	■ Select the cells or ranges to which you wish to copy the format(s).
	■ When you are finished, click the Format Painter ![icon] button to turn it off.
Apply a cell style (Quick Style) to a cell or range of cells	■ Select the cells to which you wish to apply the cell style.
	■ Choose Home→Styles→Cell Styles ![icon] from the Ribbon.
	■ Select the desired style from the list.

Task	Procedure
Create a cell style	■ Choose Home→Styles→Cell Styles ▣ →New Cell Style from the Ribbon.
	■ Click the Format button in the Style dialog box and select the desired formatting options in the Format Cells dialog box.
	■ Click OK.
	■ Name the style in the Style dialog box and select the formatting categories to be included.
Modify a cell style	■ Choose Home→Styles→Cell Styles ▣ from the Ribbon.
	■ Right-click the desired style from the list and choose Modify to edit the existing style or Duplicate to create a new style based on the existing style.
	■ Click the Format button in the Style dialog box and select the desired formatting options in the Format Cells dialog box.
	■ Click OK.
	■ Name the style in the Style dialog box, if necessary, and select the formatting categories to be included.
Import cell styles from a different workbook	■ Open the workbook from which you wish to import styles.
	■ In the destination workbook, choose Home→Styles→Cell Styles→Merge Styles from the Ribbon.
	■ Choose the source workbook name.

When you double-click Format Painter, you can scroll through the worksheet to reach the desired location(s). You can even click a sheet tab to copy formatting to a different worksheet in the workbook.

DEVELOP YOUR SKILLS 4.7.1

Change Formatting with Format Painter and Cell Styles

In this exercise, you will copy the formatting from one cell to a range of cells. You also will apply cell styles and create a custom style.

Copy Formatting with Format Painter

1. Select **cell A10**.
   You must first select the cell from which you wish to copy the formatting.

2. Choose **Home→Clipboard→Format Painter** 🖌 button from the Ribbon.

3. Select the **range A25:E25**.
   The formatting from A10 is applied to the entire range of A25:E25. Notice that the General number formatting is also applied.

4. Choose **Home→Number→Accounting Number Format** $ from the Ribbon.

5. Choose **Home→Number→Decrease Decimal** ⬚ from the Ribbon twice.

Apply Cell Styles

6. Select **cell A29**.

7. Follow these steps to apply a built-in cell style:

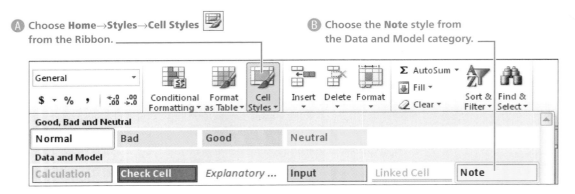

The built-in cell styles include ratings, data and model formats, titles and headings, styles matching the workbook theme, and number formats. Your styles may differ.

8. Select the **range A1:E3**.

9. Choose **Home→Styles→Cell Styles** 🖳 from the Ribbon. Then, from the Themed Cell Styles category, select **40% - Accent5**. *The cell style is in the fifth color palette from the left.*

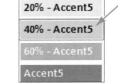

10. **Deselect** the range.

Create a Custom Cell Style

11. Choose **Home→Styles→Cell Styles** 🖳 from the Ribbon.

12. Choose **New Cell Style** at the bottom of the styles list.

13. Follow these steps to begin creating a cell style:

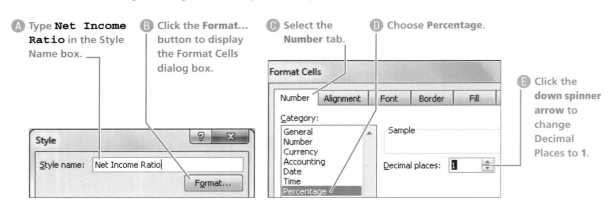

14. With the Format Cells dialog box still displayed, select the **Fill** tab.

15. Choose the **fourth color** in the **last column** of the theme colors palette.

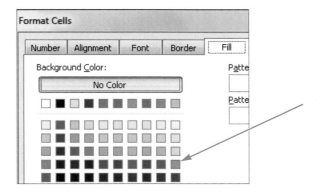

16. Follow these steps to set the text characteristics for the cell style:

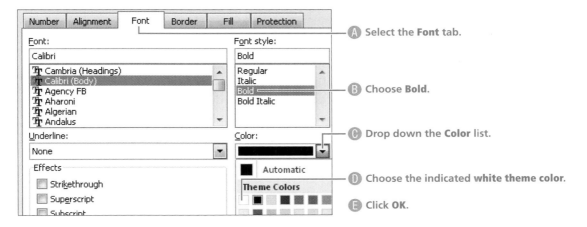

Ⓐ Select the **Font** tab.

Ⓑ Choose **Bold**.

Ⓒ Drop down the **Color** list.

Ⓓ Choose the indicated **white theme color**.

Ⓔ Click **OK**.

17. Notice that your changes are shown in the **Style** dialog box.

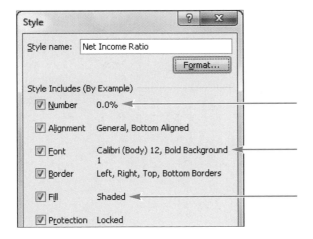

All the categories with a checkmark will be applied to the style. You can remove the checkmark from any formatting you don't want to use.

18. Click **OK** to close the Style dialog box.

19. Select the **range A27:E27**.

20. Choose **Home→Styles→Cell Styles** 📋 from the Ribbon. Then, from the Custom category, select your **Net Income Ratio** style. *With the time it took to set the formatting, you can easily understand why cell styles are useful. Using the Merge Styles command, you can also import them into other workbooks.*

21. **Deselect** the range.

22. **Save** 💾 the changes to the workbook.

4.8 Formatting with Themes

Video Lesson	labyrinthelab.com/videos

Themes allow you to apply formatting easily to your entire workbook. A variety of new theme designs are provided in Excel 2010. All themes have been developed by designers at Microsoft to help you maintain a unified design. You can, however, modify a theme by changing the font set, color palette, or graphic effect design. You can save the modifications as a custom theme that can be reused with other workbooks.

There is good advice that you should heed when using different font styles—do not use too many of them on one worksheet. You can "overformat" your worksheet! Themes allow you to choose a set of compatible fonts, one for headings and one for body text. These theme fonts for the currently selected theme are identified at the top of the Font list. Likewise, the ten theme colors display at the top of a list when you are applying colors. Individual worksheet cells to which you applied nontheme fonts do not change font when a new theme is applied to the workbook.

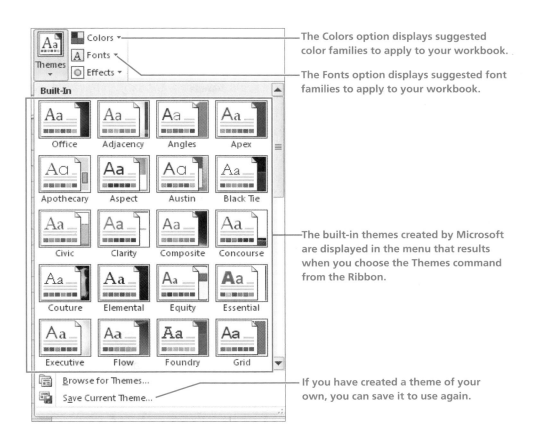

The Colors option displays suggested color families to apply to your workbook.

The Fonts option displays suggested font families to apply to your workbook.

The built-in themes created by Microsoft are displayed in the menu that results when you choose the Themes command from the Ribbon.

If you have created a theme of your own, you can save it to use again.

QUICK REFERENCE	APPLYING, MODIFYING, AND SAVING A THEME
Task	**Procedure**
Apply a theme to a workbook	■ Open the workbook to which you wish to apply the theme. ■ Choose Page Layout →Themes→Themes ![Aa] from the Ribbon. ■ Choose a theme to apply.
Modify and save a theme	■ Choose Page Layout→Themes→Themes ![Aa] from the Ribbon. ■ Choose a theme. ■ Change the Colors, Fonts, and Effect options in the Themes group of the Page Layout ribbon as desired. ■ Choose Page Layout→Themes→Themes→Save Current Theme from the Ribbon. ■ Enter a theme name and click Save.

Use Themes in a Workbook

In this exercise, you will apply a theme to the workbook. You also will modify a theme and explore how it would be saved.

Change the Theme

1. Click the **Page Layout view** ▣ button in the Status Bar at the lower-right corner of the window.
   The view buttons are to the left of the zoom slider.

2. Choose **Page Layout→Themes→Themes** Aa from the Ribbon.
   Office is the default theme applied to new workbooks.

3. Point at various **themes** and observe the effect that Live Preview displays in the worksheet.
   Notice that you can scroll down to display additional themes.

4. Choose the **Executive** theme.
   The colors and font in the workbook now correspond to those indicated in the theme.

5. Look at the left in the **Status Bar** to see that this theme displays the worksheet on one page.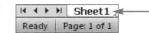

Modify and Explore Saving a Theme

6. Choose **Page Layout→Themes→** A Fonts ▾ from the Ribbon.

7. Point at various **font families** and observe the effect that Live Preview displays in the worksheet.

8. Choose the **Thatch** theme fonts.

9. Choose **Page Layout→Themes→Themes→Save Current Theme** from the Ribbon.
   The Save Current Theme dialog box displays. Notice the default folder for saving themes on your system. You could enter a filename to save the modified theme.

10. Click **Cancel** and do *not* save the theme.

11. **Save** 🖫 the changes to the workbook.

4.9 Inserting Date Functions and Formatting

Video Lesson   labyrinthelab.com/videos

As you have learned, statistical functions like SUM and AVERAGE are very useful in summarizing data. Now you will insert a function that will always display today's date. Excel will determine the date to display according to your computer's clock feature.

Working with Dates

Dates are used in workbooks in two ways. First, you can simply type and display dates in cells using various formats such as 11/20/14; November 20, 2014; or 20-Nov-14. Second, you can use dates in formulas. For example, you may want to compute the number of days an invoice is past due. You calculate this as the difference between the current date and the original invoice date.

Date Serial Numbers

When you enter a date in a cell, Excel converts the date to a serial number between 1 and 2,958,525. These numbers correspond to the 10-millennium period from January 1, 1900, through December 31, 9999. The date January 1, 1900, is assigned the serial number 1; January 2, 1900, is assigned the serial number 2; and December 31, 9999, is assigned the serial number 2,958,525. When dates are converted to numbers, you can use the numbers/dates in calculations. Best of all, serial numbers are created for you automatically!

Entering Dates

Excel performs the following steps when you enter a date in a cell:

- It recognizes the entry as a date if you enter it using a standard date format such as 11/20/14; November 20, 2014; or 20-Nov-14.
- It converts the date to a serial number between 1 and 2,958,525.
- It formats the serial number entry with the same date format you used when you entered the date.

This roundabout process occurs behind the scenes so you never see it happening. The benefit of converting dates to numbers and then formatting them with a date format is that the dates can be used in calculations.

Inserting Date and Time Functions

In this lesson, you will see the value of using date and time functions in Excel.

About Date Functions

The current date is often required in worksheets. You may also want to show the date the worksheet was created or printed. The following details apply in general to dates you insert with date functions:

- You can insert a date function rather than typing the date in a worksheet.
- Some date functions produce the current date and, depending on the specific function, can update automatically.
- You insert date functions with the Insert Function dialog box or by typing the function in the result cell.
- Date functions are not case sensitive so you can type the formula in lowercase.

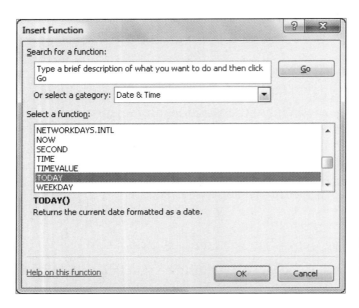

In the Date & Time function category, Excel provides a variety of functions. Notice that there is a description of the selected function displayed below the list.

The following table discusses three of the most common date and time functions.

Function	Description
TODAY( )	This function displays the current system date and calculates the serial number. The date updates automatically when the worksheet is recalculated or reopened.
NOW( )	This function displays the current system date and time and calculates the serial number. The date and time update automatically when the worksheet is recalculated or reopened.
DATE(year,month,day)	This function returns a specific date displayed in the default date format and calculates the serial number. The date does not update when the worksheet is recalculated or reopened.

DEVELOP YOUR SKILLS 4.9.1

Use the TODAY Function and Format a Date

In this exercise, you will create formulas that will calculate the current date and you will learn how to format dates.

Create Labels

1. Enter the **text labels** in the **range B29:E29** using [Alt] + [Enter], and **align right** as shown in the following illustration.

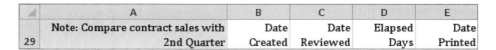

▲	A	B	C	D	E
29	Note: Compare contract sales with 2nd Quarter	Date Created	Date Reviewed	Elapsed Days	Date Printed

Type and Format a Date

2. Select **cell C30**.

3. Type **9/1/14** in the cell, and then click **Enter** ✓ on the Formula Bar.
   Look at the Number group on the Home tab of the Ribbon. The number format style displayed is Date, which Excel formatted for you when you typed the number in the date format.

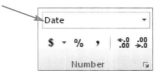

4. Display the **Home** tab of the Ribbon.

5. Click the **dialog box launcher** 🔽 in the Number group of the Home tab.
   The Format Cells dialog box will open with the Number tab displayed.

6. Follow these steps to change the date format:

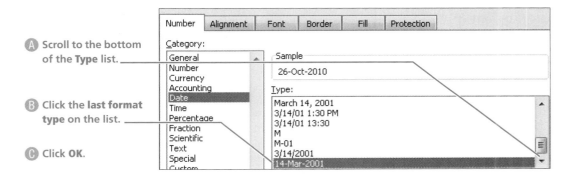

Ⓐ Scroll to the bottom of the **Type** list.

Ⓑ Click the **last format type** on the list.

Ⓒ Click **OK**.

7. Ensure that **cell C30** is still selected, and then **tap** Delete .
   Look at the Number group on the Home tab of the Ribbon and notice that even when you remove the contents of the cell (the date you typed in), the number format for the cell will remain as Date.

Use the TODAY Function and Calculate Dates

8. Follow these steps to enter the TODAY function:

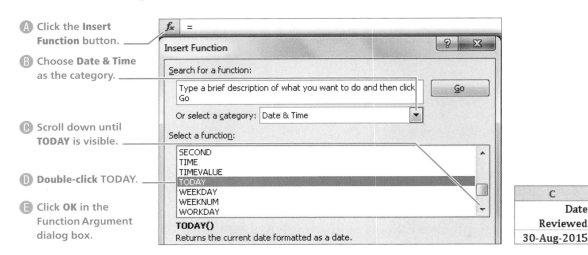

Ⓐ Click the **Insert Function** button.

Ⓑ Choose **Date & Time** as the category.

Ⓒ Scroll down until **TODAY** is visible.

Ⓓ **Double-click** TODAY.

Ⓔ Click **OK** in the Function Argument dialog box.

The date will appear with the number formatting you set for the cell.

9. Select **cell B30**, and **enter** the date that is four days prior to today.

10. Use **Format Painter** to apply the date format from **cell C30** to **cell B30**.

11. Select **cell D30**, and **enter** the formula **=C30-B30**.
    The result should equal 4. You can create formulas that calculate dates in various ways.

Use the NOW Function

12. Select **cell E30**, type **=now(** and **tap** Enter to complete the formula.
    Excel adds the ending parenthesis for the function formula for you. Number signs (###) display across the cell width. You will recall that this means the date is too long to fit.

13. **Right-click** cell E30, and choose **Format Cells** in the context menu.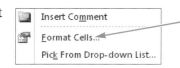

14. Select the **Alignment** tab in the Format Cells dialog box.

15. Place a **checkmark** next to Shrink to Fit and click **OK**.

The NOW function displays the current date and time, which is updated the next time you open the worksheet. Your dates will be different from those shown.

16. Save 🖫 the changes to the workbook.

4.10 Creating Custom Formats

Video Lesson labyrinthelab.com/videos

Excel's predefined number format options usually are sufficient, but occasionally you may need a modified format. For example, you may want a date to display the year as two digits instead of four. An identification or account number may need to be displayed with preceding zeros, such as 0004842. The Format Cells dialog box includes a Type box in which you can edit an existing number format or create a new one.

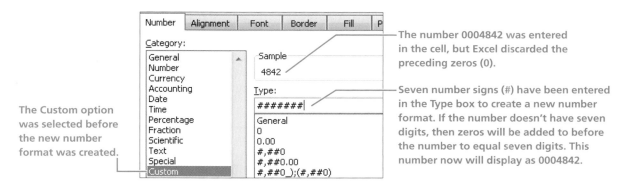

The Custom option was selected before the new number format was created.

The number 0004842 was entered in the cell, but Excel discarded the preceding zeros (0).

Seven number signs (#) have been entered in the Type box to create a new number format. If the number doesn't have seven digits, then zeros will be added to before the number to equal seven digits. This number now will display as 0004842.

QUICK REFERENCE | CREATING CUSTOM NUMBER FORMATS

Task	Procedure
Modify an existing number format to create a custom format	<ul><li>Select the cell or range to which you wish to apply a custom number format.</li><li>Click the dialog box launcher on the Number group of the Home tab.</li><li>Select the Custom category in the Format Cells dialog box.</li><li>Choose an existing format from the list that is closest to the desired formatting.</li><li>Edit the formatting in the Type box, and the Sample number displays the result.</li><li>Click OK, and the new format will be added to the bottom of the Custom list.</li></ul>

DEVELOP YOUR SKILLS 4.10.1
Modify a Date Format

In this exercise, you will edit the date format currently applied to the NOW function formula.

1. Select **cell E30**.

2. Click the **dialog box launcher** on the Number group of the Home tab.
   The Format Cells dialog box displays the Number tab.

3. Verify that the **Custom** category is selected, and **m/d/yyyy h:mm** is the currently selected format.

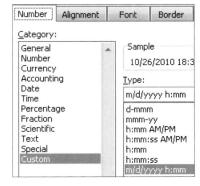

4. In the **Type** box, **edit** the format to be **m/d/yy h:mm AM/PM** and then click **OK**.

The custom date format is applied to cell E30.

5. **Save** the changes to the workbook.

E
Date
Printed
8/30/15 8:43 AM

4.11 Working with Conditional Formatting

Video Lesson   labyrinthelab.com/videos

The Conditional Formatting ⊞ command applies formatting to cells that meet criteria that you set. Conditional formats are activated only when the criteria are met. For example, you may assign a yellow fill to a cell when its value is greater than 12. You may apply conditional formatting to cells containing values, text, dates, blanks, or errors. Conditional formats are often used as alerts. They draw attention to better-than-expected results or values that fall outside an acceptable range. Conditional formatting must be set in one worksheet at a time within a workbook.

New to Excel 2010 is the ability to create conditional formatting that refers to a cell in a different sheet of the workbook. For example, you can compare a trainee's test score with the average score for all trainees located in a summary worksheet. Conditional formatting cannot refer to cells in another workbook.

Using Presets and Multiple Conditions

You can choose from conditional formatting presets on the Conditional Formatting menu for frequently used criteria, such as Greater Than, Equal To, Above Average, and Top 10 Items. You may set any number of conditional formats and create multiple rules to check for more than one condition in a cell. Do so with care to ensure that the formatting result is accurate and useful. Conditional formatting rules are applied in the priority order you set. The Stop If True option, when selected in any rule, prevents further formatting by the remaining rules after a criterion is evaluated as True.

Creating a Conditional Formatting Rule

If no preset item on the Conditional Formatting menu has your desired criteria or formatting, you may create a new conditional formatting rule. For example, you may wish to base conditional formatting on the result of a formula. The following illustration defines the parts of the New Formatting Rule dialog box. The options vary in the lower half of the dialog box depending on the rule type you select.

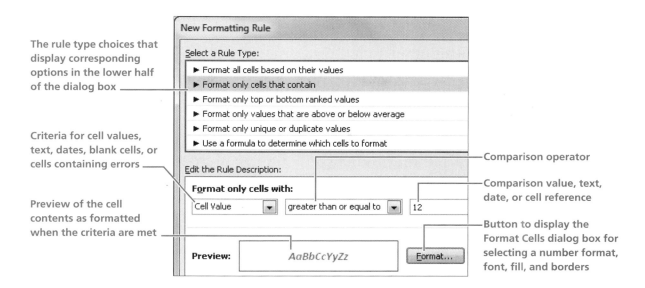

The rule type choices that display corresponding options in the lower half of the dialog box

Criteria for cell values, text, dates, blank cells, or cells containing errors

Preview of the cell contents as formatted when the criteria are met

Comparison operator

Comparison value, text, date, or cell reference

Button to display the Format Cells dialog box for selecting a number format, font, fill, and borders

Formatting with Graphics

You can choose to conditionally format cells with data bars, a color scale, or an icon set. These graphics identify values that are average, above average, and below average in the selected cell range. You may select a menu preset or create a custom rule using any of these visual aids. After bars, colors, or icons are applied with conditional formatting, you may filter to display only items that are formatted with a specific color or icon. For example, you may filter a column in a list for cells

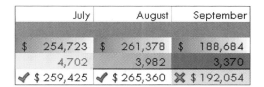

Conditional formatting with data bars, a color scale, or icons helps you to categorize data, identify trends, and highlight trouble areas.

containing a red icon to view only the cells with below-average results. You will not use filtering in this lesson.

Use consistent formatting and limit the use of data bars, color scales, and icon sets on one worksheet. Using multiple styles in adjacent rows or columns, as in the preceding figure, could confuse the reader.

The Conditional Formatting Rules Manager

Conditional formatting rules can be created, edited, rearranged, and deleted within the Conditional Formatting Rules Manager dialog box. The following illustration displays the rules set within an entire worksheet.

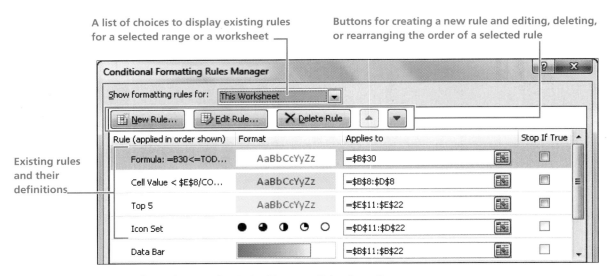

A list of choices to display existing rules for a selected range or a worksheet

Buttons for creating a new rule and editing, deleting, or rearranging the order of a selected rule

Existing rules and their definitions

The Conditional Formatting Rules Manager dialog box allows you to work with all rules applied to a selected range or a worksheet.

QUICK REFERENCE	APPLYING CONDITIONAL FORMATTING
Task	**Procedure**
Apply preset conditional formatting	▪ Select the cells to receive formatting. ▪ Choose Home→Styles→Conditional Formatting [icon] from the Ribbon, display a preset menu, and choose a command. ▪ Edit options in the preset rule dialog box, if desired.
Create a conditional formatting rule	▪ Select the cells to receive formatting. ▪ Choose Home→Styles→Conditional Formatting→New Rule from the Ribbon. ▪ Choose a rule type and formatting options in the New Formatting Rule dialog box.
Apply conditional formatting with data bars, a color scale, or an icon set	▪ Select the cells to receive formatting. ▪ Choose Home→Styles→Conditional Formatting→Data Bars or Color Scales or Icon Sets from the Ribbon. ▪ Choose a preset item on the command's submenu or More Rules to create a custom rule.
Clear conditional formatting from specific cells	▪ Select specific cells from which to remove formatting. ▪ Choose Home→Styles→Conditional Formatting→Clear Rules→Clear Rules from Selected Cells from the Ribbon.
Clear all conditional formatting from a worksheet	▪ Display the desired worksheet. ▪ Choose Home→Styles→Conditional Formatting→Clear Rules→Clear Rules from Entire Sheet from the Ribbon.
Manage conditional formatting rules	▪ Choose Home→Styles→Conditional Formatting→Manage Rules from the Ribbon to display the Conditional Formatting Rules Manager dialog box. ▪ Choose Current Selection or a worksheet from the Show Formatting Rules For list. ▪ Use buttons in the dialog box to create a new rule, or select an existing rule and edit, delete, or change its order.

Apply Conditional Formatting

In this exercise, you will apply various types of conditional formatting to cell ranges. You also will create a conditional formatting rule and remove conditional formatting from a range.

Use a Preset to Apply Highlight Formatting

1. Select the **range B8:D8**, taking care **not** to select the total in cell E8.

2. Choose **Home→Styles→Conditional Formatting→Highlight Cells Rules→Less Than** from the Ribbon.
   The Less Than dialog box appears with the suggested value $228,707. This is the average of the lowest and highest values in the range. You will change this to a formula that averages all three values in the range.

3. Follow these steps to begin the formula:
   You will build the formula =$E$8/COUNT($B$8:$D$8).

Ⓐ **Drag** the title bar of the **Less Than** dialog box so that row 8 of the worksheet is visible.

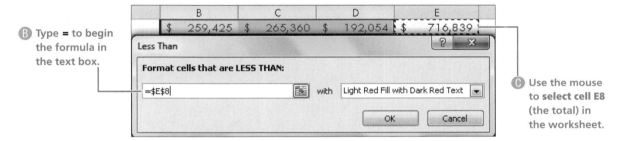

Ⓑ Type **=** to begin the formula in the text box.

Ⓒ Use the mouse to **select cell E8** (the total) in the worksheet.

4. Continue typing **/count (** in the formula.

5. Select the **range B8:D8** in the worksheet.

6. Type **)** to complete the formula.

7. Drop down the **With** list to review the other formatting choices, and leave **Light Red Fill with Dark Red Text** selected.

8. Click **OK**.

9. **Deselect** the range to see that cell D8 is formatted in red as below average.
   The color red often is used to highlight "bad" results. Yellow is used to indicate "average," and green means "good."

Create a Conditional Formatting Rule

10. Select **cell B19**, and **tap** Delete to erase its contents.

11. Taking care not to select the totals in row 23, select the **range B11:D22**.
You selected the July, August, and September expenses.

12. Choose **Home→Styles→Conditional Formatting→Highlight Cells Rules→More Rules** from the Ribbon.
The New Formatting Rule dialog box appears. Format Only Cells That Contain is the selected rule type.

13. Follow these steps to create a custom conditional formatting rule:

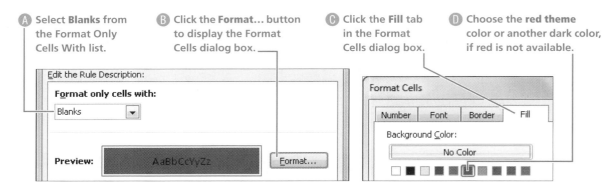

Ⓐ Select **Blanks** from the Format Only Cells With list.

Ⓑ Click the **Format...** button to display the Format Cells dialog box.

Ⓒ Click the **Fill** tab in the Format Cells dialog box.

Ⓓ Choose the **red theme** color or another dark color, if red is not available.

14. Click **OK** to exit the Format Cells dialog box.
Notice the red fill in the Preview box of the New Formatting Rule dialog box.

15. Click **OK** to exit the New Formatting Rule dialog box.
The conditional formatting is applied to cell B19, the blank cell, to draw attention to a potential error.

Format with Data Bars and Icons

You will select the expense values in one column at a time and apply conditional formatting. Selecting the entire range of July through September cells would compare each value with the Quarter Total, which is not the result you need.

16. Select the **range B11:B22** and choose **Home→Styles→Conditional Formatting→Data Bars→Blue Data Bar** from the Ribbon.
The data bars display each part of the July total expenses like a bar chart inside the cells as shown at right. Wages is a very high percentage of total expenses.

17. Select the **range C11:D22** and choose **Home→Styles→Conditional Formatting→Icon Sets→5 Quarters (black and white circles)** from the Ribbon.

	B
$	500
	14,723
	2,450
	6,750
	1,211
	8,696
	8,000
	1,263
	1,689
	17,823
	125,622
$	188,727

18. Change the value in cell C20 to **50000**.

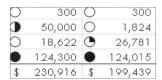

The amount of fill within each circle helps you compare expenses in relation to the total and to each other.

19. Click **Undo** ⟲ to restore the value in cell C20.

Format with a Top Rule

20. Select the **range E11:E22** and choose **Home→Styles→Conditional Formatting→ Top/Bottom Rules→Top 10 Items**.

21. Change 10 to **5** in the Top 10 Items dialog box, choose **Yellow Fill with Dark Yellow Text** from the With list, and click **OK**. *The highest five values are highlighted in the Quarter Total column. Mixing highlights, data*

bars, color scales, and icon sets on one worksheet could make the data look confusing. Normally, for consistency, you would limit the styles.

Format Using a Formula

In the next few steps, you will enter a formula that compares the date created to another date. If the result of this logical test is true, the cell's text will change to red.

22. Select **cell B30**, and choose **Home→Styles→Conditional Formatting→New Rule** from the Ribbon. *The New Formatting Rule dialog box displays.*

23. Follow these steps to create a conditional formatting rule using a formula:

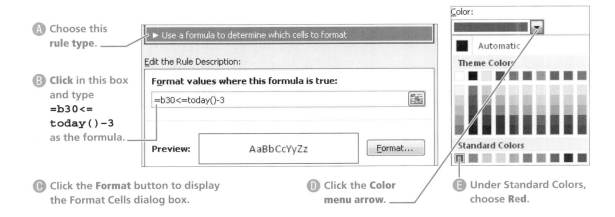

Ⓐ **Choose this rule type.**

Ⓑ **Click in this box and type =b30<= today()-3 as the formula.**

Ⓒ Click the **Format** button to display the Format Cells dialog box.

Ⓓ Click the **Color menu arrow**.

Ⓔ Under Standard Colors, choose **Red**.

24. Click **OK** in the Format Cells dialog box, and click **OK** in the Edit Formatting Rule dialog box. *The formula tests whether the creation date in cell B30 is three or more days before today's date. The logical test result is true, so red was applied to the text in cell B30.*

Remove Conditional Formatting

25. Select the **range C11:C22** and choose **Home→Styles→Conditional Formatting→ Clear Rules→Clear Rules from Selected Cells** from the Ribbon.
The icons disappear from the range. Conditional formats may be removed from a selected range or from the entire worksheet.

26. **Save** 🖫 the changes, and **close** the workbook.

4.12 Concepts Review

Concepts Review   labyrinthelab.com/excel10

To check your knowledge of the key concepts introduced in this lesson, complete the Concepts Review quiz by going to the URL listed above. If your classroom is using Labyrinth eLab, you may complete the Concepts Review quiz from within your eLab course.

Reinforce Your Skills

Format a Worksheet with the Ribbon and Mini Toolbar

In this exercise, you will format a worksheet using commands available on the Home tab of the Ribbon and on the Mini toolbar.

Format Text

1. **Open** the rs-Eco Kids Club Budget Formatting workbook from the Lesson 04 folder in your file storage location.

2. Change the **font** for the entire worksheet to one of your choice.
   Remember that cells to which a nontheme font is applied would not change font if you were to choose a different workbook theme.

3. Select **A1**, **A7**, and **A15** using the Ctrl key.

4. Choose **Home→Font→Bold** **B** from the Ribbon.

5. **Right-click** cell B25 and choose **Bold** **B** from the Mini toolbar.

Format Numbers

6. Select the **ranges B8:D8**, **B13:D13**, and **B16:D16** using the Ctrl key.

7. Choose **Home→Number→Accounting Number Format** **$** from the Ribbon.
   Leave the default two decimal places as is.

8. Select the **range B24:D25**.

9. **Right-click** a selected cell, and choose **Accounting Number Format** **$** from the Mini toolbar.

10. Select the **range B9:D12**.

11. Using the method of your choice, apply **Comma Style** with **two decimal places** to the selection.

12. Select the **range B17:D23**.

13. Use Ctrl + Y to repeat the most recent action.
    Comma Style is applied to the selection. You can use Ctrl + Y or the Mini toolbar if selecting multiple ranges is not convenient.

14. Select **cell D4**.

15. Taking care not to choose Accounting Number Format, choose **Home→Number→Number Format menu ▾** button and choose **Currency** from the list.
    Notice that the dollar sign ($) displays next to the number. Compare this to the dollar sign placement in cell C8, to which you applied Accounting Number Format.

16. **Save** 🖫 the changes, and **close** the workbook.

REINFORCE YOUR SKILLS 4.2

Align Data and Copy Formats

In this exercise, you will change the alignment within cells and copy formatting from one cell to others.

1. **Open** the rs-Eco Kids Club Budget Alignment workbook from the Lesson 04 folder in your file storage location.

2. Select **cell A4** and **right-align** the entry.

3. Select **cell B24**.

4. Choose **Home→Clipboard→Format Painter** from the Ribbon.

5. Select the **range B25:D25**.
   The formatting from cell B24 is applied to the range B25:D25.

6. **Save** the changes and **close** the workbook.

REINFORCE YOUR SKILLS 4.3

Work with Text Control Options

In this exercise, you will merge and center entries, use the Shrink to Fit feature, and insert line breaks to control text.

Merge and Center Titles and Split Cells

1. **Open** the rs-Eco Kids Club Budget Text Control workbook.

2. Select the **range A1:D1**.

3. Choose **Home→Alignment→Merge & Center** from the Ribbon.

4. With the range still selected, choose **Home→Alignment→Merge & Center**.
   Choosing the command again splits, or unmerges, the cells.

5. Select the **range A1:D2**.

6. Choose **Home→Alignment→Merge & Center menu ▾→Merge Across** from the Ribbon.
   The Merge Across command allows you to merge multiple rows at once.

7. **Center-align** the selection.

Use Shrink to Fit

8. Select the **range B6:D6**.

9. Choose **Home→Alignment→dialog box launcher** from the Ribbon.

10. Place a checkmark in the **Shrink to Fit** box under Text Control, as shown at right, and then click **OK**.
    The contents of the cells shrunk to fit into the cells with the current width, but the text is hard to read.

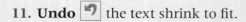

11. **Undo** the text shrink to fit.

Insert Line Breaks

12. **Double-click** cell B6 to begin in-cell editing.

13. Move the **insertion point** just to the left of the *A* in *Actual*, and **tap** ‎Backspace‎ to remove the space between words.

14. Use ‎Alt‎+‎Enter‎ to insert a line break.

15. Repeat the above steps to insert a line break in the text of **cells C6** and **D6**.

16. **Align** the text in the **range B6:D6** with the numbers in the columns.

17. **Save** 💾 the changes, and **close** the workbook.

REINFORCE YOUR SKILLS 4.4

Work with Dates, Cell Styles, and Themes

In this exercise, you will enter a date function that will calculate the current date for you. You will apply cell styles to worksheet cells and change the fonts in the workbook theme.

Insert and Format Today's Date

1. **Open** the rs-Eco Kids Club Budget Date Function workbook.

2. Select **cell B4**.

3. Click the **Insert Function** *ƒx* button.

4. Choose the **Date & Time** category if you do not see the TODAY function in the Most Recently Used category.

5. **Scroll down**, and then click to select the **TODAY** function.

6. Click **OK**.

7. Click **OK** again in the Function Arguments window.
The date will be returned in the default MM/DD/YYYY format.

8. Choose **Home→Number→dialog box launcher** ▢ from the Ribbon.

9. Display the **Number** tab in the Format Cells dialog box, **scroll down** if necessary, and then choose the format that will display the date as in the example **1-Jan-15.**
Excel uses March 14, 2001, as its "example date" in the Type list of the Format Cells dialog box. Rest assured that the date displayed will not be March 14, 2001, unless that is the date entered in the cell or the date resulting from a formula you may have created.

Apply Cell Styles

10. Make certain that **cell B4** is still selected, and then choose **Home→Styles→Cell Styles** from the Ribbon.

11. Choose an appropriate **Quick Style** from the list to draw attention to the date.

12. Select the **ranges A7:D7, A15:D15, and A25:D25** using the ‎Ctrl‎ key.

13. Choose **Home→Styles→Cell Styles from the Ribbon**, and then choose an appropriate **Themed Cell Style** from the list.

Change the Theme Fonts

14. Choose **Page Layout→Themes→Fonts** $\boxed{A}$ from the Ribbon.

15. Point at various **font themes** to preview the workbook, and then choose a **font** theme.
    Remember that you can scroll to view all the font themes.

16. Evaluate how the data appear, and change the **font theme**, if necessary, until you are satisfied.

17. Add any **formatting** that you think enhances the workbook design.

18. **Save**  the changes, and **close** the workbook.

REINFORCE YOUR SKILLS 4.5

Apply Conditional Formatting and Manage Rules

In this exercise, you will apply conditional formatting to cell ranges to analyze trends. You will use the Conditional Formatting Manager to edit, rearrange, and delete conditional formatting rules.

Create Formulas

1. **Open** the rs-Shipping Fee Analysis workbook.

2. Select **cell F4**, and **enter** the formula **=d4-e4**.
   The result should be (37.00). The formula calculates the amount that the estimated shipping fee collected from the customer was over or under the actual fee paid.

3. **Copy** the difference formula in **cell F4** down the column for all orders in **rows 5 through 18**.

4. Select the **range D19:F19**, and use **AutoSum** to total the values in each column. **Bold** all entries in **row 19**.

5. **Right-align** the **column headings** in **row 3**.

Use a Date Preset

6. Select the **range B4:B18**.

7. Choose **Home→Styles→Conditional Formatting→Highlight Cells Rules→A Date Occurring** from the Ribbon.
   The A Date Occurring dialog box appears with the Yesterday option displayed.

8. Choose in **In the Last 7 Days** from the date list, and choose **Green Fill with Dark Green Text** from the With list.
   The last four dates are highlighted in column B of the worksheet.

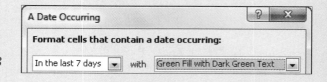

Apply and Customize an Icon Set

9. Select the **range F4:F18**.

10. Choose **Home→Styles→Conditional Formatting→Icon Sets→3 Symbols (Circled)** from the Ribbon.
    Displaying three icons makes the list look cluttered. You want to draw attention to the largest negative amounts.

11. With the **range F4:F18** still selected, follow these steps to remove two icons from the display:

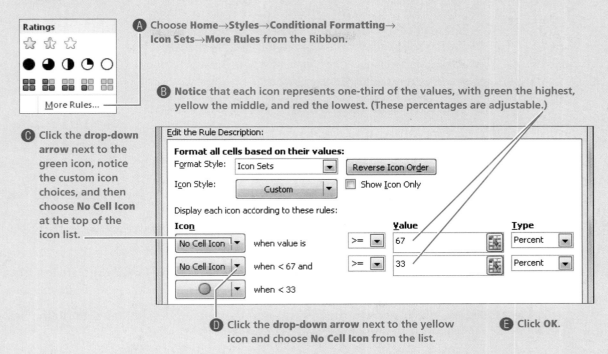

Ⓐ Choose **Home→Styles→Conditional Formatting→ Icon Sets→More Rules** from the Ribbon.

Ⓑ **Notice** that each icon represents one-third of the values, with green the highest, yellow the middle, and red the lowest. (These percentages are adjustable.)

Ⓒ Click the **drop-down arrow** next to the green icon, notice the custom icon choices, and then choose **No Cell Icon** at the top of the icon list.

Ⓓ Click the **drop-down arrow** next to the yellow icon and choose **No Cell Icon** from the list.

Ⓔ Click **OK**.

Now only red icons display to focus attention on three undesirable amounts in cells F4, F6, and F16.

Apply a Color Scale

12. Select the **range E4:E18**.

13. Choose **Home→Styles→ Conditional Formatting→Color Scales→Green-White Color Scale** from the Ribbon. *The Actual Shipping values are highlighted with shades of green. The darkest green highlights the highest value, the shades become lighter as the values decrease, and the lowest value displays a white background.*

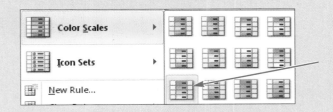

Create a Text Rule

14. Select the **range C4:C18**.

15. Choose **Home→Styles→Conditional Formatting→Highlight Cells Rules→Text That Contains** from the Ribbon.

16. Type **11** in the Format Cells that Contain the Text box, choose **Yellow Fill with Dark Yellow Text** from the With list, and then click **OK**.

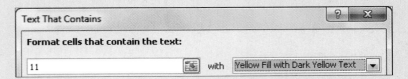

17. Deselect the range, and analyze the results.

Notice that the highlighted cells indicate a pattern. The three worst values marked in the Difference column also are highlighted in dark green as the highest Actual Shipping charges. The yellow highlights in the Shipped Via column show that vendor 11 shipped these three orders. Conditional formatting makes important data and trends clear.

	C	D	E	F
3	Shipped Via	Estimated Shipping	Actual Shipping	Difference
4	11	125.00	162.00	(37.00)
5	22	10.00	8.95	1.05
6	11	100.00	142.65	(42.65)
7	33	50.00	50.00	-
8	44	10.00	17.45	(7.45)
9	44	16.00	13.25	2.75
10	33	82.00	64.00	18.00
11	22	40.00	23.75	16.25
12	33	5.00	4.95	0.05
13	22	42.00	48.75	(6.75)
14	11	100.00	100.00	-
15	44	52.50	46.25	6.25
16	11	200.00	240.00	(40.00)

Apply, Edit, and Rearrange Multiple Rules

18. Select the **range C4:C18**.

19. Choose **Home→Styles→Conditional Formatting→Highlight Cells Rules→Duplicate Values** from the Ribbon, choose options to **format duplicate values with a green fill with dark green text**, and click **OK**.

All vendor numbers in column C are duplicates. The second rule overwrites the yellow highlighting created by the first rule. You will arrange rules to prevent this.

20. Choose **Home→Styles→Conditional Formatting→Manage Rules** from the Ribbon.
The Manage Rules command is at the bottom of the Conditional Formatting menu.

21. Follow these steps in the Conditional Formatting Rules Manager dialog box to rearrange the two rules applied to range C4:C18:

A **Drop down** the Show Formatting Rules For list and choose **This Worksheet** to display all conditional formatting rules.

B Select the **Cell Value Contains '11'** rule (the second rule in the list), and then click the **Move Up** button.

Conditional Formatting Rules Manager

Show formatting rules for: This Worksheet

New Rule... | Edit Rule... | Delete Rule

Rule (applied in order shown)	Format	Applies to	Stop If True
Cell Value = 11	AaBbCcYyZz	=$C$4:$C$18	☑
Duplicate Values	AaBbCcYyZz	=$C$4:$C$18	☐
Graded Color Scale		=$E$4:$E$18	☐
Icon Set		=$F$4:$F$18	☐
Icon Set		=$F$4:$F$18	☐

C Click to add a checkmark in the **Stop If True** box for the Cell Value Contains '11' rule.

D Click **OK**.

Conditional Formatting rules are applied in the order listed. The Stop If True option in the first rule prevents the green formatting from being applied by the Duplicate Values rule.

Delete a Conditional Formatting Rule

22. Choose **Home→Styles→Conditional Formatting→Manage Rules** from the Ribbon.

23. Drop down the Show Formatting Rules For list and choose **This Worksheet**.

24. Select the Icon Set rule that displays **three icons**.

Icon Set	● ○ ○	=$F$4:$F$18	

This rule is no longer needed because you customized the icons.

25. Click the **Delete Rule** button at the top of the dialog box, and then click **OK**.
Your worksheet should resemble the following illustration. Your dates in column B will differ.

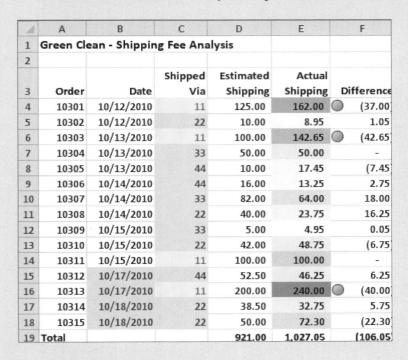

	A	B	C	D	E	F
1	Green Clean - Shipping Fee Analysis					
2						
3	Order	Date	Shipped Via	Estimated Shipping	Actual Shipping	Difference
4	10301	10/12/2010	11	125.00	162.00 ○	(37.00)
5	10302	10/12/2010	22	10.00	8.95	1.05
6	10303	10/13/2010	11	100.00	142.65 ○	(42.65)
7	10304	10/13/2010	33	50.00	50.00	–
8	10305	10/13/2010	44	10.00	17.45	(7.45)
9	10306	10/14/2010	44	16.00	13.25	2.75
10	10307	10/14/2010	33	82.00	64.00	18.00
11	10308	10/14/2010	22	40.00	23.75	16.25
12	10309	10/15/2010	33	5.00	4.95	0.05
13	10310	10/15/2010	22	42.00	48.75	(6.75)
14	10311	10/15/2010	11	100.00	100.00	–
15	10312	10/17/2010	44	52.50	46.25	6.25
16	10313	10/17/2010	11	200.00	240.00 ○	(40.00)
17	10314	10/18/2010	22	38.50	32.75	5.75
18	10315	10/18/2010	22	50.00	72.30	(22.30)
19	Total			921.00	1,027.05	(106.05)

26. Save 🖫 the changes, and **close** the workbook.

Apply Your Skills

Format Text and Numbers

In this exercise, you will format text and numbers.

1. **Open** the as-Green Clean Inventory workbook from the Lesson 04 folder in your file storage location.

2. Format **cell D5** in **Currency Style** with **two decimals**.

3. Format the **range D6:D9** in **Number** style from the Number Format list in the Ribbon.

4. Format the **range E5:E10** in **Comma Style** with **zero decimals**.

5. Apply **bold** formatting to the entries in **rows 4** and **10**.

6. Format the title in **cell A1** with **bold**, and change the font size to **14**.

7. **Save** 💾 the changes to the workbook, and continue with the next exercise.

▲	A	B	C	D	E
1	**Green Clean Inventory**				
2	Carpet Products				
3					
4	**CARPET CLEANING SOLUTIONS**	**Type**	**Size**	**Price**	**Quantity**
5	EarthWise Carpet Cleaner	Concentrate	64 ounces	$17.50	224
6	EarthWise Carpet Cleaner	Concentrate	32 ounces	9.85	468
7	EarthWise Carpet Cleaner	Spray	16 ounces	4.50	201
8	GBS All Purpose Carpet	Liquid	120 ounces	11.95	53
9	GBS Dry Powder Cleaner	Powder	16 ounces	4.25	134
10	**Total Inventory**				**1,080**
11					
12	CARPET STAIN REMOVERS	Type	Size	Retail Price	Quantity
13	EarthWise Carpet Stain Remover	Concentrate	64 ounces	9.95	251
14	EarthWise Carpet Stain Remover	Concentrate	32 ounces	5.5	131
15	EarthWise Carpet Stain Remover	Spray	16 ounces	4.65	192
16	Carpet Bright Stain Eliminator	Spray	32 ounces	7.35	62
17	Total Inventory				636

Align and Control Text, Add Borders, and Use Format Painter

In this exercise, you will center the titles across worksheet columns, insert line breaks to wrap text, apply borders to a cell, and use Format Painter.

Before You Begin: You must have completed Apply Your Skills 4.1, and the as-Green Clean Inventory workbook should be open.

1. **Merge** and **center** the titles in **cells A1** and **A2** across **columns A through E**.

2. Change **cell D4** to **Retail Price** and insert a **line break** so that each word is on a separate line in the entry.

3. **Right-align** the entries in **cells D4** and **E4**.

4. Place a **single border** along the top of the **cell E10** and a **double line border** along the bottom.

5. Use **Format Painter** to apply the formatting from the **range A4:E4** to the **range A12:E12**.

6. Use **Format Painter** to apply the following formatting:
   - From cell D5 to **cell D13**
   - From cell D6 to the **range D14:D16**
   - From cell E5 to the **range E13:E16**
   - From cell E10 to **cell E17**

7. **Save** 💾 the changes to the workbook, and continue with the next exercise.

▲	A	B	C	D	E
1	**Green Clean Inventory**				
2	Carpet Products				
3					
4	**CARPET CLEANING SOLUTIONS**	**Type**	**Size**	**Retail Price**	**Quantity**
5	EarthWise Carpet Cleaner	Concentrate	64 ounces	$17.50	224
6	EarthWise Carpet Cleaner	Concentrate	32 ounces	9.85	468
7	EarthWise Carpet Cleaner	Spray	16 ounces	4.50	201
8	GBS All Purpose Carpet	Liquid	120 ounces	11.95	53
9	GBS Dry Powder Cleaner	Powder	16 ounces	4.25	134
10	**Total Inventory**				**1,080**
11					
12	**CARPET STAIN REMOVERS**	**Type**	**Size**	**Retail Price**	**Quantity**
13	EarthWise Carpet Stain Remover	Concentrate	64 ounces	$9.95	251
14	EarthWise Carpet Stain Remover	Concentrate	32 ounces	5.50	131
15	EarthWise Carpet Stain Remover	Spray	16 ounces	4.65	192
16	Carpet Bright Stain Eliminator	Spray	32 ounces	7.35	62
17	**Total Inventory**				**636**

Change the Theme, Apply Color to Cells, and Create Conditional Formatting

In this exercise, you will indent cell entries, center the title across worksheet columns, apply a border to cells, and use Format Painter. You will apply a conditional formatting rule to highlight low quantities of products in the inventory.

Before You Begin: *You must have completed Apply Your Skills 4.2, and the as-Green Clean Inventory workbook should be open.*

1. Apply the **fill color** of your choice to the **merged range A1:A2**.

2. Change the **font color** in the **ranges A5:C9** and **A13:C16**.

3. Apply the **Sketchbook** theme to the workbook. (This theme is in the From Office.com group of the menu. If unavailable, choose an appropriate theme from the Built-In group.)

4. Use **Page Layout view** or the **Print** tab in Backstage view to ensure that the worksheet fits on one page.

5. Create a **conditional formatting rule** that highlights any values below 150 in the Quantity column, but do not include the total inventory cells.

6. **Save** 🖫 the changes, and **close** the workbook.

	A	B	C	D	E
1	**Green Clean Inventory**				
2	Carpet Products				
3					
4	**CARPET CLEANING SOLUTION!**	**Type**	**Size**	**Retail Price**	**Quantity**
5	EarthWise Carpet Cleaner	Concentrate	64 ounces	$17.50	224
6	EarthWise Carpet Cleaner	Concentrate	32 ounces	9.85	468
7	EarthWise Carpet Cleaner	Spray	16 ounces	4.50	201
8	GBS All Purpose Carpet	Liquid	120 ounces	11.95	53
9	GBS Dry Powder Cleaner	Powder	16 ounces	4.25	134
10	**Total Inventory**				**1,080**
11					
12	**CARPET STAIN REMOVERS**	**Type**	**Size**	**Retail Price**	**Quantity**
13	EarthWise Carpet Stain Remover	Concentrate	64 ounces	$9.95	251
14	EarthWise Carpet Stain Remover	Concentrate	32 ounces	5.50	131
15	EarthWise Carpet Stain Remover	Spray	16 ounces	4.65	192
16	Carpet Bright Stain Eliminator	Spray	32 ounces	7.35	62
17	**Total Inventory**				**636**

Critical Thinking & Work-Readiness Skills

In the course of working through the following Microsoft Office-based Critical Thinking exercises, you will also be utilizing various work-readiness skills, some of which are listed next to each exercise. Go to labyrinthelab.com/ workreadiness to learn more about the work-readiness skills.

4.1 Format Text in an Excel Spreadsheet

Green Clean (and any organization in which you may be employed) has design preferences and standards. This exercise will help you build your formatting ability according to Green Clean's standards. Open ct-Customer Base (Lesson 04 folder). Practice the following skills:

- Right-align the column headings in columns B-F.
- Indent companies A-K in column A.
- Merge the range A1:F1, and type **First Quarter Sales** in the merged cell. Apply appropriate text formatting to this title.
- Text wrap your full name and today's date in cell A20.

Save your work as **ct-Customer Base1** in your Lesson 04 folder.

4.2 Display Numbers in an Excel Spreadsheet

Green Clean uses numbers in spreadsheets for a variety of purposes: currency style for their price lists, quantities for order forms, and accounting styles and negative numbers for budgeting. Open ct-Customer Base1, if necessary, and resave it as **ct-CustomerBase2**. You realize that to work with all of the company's spreadsheets, you need to practice formatting numbers, noting accounting, currency, percent, and negative numbers styles. Select the range D4:D18. From the Number group on the Home tab of the Ribbon, select different number styles. Note the various foreign currency styles on the Accounting Number Format menu. Remember these styles do not calculate exchange rates. Select the range F3:F18 and format the range to show tenths of a percent (0.1%). Select cell D18.

4.3 Use Format Painter and Insert the Date

Green Clean plans to acquire several small cleaning companies. In anticipation of adding a lot of data to Customer Base spreadsheet you decide to hone your spreadsheet skills. Open ct-Customer Base2, if necessary, and save it as **ct-CustomerBase3**. Using the Format Painter, change the column C entries to look like those in column B. Think about how Format Painter can help you be consistent and efficient. Then, returning to the Excel spreadsheet, insert today's date in cell B20 and the time in cell C20. Practice inserting date and time functions. If working alone, format the date and time at least three different ways. If working in a group, discuss the usefulness of date and time stamping. Save the changes to your spreadsheet and close the file.

Changing the Appearance of Worksheets

LESSON OUTLINE

LEARNING OBJECTIVES

After studying this lesson, you will be able to:

- Insert, delete, move, copy, and rename worksheets in a workbook
- Modify column width and row height
- Insert, delete, hide, and unhide columns and rows
- Set the vertical alignment and rotate text
- Find and replace data and formatting, and use AutoCorrect effectively

In this lesson, you will learn techniques for changing the structure of worksheets as it relates to worksheet tab order, rows, columns, and additional cell alignment options. In addition, you will learn about time-saving features such as Find and Replace. After you complete this lesson, you will have learned many basics you need to work with Excel.

CASE STUDY

Changing Workbook Tabs, Columns, and Rows

Safety is an important concern at Green Clean, the janitorial product supplier and cleaning service contractor. Isabella Riso-Neff is the risk management director. She prepares company policies and procedures for legal compliance, contracts, insurance, Worker's Compensation, and workplace safety. Isabella is coordinating with Ken Hazell, the human resources director, to formalize the safety training program at Green Clean.

Isabella will organize the structure of a workbook containing multiple worksheets. A worksheet will contain a list of learning objectives for the training topic. Test questions will be created for each objective to assess an employee's knowledge and performance regarding the objective. The worksheet will show the number of test questions in each category as well as the total and percentage. Isabella will work with entire rows and columns to organize the worksheet, find and replace text and formats, and vertically align and rotate headings.

	A	B	C	D	E	F	G	H
1		Green Clean						
2		Safety Training - Chemicals						
3			Exam Categories					
4		Performance Objectives	Knowledge	Comprehension	Performance	Analysis	Total	Percentage
5			(Number of Items)					
6	1.	*Identify and mix hazardous materials safely.*						
7		a. Understand and follow steps on material safety data sheets (MSDS) correctly.	2	1	2		5	10%
8		b. Identify hazardous materials		2	2	1	5	10%

Column widths and row heights are adjusted to display the cell contents. The text for the exam categories is rotated 90 degrees to fit the columns on one page.

24		a. Demonstrate first aid procedures for various given incidents.	2	2	2	0	0%
25		b. Demonstrate the use of an emergency wash station.	2	2	2	2	4%
26		Total	7	20	29	11	52	100%
27		Percentage	13%	38%	56%	21%	100%	
28								

⊮ ◀ ▶ ⊯ **Chemicals** ╱ Lifting ╱ Garbage ╱ Floors ╱ Notes ╱ ⌁ ╱

Worksheet tabs are copied, rearranged, and colored to clearly identify the workbook structure.

5.1 Managing Worksheets

Video Lesson   labyrinthelab.com/videos

As you begin to work with more complex workbooks, you will need to be comfortable with workbook management and navigating among multiple worksheets. You can organize a workbook by inserting, deleting, and rearranging worksheets. You also can rename worksheet tabs and apply colors to them.

Inserting and Deleting Worksheets

FROM THE KEYBOARD

Shift + F11 to insert a worksheet

Although Excel displays three worksheets in a new workbook by default, you can insert as many new worksheets as your available computer memory allows. Excel makes it very easy to insert a new worksheet with the Insert Worksheet button located at the far right corner of the worksheet tabs. You may also insert multiple worksheets before any worksheet tab. To clean up the appearance of your workbook, you may wish to delete unused worksheets. You may also select multiple worksheets for deletion at one time. Realize, though, that deleting a worksheet cannot be undone!

Rearranging, Copying, Renaming, and Coloring Worksheet Tabs

Sheet tabs can be placed in any order simply by dragging. You can duplicate a worksheet by holding Ctrl and dragging its tab to the desired location. This copying feature is useful in creating sheets for recurring time periods, such as quarters of the year, or categories, as you will do in this lesson. You can also rename a worksheet tab to give it a more descriptive name. If you want to organize your workbook a bit more, you can change the color of the tabs. The active worksheet tab name will be displayed in bold. Take a look at the following figure to learn more about worksheet tabs.

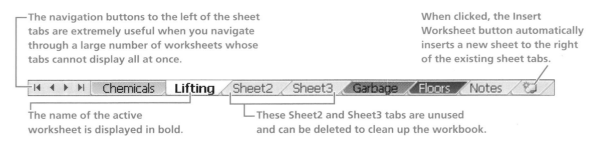

The navigation buttons to the left of the sheet tabs are extremely useful when you navigate through a large number of worksheets whose tabs cannot display all at once.

When clicked, the Insert Worksheet button automatically inserts a new sheet to the right of the existing sheet tabs.

The name of the active worksheet is displayed in bold.

These Sheet2 and Sheet3 tabs are unused and can be deleted to clean up the workbook.

You cannot undo the Delete worksheet command. If you issue the command by mistake, however, you can close the workbook without saving it and then reopen it to recover the lost worksheet.

Hiding and Unhiding Worksheets

You can hide a worksheet from view. For example, you may temporarily want to work with only certain sheets or prefer not to call attention to data on a specific worksheet. Be aware, however, that anyone using your workbook could unhide the sheet. You can hide and unhide worksheets using commands on the Ribbon or from the context menu that displays after you right-click a sheet tab.

QUICK REFERENCE   MANAGING WORKSHEETS

Task	Procedure
Activate a worksheet	■ Click the desired worksheet tab.
Rename a worksheet	■ Double-click the worksheet tab to be renamed. ■ Type a new name and tap [Enter].
Change the worksheet tab color	■ Right-click the desired sheet tab. ■ Choose Tab Color from the context menu and click the desired color.
Insert a worksheet to the right of existing sheet tabs	■ Click the Insert Worksheet button to the right of the last tab displayed.
Insert a worksheet before the active sheet tab	■ Choose Insert→Cells→Insert→Insert menu ▼→Insert Sheet from the Ribbon.
Insert multiple worksheets before the active sheet tab	■ Select the desired worksheet tab, hold down [Shift], and then click a sheet tab at the right to equal the number of worksheets that you wish to insert. ■ Choose Home→Cells→Insert menu ▼→Insert Sheet from the Ribbon.
Delete a worksheet	■ Right-click the tab of the worksheet you wish to delete. ■ Choose Delete from the context menu.
Delete multiple worksheets	■ Select the first worksheet tab to be deleted, hold down [Ctrl], and then click each additional sheet tab that you wish to delete. (Or, hold down [Shift] and select the last in a range of tabs.) ■ Choose Home→Cells→Delete menu ▼→Delete Sheet from the Ribbon. ■ Click Delete in the dialog box that appears.
Move a worksheet	■ Drag the worksheet tab to the desired position in the worksheet order.
Copy a worksheet	■ Select the sheet to be copied. ■ Hold down [Ctrl] while dragging the tab of the sheet you wish to copy. ■ Release the mouse button, and then release [Ctrl] when the new tab is in the desired position.
Hide a worksheet	■ Select the worksheet tab. ■ Choose Home→Cells→Format→Hide & Unhide→Hide Sheet from the Ribbon, or right-click the sheet tab and choose Hide from the context menu.
Unhide a worksheet	■ Choose Home→Cells→Format→Hide & Unhide→Unhide Sheet from the Ribbon (or right-click the sheet tab and choose Unhide from the context menu), and choose the sheet to be unhidden.

Modify Workbook Sheet Order and Sheet Tabs

In this exercise, you will insert and move a new worksheet, delete a sheet, and copy a sheet. You will rename worksheet tabs and change their color. Finally, you will hide and unhide a worksheet.

Rename Sheet Tabs

1. **Open** the Safety Training workbook from the Lesson 05 folder in your file storage location.

2. Follow these steps to rename Sheet1:

Ⓐ **Double-click** the Sheet1 tab at the bottom of the worksheet to select its name.　　Ⓑ Type **Chemicals**.

Ⓒ **Tap** Enter to complete the name change.

3. **Rename** Sheet2 to **Lifting**.

Insert, Move, and Delete Sheets

4. Click the **Insert Worksheet** button to the right of the sheet tabs.
   A new sheet appears to the right of the existing sheets.

5. **Rename** the new sheet as **Notes**.

6. Drag the **Notes** sheet to the left of **Sheet3**.

   Notice that the mouse pointer displays an empty sheet icon as you drag to the desired position indicated by the small triangle ▼. Drag again if the Notes sheet does not display between Lifting and Sheet3 after you release the mouse button.

7. **Right-click** Sheet3, and choose **Delete** from the context menu.
   Excel does not ask you to confirm the deletion because the worksheet is empty.

8. Click the **Lifting** sheet tab to select the sheet.

9. **Hold down** Shift and select the **Notes** tab.
   Both tabs are selected. Next, you will insert two sheets, the number of sheets selected.

10. Choose **Home→Cells→Insert menu ▼→Insert Sheet** from the Ribbon.

   Two new sheets were inserted before the Lifting sheet. Your sheet numbers may be different.

11. With Sheet5 currently selected, **hold down** Ctrl and select the **Sheet6** tab.
   The Ctrl key allows you select nonadjacent sheets for deletion, while the Shift key selects all sheets between the active sheet tab and the next tab you select.

12. Choose **Home→Cells→Delete menu ▾→Delete Sheet** from the Ribbon.
    The two sheets are deleted.

13. **Save**  the changes to the workbook.

Copy the Lifting Sheet

14. Click the **Lifting** sheet tab to select the sheet.

15. **Hold down** Ctrl, drag the **Lifting** tab to the right to position it between Lifting and Notes, and **release** Ctrl.

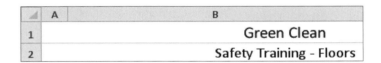

Notice that the mouse pointer displays a sheet icon containing a plus sign (+) as you drag, indicating that you are copying the sheet. The duplicated sheet is named Lifting (2).

16. **Rename** Lifting (2) to `Garbage`.

17. Repeat **steps 8–10** to copy the **Garbage** sheet and **rename** it to `Floors`.

18. In **cell A2** of the Floors sheet, edit *Lifting and Motion* to read `Floors`.

	A	B
1		Green Clean
2		Safety Training - Floors

19. Select the **Garbage** sheet.

20. In **cell A2**, edit *Lifting and Motion* to read `Garbage`.

Change the Sheet Tab Color

21. **Right-click** the Chemicals sheet, point to Tab Color in the context menu, and choose the **orange theme color** from the palette, as shown.

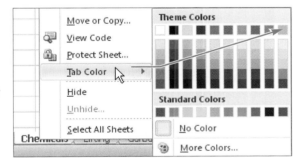

22. Repeat the above step to apply a **blue theme shade** to the **Lifting sheet** tab.

23. Apply a **green theme shade** to the **Garbage** sheet tab.

24. Apply a **brown theme shade** to the **Floors** tab.
    You will leave the Notes tab in its original gray shade.

25. Select the **Chemicals** tab.
    Notice that the text of the currently selected tab turns bold and its color reduces to a subtle orange band below the text.

Hide and Unhide a Worksheet

26. **Right-click** the Notes sheet tab and choose **Hide** from the context menu, as shown at right.
    The worksheet and its tab disappear.

27. Choose **Home→Cells→Format** from the Ribbon.

28. Trace down to **Visibility**, point to **Hide & Unhide**, and choose **Unhide Sheet** from the submenu that appears.

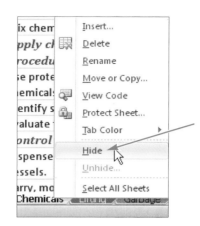

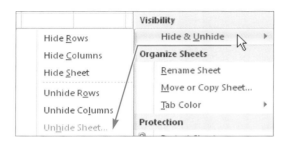

The Unhide dialog box displays. The Notes sheet already is selected because it is the only one available to be unhidden.

29. Click **OK**.

30. **Save** 💾 the changes to the workbook and continue with the next topic.

5.2 Modifying Columns and Rows

Video Lesson   labyrinthelab.com/videos

As you have seen, many entries do not fit within the default column width. Worksheets can also appear overcrowded with the standard row heights, which may tempt you to insert blank rows to make the worksheet more readable. The problem with this "fix," though, is that it can cause problems down the road when you begin to use some of Excel's more powerful features. In this lesson, you will use more time-saving techniques to fix column width and row height issues, such as changing multiple columns and rows at the same time and using AutoFit to let Excel figure out the best width or height. Both of these commands simply require you to select multiple columns or rows before issuing the command.

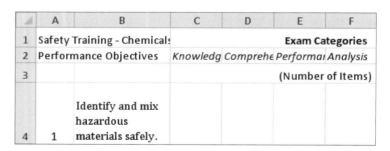

You can see that you have a lot of work to do here in resizing rows and columns!

Column Widths and Row Heights

There are a variety of methods for changing widths of columns and heights of rows. They can be performed on either one or multiple columns or rows. One efficient way to adjust widths and heights is to simply drag the heading lines of the column(s) or row(s).

Standard Column Widths and Row Heights

Each column in a new worksheet has a standard width of 8.43 characters, where the default text setting is Calibri 11 point. Each row has a standard height of 15 points, which is approximately one-fifth of an inch.

AutoFit

You can adjust both column widths and row heights with the AutoFit command. AutoFit adjusts column widths to fit the widest entry in a column. Likewise, AutoFit adjusts row heights to accommodate the tallest entry in a row. The following Quick Reference table discusses AutoFit options and other commands for setting column widths and row heights.

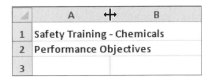

When you point to the border between columns or rows, a double-pointed arrow lets you know you can manually drag to change its size or double-click to issue the AutoFit command.

QUICK REFERENCE	CHANGING COLUMN WIDTHS AND ROW HEIGHTS
Technique	**Procedure**
Set a precise column width	■ Select the column for which you wish to change the width. ■ Choose Home→Cells→Format→Column Width from the Ribbon. ■ Type the column width you desire.
Set column widths with AutoFit using the Ribbon	■ Select the column(s) for which you wish to change the width. ■ Choose Home→Cells→Format→AutoFit Column Width from the Ribbon.
Set column widths with AutoFit by double-clicking	■ Select a single column or multiple columns for which you wish to change the width. ■ Position the mouse pointer between any two selected headings or to the right of the selected single column heading. Double-click only when you see the double arrow mouse pointer to AutoFit all selected columns.
Set a precise row height	■ Select the row for which you wish to change the height. ■ Choose Home→Cells→Format→Row Height from the Ribbon. ■ Type the row height you desire.
Set row heights with AutoFit	■ Select the row for which you wish to change the height. ■ Choose Home→Cells→Format→AutoFit Row Height from the Ribbon. You can also select multiple rows and double-click between any two selected headings to AutoFit all selected rows.
Manually adjust column widths and row heights	■ Select one or more columns or rows and drag the column or row heading line instead of double-clicking it.

Change Column Width and Row Height

In this exercise, you will change the column width and row height to ensure that the cell entries fit properly.

1. Display the **Chemicals** worksheet of the Safety Training workbook.

Adjust Column Widths

2. Follow these steps to resize column A:

Ⓐ Place the **mouse pointer** to the right of column A until the double-arrow mouse pointer appears, and then **double-click**.

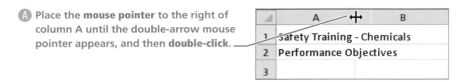

Notice that the column is resized to fit the widest entry, which is in row 1. You will be merging and centering the title in row 1, so this column is too wide for your use.

Ⓑ Point to the border between **columns A and B** until the double-arrow appears.

Ⓒ **Click** and **drag** with the mouse to the left.

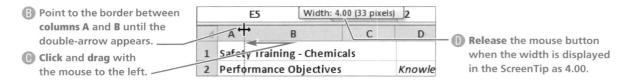

Ⓓ **Release** the mouse button when the width is displayed in the ScreenTip as 4.00.

Set a Precise Column Width

3. Click the **column B heading** to select the entire column.

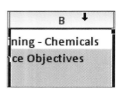

4. Follow these steps to precisely set the column width:

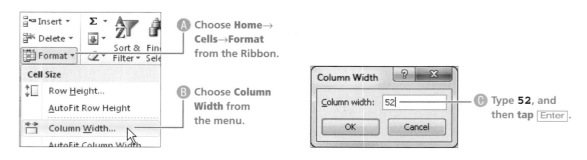

Ⓐ Choose **Home→ Cells→Format** from the Ribbon.

Ⓑ Choose **Column Width** from the menu.

Ⓒ Type **52**, and then tap Enter.

The column has been sized much larger to accommodate the larger cell entries, which have "spread out" because the cells are formatted to wrap text.

5. Click the **heading** for **row 4** and drag down through **row 23**.

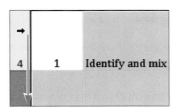

Rows 4 through 24 should now be selected. Any command issued will apply to all selected rows.

6. **Point** between two of the selected rows to display the double-arrow pointer and **double-click**.
All of the selected rows shrink to fit the tallest entry. You can choose Home→ Cells→Format→AutoFit Row Height from the Ribbon if you have difficulty keeping the mouse still while double-clicking.

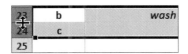

7. **Save** 💾 the changes to the workbook.

5.3 Inserting and Deleting Columns, Rows, and Cells

| Video Lesson | labyrinthelab.com/videos |

You can insert and delete columns, rows, and cells as needed in your worksheets. You probably figure that you will have plenty of rows and columns because you start out with more than 1,000,000 and 16,000 of them, respectively. The ability to insert and delete will come in handy when you want to restructure your worksheet after it has been created.

Inserting and Deleting Rows and Columns

Excel lets you insert and delete rows and columns. This feature gives you the flexibility to restructure your worksheets after they have been set up. The Quick Reference table in this section discusses the various procedures used to insert and delete rows and columns.

Formulas using SUM, AVERAGE, and other similar functions will update automatically to take into account inserted and deleted rows and columns with two exceptions. If you insert a row above the first row in the range and its formula, you will need to edit the formula to include that row. Likewise, you will need to edit the formula if you insert a column to the left of the first column in the formula range. The following illustration shows how the inserted row has no effect on the SUM formulas.

	A	B	C	D	E
1		Solvents	Cleaners	Polishes	Total
2		2	2	2	
3	In Stock	2	2	2	6
4	Ordered	2	2	2	6
5	Damaged	2	2	2	6
6	Total	=SUM(B3:B5)		6	18

A new row 2 was inserted above the range included in the original SUM formula. Notice that the SUM formula does not include the new row because it is above the cell that began the original range. The totals are still 6 rather than 8. If a new row were inserted between rows 3 and 4, the function would be automatically updated to include the new row because it is within the range of the formula. The totals would then be 8.

Excel does not alert you to an inserted row or column outside the original range used in a formula.

Inserting and Deleting Cells

If you want to insert or delete only cells, not entire rows or columns, you need to issue a command to insert or delete cells. This command will allow you to add or remove a "chunk" or range of cells from your worksheet. However, this command may cause problems because it alters the structure of your entire worksheet. For this reason, use this feature cautiously.

Shift Cells Option

When you add or remove a range of cells from your worksheet, you will need to tell Excel how to shift the surrounding cells to either make room for the addition or fill the space from the deletion.

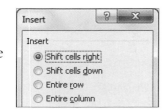

There are four Shift Cells options for you to choose from when you insert cells.

The Appearance of the Cells Group Commands

The buttons in the Cells group of the Home tab of the Ribbon will appear differently depending on the size of your Excel window (which may be determined by the size of your monitor).

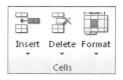

The figure on the left displays how the Cells group buttons will be displayed in a larger window, whereas the figure on the right displays the buttons as displayed in a smaller window. In the exercise steps, you will see the illustrations depicting the larger Ribbon buttons.

QUICK REFERENCE	INSERTING AND DELETING ROWS, COLUMNS, AND CELLS
Task	**Procedure**
Insert rows	■ Select the number of rows you wish to insert (the same number of new rows will be inserted above the selected rows).
	■ Choose Home→Cells→Insert from the Ribbon, or right-click the selection and choose Insert from the context menu.
Insert columns	■ Select the number of columns you wish to insert (the same number of new columns will be inserted to the left of the selected columns).
	■ Choose Home→Cells→Insert from the Ribbon, or right-click the selection and choose Insert from the context menu.
Delete rows	■ Select the rows you wish to delete.
	■ Right-click the selection and choose Delete.

Task	Procedure
Delete columns	■ Select the columns you wish to delete. ■ Right-click the selection and choose Delete.
Insert cells	■ Select the cells in the worksheet where you want the inserted cells to appear. ■ Choose Home→Cells→Insert from the Ribbon, or right-click the selection and choose Insert from the context menu. ■ Choose the desired Shift Cells option.
Delete cells	■ Select the cells you wish to delete. ■ Choose Home→Cells→Delete from the Ribbon, or right-click the selection and choose Delete from the context menu. ■ Choose the desired Shift Cells option.

DEVELOP YOUR SKILLS 5.3.1

Add and Remove Rows, Columns, and Cells

In this exercise, you will insert and delete rows, as well as insert cells into the worksheet.

Delete Unnecessary Rows

1. Select **rows 15** and **24**, using the ⎡Ctrl⎤ key to select **nonadjacent** rows.
   The rows in which there are no objectives listed are now selected.

2. With both rows still selected, **right-click** row 24 and choose **Delete** from the context menu.
   The data below a deleted row moves up one row.

Add Another Row to the Sheet

3. Select **row 6**.
   When you choose to insert a row, the new row will be placed above the row you have selected.

4. **Point** (don't click) over the **Home→Cells→Insert** button on the Ribbon as shown.
   Notice that when you place the mouse pointer over the Insert button, there is a line that divides it into two halves. If you click above or to the left of the line (depending on how large the Ribbon appears on your computer), a new cell, row, or column will be inserted above or to the left of your selection. If you click below or to the right of the line, a menu appears from which you can select a command.

5. Click the **Insert** button (not the menu ▼ button).

6. **Enter** the text in the following illustration into the appropriate cells.

⫟	A	B	C	D	E	F
8	b.	Identify hazardous materials.		2	2	1

7. Follow these steps to copy the necessary formulas:

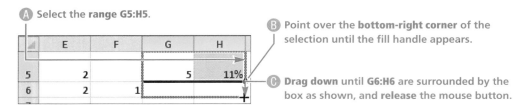

Ⓐ Select the **range G5:H5**.

Ⓑ Point over the **bottom-right corner** of the selection until the fill handle appears.

Ⓒ **Drag down** until **G6:H6 are surrounded by the** box as shown, and **release** the mouse button.

All of the formulas and functions have automatically been updated to include the correct cell addresses because cell references were used in creating the worksheet formulas. The percentages in column H recalculated to include the new values, and cell H5 now displays 10%.

Insert a Row Outside a Formula Range

8. Select **cell C24** and view its formula in the Formula Bar, and then select **cell C25** and view its formula.
   The C24 formula is =SUM(C4:C23), and the C25 formula is =C24/$G$24. The related worksheet formulas have automatically been updated as a result of the previous steps. The formulas include the correct cell addresses because the deleted and inserted rows were within the original ranges of the formulas.

9. Insert a **new row** at **row 4**.

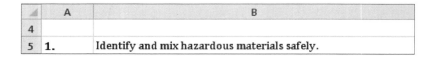

10. Select **cell C25** and view its formula in the Formula Bar.
    The formula adjusted to =SUM(C5:C24) because the data moved down one row. However, the formula did not update to include cell C4 from the newly created row. That row is above the first cell of the original range in the formula. You would need to edit formulas if you wanted to include row 4.

11. **Undo** 🔄 the inserted row 4.

Insert Cells into the Worksheet

You have discovered that you want to merge and center the contents of cell A1 over the entire worksheet. You will need to "bump" everything in columns C through H down one row.

12. Select the **range C1:H1**.

13. Follow these steps to insert the cells and shift your existing data down:

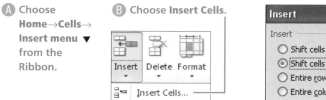

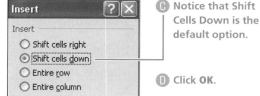

Ⓐ Choose **Home→Cells→ Insert menu ▼** from the Ribbon.

Ⓑ Choose **Insert Cells.**

Ⓒ Notice that Shift Cells Down is the default option.

Ⓓ Click **OK.**

14. Select the **range A3:B3**.

15. Choose **Home→Cells→Insert** ⊞ from the Ribbon.
    Everything in columns A and B, below cells A3 and B3, is shifted down one cell.

16. Select **row 1** and choose **Home→Cells→Insert** ⊞ from the Ribbon again.
    Because you selected an entire row first, a new row is inserted.

Time to Format!

Now that you have changed the structure of the worksheet a bit, you will do some formatting to make it more presentable.

17. Follow these steps to merge and center a range:
    - Select the **range A1:H1**.
    - Choose **Home→Alignment→Merge & Center** ⊞ from the Ribbon.
    - While the merged range is still selected, change the font size to **16**.

    There is nothing in this cell at this time, but you will add a text title later.

18. **Merge & Center** ⊞ the **range A2:H2** and change the font size to **14**.

19. **Merge & Center** ⊞ the **range A3:B5** and change the font size to **14**.
    Notice that the Merge & Center command works to merge both columns and rows at once.

20. **Merge & Center** ⊞ the **range C3:H3** and place a **border** along the bottom of the cells.

21. **Merge & Center** ⊞ the **range C5:H5**.

22. **Right-align** ≡ the **range B26:B27**.
    Once you are done formatting, your worksheet should resemble the following figure.

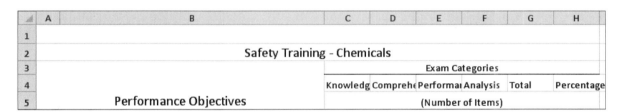

23. Use ⎡Ctrl⎤+⎡S⎤ to **save** the changes to the workbook.

5.4 Formatting and Hiding Columns and Rows

Video Lesson labyrinthelab.com/videos

You can format, hide, and unhide columns and rows by first selecting the desired columns or rows. You can make your selection in several ways: clicking a single column or row heading, dragging to select adjacent headings, or holding the Ctrl key while you click each nonadjacent heading.

Formatting All Cells in a Column or Row Simultaneously

Once you have selected the desired row or column, you apply any formatting just as you would to a single cell or range. The formatting is applied to every cell across the row or down the column to the end of the worksheet. The advantage to formatting entire rows or columns is that the formatting already is applied consistently to every cell when you enter data. Some settings, such as column width or row height, automatically apply to every cell in the column or row.

Hiding Columns and Rows

There may be times when you wish to hide certain rows or columns from view. The hidden rows and columns will not be visible, nor will they print. However, the hidden rows and columns will still be part of the worksheet, and their values and formulas could still be referenced by other formulas in the visible rows and columns. Hiding rows and columns can be useful when you want to focus attention on other parts of the worksheet.

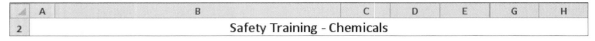

Notice that column F and row 1 are not visible once the Hide command is issued.

Unhiding Columns and Rows

After rows or columns have been hidden, you must issue an Unhide command to make them visible once again. Before the command to unhide rows is issued, you must select at least one row above and one row below the hidden ones. Likewise, you must select at least one column to the left and one to the right of the hidden ones before issuing the Unhide command. If you have hidden column A or row 1, you will need to drag to select from row 2 up to the column headings or from column B left through the row headings.

Task	Procedure
Hide columns or rows	■ Select the column(s) or row(s) you wish to hide. ■ Choose Home→Cells→Format→Hide & Unhide→Hide Columns or Hide Rows from the Ribbon, or right-click the column heading and choose Hide from the context menu.
Unhide columns or rows	■ Select the columns to the left and right or the rows above and below the column(s) or row(s) you wish to unhide. ■ Choose Home→Cells→Format→Hide & Unhide→Unhide Columns or Unhide Rows from the Ribbon, or right-click the column heading and choose Unhide from the context menu.

Hide, Unhide, and Format Columns and Rows

In this exercise, you will hide and unhide rows and columns. You also will format all cells in a column simultaneously.

Hide Multiple Columns and a Row

You will hide the number of questions in individual categories so that only the total and percentage columns display. You will also hide row 1 because you have yet to enter anything in it.

1. Follow these steps to hide columns C through F:

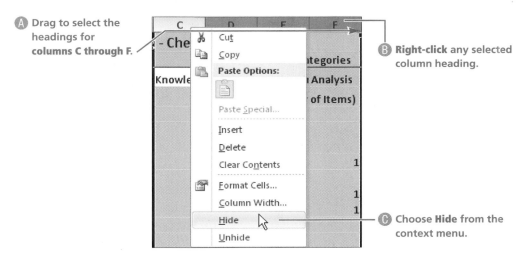

Ⓐ Drag to select the headings for **columns C through F.**

Ⓑ **Right-click** any selected column heading.

Ⓒ Choose **Hide** from the context menu.

Columns C through F are no longer visible. They are still a part of the worksheet and can be revealed again with a simple Unhide command.

2. **Right-click** the row 1 heading, and then choose **Hide** from the context menu.

Unhide the Hidden Columns and Row

3. Follow these steps to unhide columns C through F:

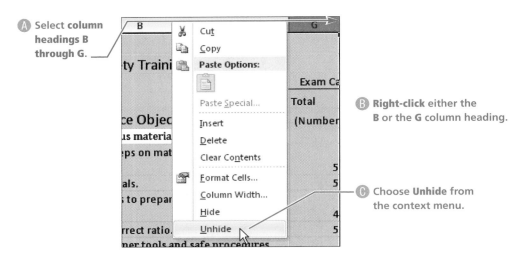

Ⓐ Select **column headings B through G**.

Ⓑ **Right-click** either the **B** or the **G** column heading.

Ⓒ Choose **Unhide** from the context menu.

Remember that to unhide a column you must first select the columns to the left and right of the hidden column (or the rows above and below a hidden row).

4. Follow these steps to unhide row 1:

Ⓐ Select from **row heading 2** up to the **Select All** button.

Ⓑ **Right-click** over row heading 2.

Ⓒ Choose **Unhide** from the context menu.

Row 1 is visible once again.

Apply Percent Style to All Cells in a Column

5. Click the **column heading** for **column H**.
   Notice that the Number Format box in the Number group of the Home tab indicates that the column currently is in General number format, except for cells that have been formatted manually in rows 7–27.

6. Choose **Home→Number→Percent Style** % from the Ribbon.
   The Number Format box in the Number group of the Home tab now displays Percentage. All numbers in the column are formatted as percentages, but text entries are unaffected.

7. Enter **50** in cell H29 to verify that the percentage format is applied.

8. **Undo** 🔄 the entry.

9. **Save** 💾 the changes to the workbook.

5.5 Changing Vertical Alignment and Rotating Text

Video Lesson labyrinthelab.com/videos

You have already learned many techniques for arranging data. Now you will be expanding on that knowledge and learning how to change the vertical alignment and rotate the contents of cells.

Setting Vertical Alignment

Vertical alignment positions the cell contents between the top and bottom of the cell. Vertical alignment options include top, bottom, center, and justify. The default alignment is bottom. The Justify option is useful with multiple-line entries. For example, the Justify option evenly distributes unused space between lines in a multiple-line entry so text fills the cell from the top edge to the bottom edge. Vertical alignment is set by choosing the Top Align, Middle Align, and Bottom Align buttons in the Alignment group on the Home tab of the Ribbon. You can also choose those options and Justify via the Alignment dialog box launcher button in the Ribbon.

Rotating Text

The Orientation option on the Ribbon has several rotation options that you can apply to text in a cell. When column headings are extra wide, making the worksheet spread out too far horizontally, you might consider rotating the text to save room. The decision to rotate text to improve a worksheet's appearance must be balanced with how easily the text may be read. Text can be rotated more precisely from 0 to 90 degrees using the Orientation option on the Alignment tab in the Format Cells dialog box. Excel increases the row height to accommodate the rotated text.

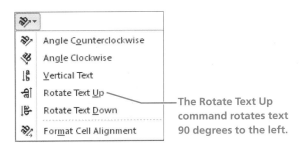

The Rotate Text Up command rotates text 90 degrees to the left.

Orienting the column headings allows the column widths to be narrower.

Task	Procedure
Set cell content to align vertically with the top, middle, or bottom of a cell	▪ Select the cell(s) in which you wish to change the vertical alignment. ▪ Choose Home→Alignment→Top Align, Middle Align, or Bottom Align from the Ribbon.
Set cell content to justify vertically within a cell	▪ Select the cell(s) in which you wish to change the vertical alignment. ▪ Choose Home→Alignment dialog box launcher ⬚ from the Ribbon. ▪ Click the Vertical drop-down arrow under Text Alignment and choose Justify from the list.
Rotate text within a cell using a preset option	▪ Select the cell(s) in which you wish to rotate text. ▪ Choose Home→Alignment→Orientation ⬚ from the Ribbon and select the desired preset from the list.
Rotate text within a cell using a precise number of degrees	▪ Select the cell(s) in which you wish to rotate text. ▪ Choose Home→Alignment dialog box launcher ⬚ from the Ribbon. ▪ Choose the desired text rotation in the Orientation section of the Alignment tab in the Format Cells dialog box.

DEVELOP YOUR SKILLS 5.5.1

Rotate Text and Change Its Vertical Alignment

In this exercise, you will rotate the categories at the top of the worksheet as well as change the vertical alignment in cells.

Rotate Text

1. Select the **range C4:H4**.

2. Choose **Home→Alignment→Orientation** ⬚ →**Rotate Text Up** from the Ribbon.

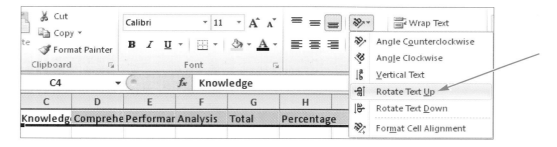

The headings are rotated in their cells. Normally, the row height would increase automatically to AutoFit the headings. The merged text in row 3 prevented that from happening in this case.

3. Point at the bottom of the **row 4 header** until the double-arrow pointer displays and then **double-click**. *The row height increases so that all rotated text is visible. If you have difficulty positioning the mouse pointer precisely, you may select row 4 and then choose Home→Cells→Format→AutoFit Row Height from the Ribbon.*

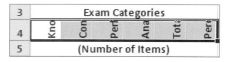

4. Follow these steps to AutoFit columns C through H:

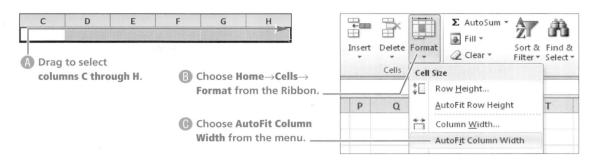

Ⓐ Drag to select columns C through H.

Ⓑ Choose **Home→Cells→Format** from the Ribbon.

Ⓒ Choose **AutoFit Column Width** from the menu.

Change Vertical Alignment

5. Select **cell A3**.
   Remember, this is a vertically and horizontally merged cell so it is quite large.

6. Choose **Home→Alignment→Middle Align** ≡ from the top row of the Ribbon.

7. Select the **range A6:H25**.

8. Choose **Home→Alignment→Top Align** ≡ from the Ribbon.
   The text in the performance objective rows now aligns at the top of cells, which makes it easier to read across the rows. You have decided that the alphabet letters in column A should be aligned at the right of their cells.

9. Select the **range A7:A10**.

10. Choose **Home→Alignment→Align Text Right** ≡ from the Ribbon.

11. Use **Format Painter** to copy the formatting from **cell A10** to the other alphabet letters in **ranges A12:A14, A16:A17, A19:A22,** and **A24:A25.**
    Rows 3 through 7 of your worksheet should resemble the following illustration.

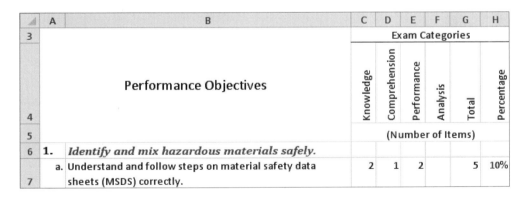

12. **Save** 💾 the changes to the workbook.

5.6 Using Excel's Find and Replace Commands

Video Lesson   labyrinthelab.com/videos

Excel's Find command performs searches on a worksheet or an entire workbook. It can search for a particular word, number, cell reference, formula, or format. Find is often the quickest way to locate an item in a workbook. The Replace feature helps you to find an item and replace it with a specified item.

Excel searches for text without regard to case. For example, a search for *green* will find all occurrences of *green* and *Green*. Unlike Microsoft Word in the Office Suite, Excel replaces text only with the exact case you type. Replacing *Green* with *blue* does not capitalize the "b" to match case in the original word. This is one reason you will want to use the Replace All command with care.

Replacing Cell Formats

FROM THE KEYBOARD

Ctrl + F to find
Ctrl + H to replace

Excel lets you find and replace not just text but also cell formats. For example, you may want to search all worksheets and workbooks for cells formatted with Currency style with no decimals and replace that format with Currency style with two decimals. Finding and replacing cell formats can be a big time-saver, especially with large worksheets and multiple-sheet workbooks.

TIP Find and replace options remain set after the Find and Replace dialog box is closed unless you have cleared the options. If Excel does not find the text you want, check that you have removed any undesired formatting options.

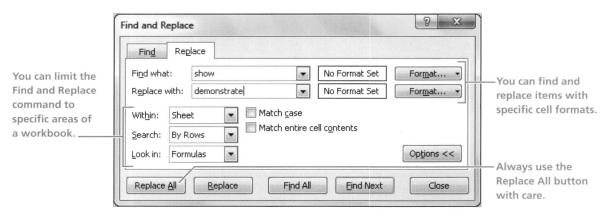

You can limit the Find and Replace command to specific areas of a workbook.

You can find and replace items with specific cell formats.

Always use the Replace All button with care.

Task	Procedure
Find text or formatting	■ Choose Home→Editing→Find & Select →Find from the Ribbon. ■ Type in the text you wish to find, or choose the appropriate formatting. ■ Choose either to find the next instance of the text or formatting by clicking Find Next or to find all instances by clicking Find All. ■ Click Close when you are through with the Find feature
Find and replace text or formatting	■ Choose Home→Editing→Find & Select →Replace from the Ribbon. ■ Type in or choose the formatting that you wish to find and have replaced. ■ Type in the text or choose the formatting that will replace the indicated text or formatting. ■ Click Close when you are through with the Replace feature.
Clear all find and replace options	■ Delete the Find What and Replace With entries in the Find and Replace dialog box. ■ Click the drop-down arrow on the top Format button, and choose Clear Find Format. ■ Click the drop-down arrow on the bottom Format button, and choose Clear Replace Format.

Find and Replace Entries

In this exercise, you will find and replace text as well as formatting.

Find and Replace Text

1. Choose **Home→Editing→Find & Select** [icon]**→Replace** from the Ribbon.
The Find and Replace dialog box opens.

2. Follow these steps to prepare to replace all instances of *Show* with *Demonstrate*.

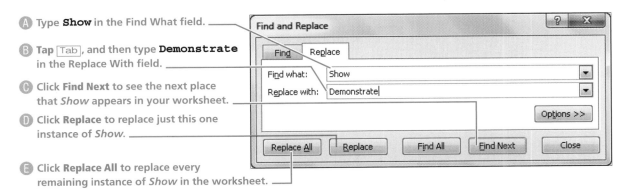

Ⓐ Type **Show** in the Find What field.

Ⓑ Tap Tab, and then type **Demonstrate** in the Replace With field.

Ⓒ Click **Find Next** to see the next place that *Show* appears in your worksheet.

Ⓓ Click **Replace** to replace just this one instance of *Show*.

Ⓔ Click **Replace All** to replace every remaining instance of *Show* in the worksheet.

3. Click **OK** to acknowledge the total number of replacements.

After replacing all, Excel will let you know the total number of replacements. Leave the Find and Replace dialog box open for the next step.

Find and Replace Formatting

4. Click the **Options** button in the Find and Replace dialog box.
   Excel expands the dialog box to display additional Find and Replace settings.

5. Follow these steps to set the formatting to be found:

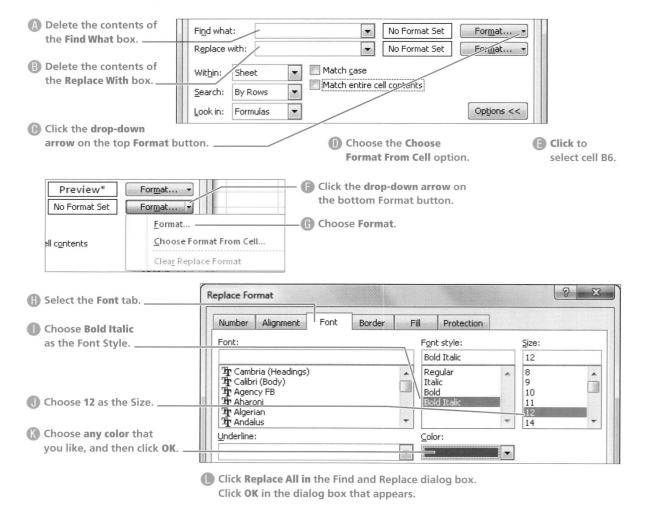

Ⓐ Delete the contents of the **Find What** box.

Ⓑ Delete the contents of the **Replace With** box.

Ⓒ Click the **drop-down arrow** on the top **Format** button.

Ⓓ Choose the **Choose Format From Cell** option.

Ⓔ **Click** to select cell B6.

Ⓕ Click the **drop-down arrow** on the bottom Format button.

Ⓖ Choose **Format**.

Ⓗ Select the **Font** tab.

Ⓘ Choose **Bold Italic** as the Font Style.

Ⓙ Choose **12** as the Size.

Ⓚ Choose **any color** that you like, and then click **OK**.

Ⓛ Click **Replace All in** the Find and Replace dialog box. Click **OK** in the dialog box that appears.

All instances of formatting that are the same as that in cell B6 are replaced with the new formatting that you have chosen.

Clear Find and Replace Criteria

The find and replace criteria remain set even after the dialog box is closed. You must clear the criteria from the dialog box before performing another find or replace operation. (Exiting Excel also clears the dialog box.)

6. Click the **drop-down arrow** on the top Format button and choose **Clear Find Format**.

7. Click the **drop-down arrow** on the bottom Format button and choose **Clear Replace Format**.

8. Click **Close** to exit the Find and Replace dialog box.

9. **Save** the changes to the workbook.

5.7 Using AutoCorrect

Video Lesson   labyrinthelab.com/videos

Excel's AutoCorrect feature can improve the speed and accuracy of entering text. AutoCorrect is most useful for replacing abbreviations with a full phrase of up to 255 characters. For example, you could set up AutoCorrect to substitute *United States Government* whenever you type *usg*. AutoCorrect also automatically corrects common misspellings and typographical errors. For example, the word *the* is often misspelled as *teh*, and the word *and* is often misspelled as *adn*. These and other common spelling mistakes are fixed automatically. Auto-Correct also automatically capitalizes the first letter of a day if you type it in lowercase. For example, if you type *sunday* and complete the entry, AutoCorrect will enter *Sunday* in the cell. Finally, AutoCorrect fixes words that have two initial capital letters by switching the second letter to lowercase.

The AutoCorrect dialog box allows you to customize how the AutoCorrect feature will work for you.

AutoCorrect entries are shared by all programs in the Microsoft Office Suite, so if you've already added some in Word, they are available for you to use in Excel as well.

Expanding AutoCorrect Entries

AutoCorrect goes into action when you type a word in a text entry and tap ⎡Spacebar⎤ or when you complete a text entry. The word or entry is compared with all entries in the AutoCorrect table. The AutoCorrect table contains a list of words and their replacement phrases. If the word you type matches an entry in the AutoCorrect table, a phrase from the table is substituted for the word. This is known as expanding the AutoCorrect entry.

Undoing AutoCorrect Entries

There may be times that AutoCorrect replaces an entry against your wishes. AutoCorrect is treated as a single "character," meaning that it is viewed by the Undo feature the same as if you typed an "a" or tapped ⎡Delete⎤. Therefore, you can use Undo to reverse an AutoCorrect entry.

Creating and Editing AutoCorrect Entries

The AutoCorrect dialog box allows you to add entries to the AutoCorrect table, delete entries from the table, and set other AutoCorrect options. To add an entry, type the desired abbreviation in the Replace box and the desired expansion for the abbreviation in the With box.

If you create the abbreviation using uppercase letters, it will not work if you type it in lower-case letters later. Type all abbreviations in lowercase so you don't have to remember to type them in upper- or lowercase in the worksheet.

QUICK REFERENCE	USING AUTOCORRECT
Task	**Procedure**
Modify AutoCorrect options	▪ Choose File→Options [icon].
	▪ Click the Proofing option from the left-side menu.
	▪ Click AutoCorrect Options.
	▪ Make any desired changes to the AutoCorrect feature.
	▪ Click OK.
	▪ Click OK to close the Excel Options window.

DEVELOP YOUR SKILLS 5.7.1
Use AutoCorrect

In this exercise, you will train AutoCorrect to replace an abbreviation with a phrase and learn how to override AutoCorrect.

Observe How AutoCorrect Works

1. Select **cell A1**.

2. Type **teh cat adn dog ran fast**, and then **tap** ⎡Enter⎤.
   Notice that both of the spelling errors have been corrected by AutoCorrect.

Override an AutoCorrect Command

3. Click **cell A1**, type **adn** and **tap** Spacebar.
   AutoCorrect has corrected the misspelling.

4. Use Ctrl + Z to **undo** the last command.
   Undo will reverse the last command, in this case AutoCorrect.

5. **Tap** Esc to cancel the entry.

Create an AutoCorrect Entry

6. Choose **File→Options** 🔲 .

7. Follow these steps to display the AutoCorrect dialog box:

Ⓐ Display the **Proofing** tab.

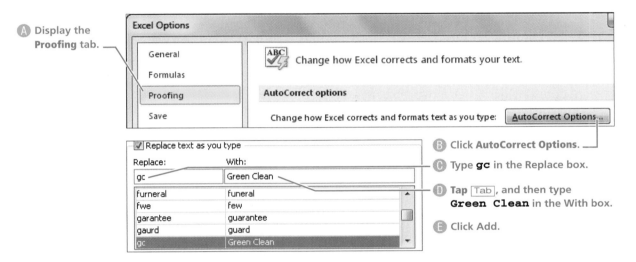

Ⓑ Click **AutoCorrect Options**.

Ⓒ Type **gc** in the Replace box.

Ⓓ Tap Tab, and then type **Green Clean** in the With box.

Ⓔ Click Add.

Your entry will be added to the list.

8. Click **OK** in the AutoCorrect dialog box.

9. Click **OK** in the Excel Options dialog box.

Use an AutoCorrect Entry

10. Ensure that **cell A1** is still selected, type **gc** and **tap** Enter.
    The AutoCorrect entry that you created is entered into the cell.

Delete an AutoCorrect Entry

It is important for you to delete the AutoCorrect entry you just created. Otherwise it will still be there when the next student uses the computer.

11. Choose **File→Options**, and display the **Proofing** tab.

12. Click **AutoCorrect Options**.

13. Follow these steps to delete the AutoCorrect entry you have created:

(A) Type **gc** in the Replace box.

Replace: | With:
gc | Green Clean

furneral	funeral
fwe	few
garantee	guarantee
gaurd	guard
gc	Green Clean

| Replace | Delete |

(B) Click **Delete**, and then **tap** Enter.

(C) Click **OK**.

14. **Save** 🖫 the changes and **close** the workbook.

5.8 Concepts Review

Concepts Review   labyrinthelab.com/excel10

To check your knowledge of the key concepts introduced in this lesson, complete the Concepts Review quiz by going to the URL listed above. If your classroom is using Labyrinth eLab, you may complete the Concepts Review quiz from within your eLab course.

Reinforce Your Skills

Manage Worksheets

In this exercise, you will start with a new, blank workbook. You will organize the workbook by renaming, inserting, deleting, rearranging, and copying its worksheets.

Rename Sheet Tabs

1. Use Ctrl + N to start a **new**, blank workbook if one is not already displayed.

2. **Double-click** the Sheet1 tab, type **April**, and **tap** Enter.

3. **Rename** the Sheet3 tab to **March**.

Delete a Sheet

4. **Right-click** the Sheet2 tab and select **Delete** from the context menu.

Insert and Move Sheets

5. Choose **Home→Cells→Insert menu ▾→Insert Sheet** from the Ribbon.
   The new sheet is added before the currently active sheet.

6. **Rename** the new sheet to **February**.

7. Click the **Insert Sheet** button at the right of the sheet tabs.
   The new sheet is added as the last sheet.

8. **Rename** the new sheet to **January**.

9. **Drag and drop** the sheet tabs to arrange them in month sequence from January through April.

Copy a Sheet

10. **Hold down** the Ctrl key and **drag** the April sheet tab to the right.
    A new April (2) sheet tab should display when you release the mouse and Ctrl.

11. **Rename** the April (2) sheet tab to **May**.

12. **Copy** the May sheet to create a **June** sheet.

13. **Save** 💾 as **rs-Tabs** in the Lesson 05 folder and **close** the workbook.

Insert and Delete Rows

In this exercise, you will modify a sales invoice worksheet by removing and inserting line items.

1. **Open** the rs-Sales Invoice workbook from the Lesson 05 folder in your file storage location.

Create Formulas

2. Select **cell D7**, and **enter** a formula that calculates the Extension as the Quantity multiplied by the Unit Price.
   The result should be 122.5.

3. **Copy** the Extension formula down through **rows 8–11**.

4. Use **AutoSum** to compute the subtotal for the extension in **column D**.

5. Calculate the **Sales Tax** as the Subtotal multiplied by 7.75%.

6. Calculate the **Total** as the Subtotal plus the Sales Tax.

7. Select all of the numbers in **columns C–D** and change the number format to **Comma Style** with **two decimals**.

8. Apply **Accounting Number Format** to **cell D14** so the total contains a dollar sign ($).

Delete a Row and Insert New Rows

The customer has decided to cancel one product from the order and add two other products.

9. Select **row 9** by clicking the row heading.

10. Choose **Home→Cells→Delete** ⊟ (taking care not to click the menu ▾ button) from the Ribbon.
    Notice that if you select the entire row, you can simply click the Delete command without having to choose the menu button and the Delete Sheet Rows command. The Subtotal, Sales Tax, and Total automatically recalculated to omit the deleted row.

11. **Drag** to select the **row headings** for **rows 10** and **11**.

12. Choose **Home→Cells→Insert** ⊞ from the Ribbon.
    Notice that the first blank record was inserted at row 10 and the prior contents of row 10 shifted down two rows.

13. Add the following two items:

⊿	A	B	C
10	GBS All Purpose Carpet	3	11.95
11	Handy Trash Liners	24	2.85

14. Use the **fill handle** to copy the formula in **cell D9** to **cells D10** and **D11**.

15. Select **cell D13** and notice that the **SUM** function has been updated automatically to include the values in cells D10 and D11 that were added when you inserted the rows.
    Excel adjusted the formula reference because the rows inserted were within the range referenced in the formula.

Enter the Current Date

16. Use the **TODAY** function to insert the current date in **A3**.

17. Format the date with the **date format** of your choice.

18. Insert a **blank row** between the date and the customer name.
    Your workbook should resemble the following illustration.

	A	B	C	D
1	**Green Clean**			
2	*Sales Invoice*			
3	October 22, 2010			
4				
5	*Customer:*	**Heartwell Laboratories**		
6				
7	**Item**	**Quantity**	**Unit Price**	**Extension**
8	EarthWise Carpet Clea	7	17.50	122.50
9	EarthWise Carpet Clea	16	9.85	157.60
10	EarthWise Carpet Stair	10	5.50	55.00
11	GBS All Purpose Carpe	3	11.95	35.85
12	Handy Trash Liners	24	2.85	68.40
13	Carpet Bright Stain Elir	6	7.35	44.10
14	**Subtotal**			483.45
15	**Sales Tax**			37.47
16	**Total**			**$ 520.92**
17				
18	*Thank you for your business!*			

19. **Save** 💾 the changes to the workbook and continue to the next exercise.

Adjust Column and Row Properties

In this exercise, you will insert and format a column, adjust column widths, and hide a row.

Before You Begin: You must have completed Reinforce Your Skills 5.2. The rs-Sales Invoice workbook should be open.

Insert and Format a Column

1. Select **column A** by clicking the column heading.

2. Choose **Home→Cells→Insert** 📋 from the Ribbon.
   To accommodate the new column A, the previous column headings increased by one letter. The titles that were in the range A1:A3 now are in the range B1:B3.

	A
7	**Item No.**
8	14335
9	14043
10	29322
11	29566
12	35800
13	38720

3. While **column A** is still selected, **center-align** all the cells in the column.
   All entries that you type in the next step will be center aligned.

4. **Enter** the following data in **column A**, as shown at right.

Change Column Widths

5. **Point** at the border to the right of the **column B heading** until the pointer displays a two-headed arrow and **double-click**. *You just AutoFit the column width, and all text in column B should be visible.*

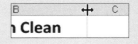

6. **Center-align** the titles and date in the **range B1:B3**.

7. Select **columns C through E**.

8. Point at the border between the **column D** and E **headings** and **double-click**. *The columns are sized to fit the widest entry. The customer name in Column C is a long entry that made the column too wide, so you will adjust the column width manually.*

9. **Point** at the border to the right of the **column C heading** and drag until the ScreenTip indicates that the width is approximately 10.00.

Hide a Row

10. Select **row 5**.

11. Choose **Home→Cells→Format** [icon] **→Hide & Unhide→Hide Rows** from the Ribbon. *The company name in row 5 is now hidden from view.*

12. **Save** [icon] the changes and **close** the workbook.

REINFORCE YOUR SKILLS 5.4

Use Find and Replace

In this exercise, you will experiment with finding and replacing contents and formats.

Find and Replace Contents

1. **Open** the rs-Quarterly Sales workbook from the Lesson 05 folder. *You wish to change* Region *to* Area *in headings but not in region numbers, such as Region 1.*

2. Choose **Home→Editing→Find & Select** [icon] **→Replace** from the Ribbon.

3. Enter **region** in the Find What box and **Area** in the Replace With box. *You do not have to use a capital "R" in the Find What box. If you want the replacement text to be capitalized, though, you must type it that way in the Replace With box.*

4. Click **Find Next**. *Using the Replace All command would not give the correct result because you want to leave the Region 1, Region 2, and Region 3 entries as is. If the dialog box covers the worksheet data, you may drag the title bar at the top of the dialog box to move it out of the way.*

5. Replace only the entries in **cells B4** and **E4**; leave the dialog box **open**.

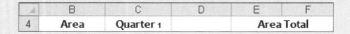

	B	C	D	E	F
4	**Area**	**Quarter 1**		**Area Total**	

If you replaced an entry that you did not want to change, you can click Undo in the Quick Access toolbar without closing the Find and Replace dialog box.

6. Enter **region 1** in the Find What box and **East** in the Replace With box.

7. Click the **Find All** button, and then **click** each of the occurrences at the bottom of the dialog box to review the contents of each cell.

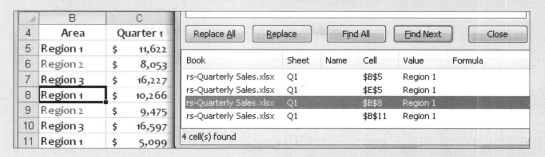

The Find All command reports that four occurrences were found. You may enlarge the dialog box by dragging its bottom border down. After reviewing the possible replacements, you decide that using Replace All is acceptable.

8. Click **Replace All**. Then, click **OK** to acknowledge the number of replacements made.

9. Make the following additional replacements:
   - Replace *Region 2* with **Central**.
   - Replace *Region 3* with **West**.

10. **Close** the **Find and Replace** dialog box, and review the replacements.

Find and Replace Formats

11. Use Ctrl + H to display the **Find and Replace** dialog box.

12. **Delete** the entries in the **Find What** and **Replace With** boxes.

13. Click the **Options** button to expand the dialog box, if necessary.

14. Click the **drop-down arrow** on the Format button in the Find What row, and then click the **Choose Format From Cell** command on the menu.

15. Select **cell B6**.

16. Click the **Format** button for the Replace With box (not the drop-down button) to display the **Replace Format** dialog box.

17. Display the **Font** tab, choose to make the Font style **Regular** and the color **black**, if not already selected, and then click **OK**.

18. Choose to **Replace All**.

19. Click **OK** to acknowledge the number of replacements made.

Clear All Find and Replace Settings

20. Use the **Format** menus to clear all find and replace settings.
    The two preview boxes should display No Format Set when you are finished.

21. **Close** the Find and Replace dialog box.

22. **Save** 🖫 the changes to the workbook and continue to the next exercise.

Use AutoCorrect

In this exercise, you will edit a worksheet by creating, using, and deleting AutoCorrect entries.

Before You Begin: You must have completed Reinforce Your Skills 5.4. The rs-Quarterly Sales workbook should be open.

Create AutoCorrect Entries

1. Choose **File→Options** [icon].

2. Click the **Proofing** option along the left-side menu, and then click **AutoCorrect Options**.

3. In the Replace box, type **aw** and **tap** Tab.
   Remember to type the abbreviation in lowercase.

4. In the With box, type **Amy Wyatt**.

5. Click the **Add** button.
   Do not click the OK button right now as you are going to create a few more AutoCorrect entries.

6. **Create** the following entries. Click **OK** when you are finished.

lm	**Leisa Malimali**
bs	**Brian Simpson**

7. Click **OK** to close the Excel Options window.

Use AutoCorrect Entries

8. Select **cell A5**.

9. Type **aw** and **tap** Spacebar.
   The sales rep's name appears in the cell.

10. Select **cell A8**.

11. Type **bs** and **tap** Tab.

12. Using **AutoCorrect**, enter Leisa Malimali's name in **cell A11**.

13. Using the method of your choice, either AutoCorrect or the fill handle, **enter** the same sales rep's name in the two blank cells below each name.

14. AutoFit **column A** so the names are visible.

4	Sales Rep	Area
5	Amy Wyatt	East
6	Amy Wyatt	Central
7	Amy Wyatt	West
8	Brian Simpson	East
9	Brian Simpson	Central
10	Brian Simpson	West
11	Leisa Malimali	East
12	Leisa Malimali	Central
13	Leisa Malimali	West

Delete AutoCorrect Entries

Remember that the AutoCorrect entries that you create can be used in all Office applications. You may find that you do not want a name to appear each time you type its shortcut. You will now delete the AutoCorrect entries that were created.

15. Choose **File→Options**.

16. Click the **Proofing** option along the left-side menu, and then click **AutoCorrect Options**.

17. In the **Replace** box, type **aw**.
    The AutoCorrect entry appears in the With box next to its abbreviation in the Replace box.

18. Click the **Delete** button under the AutoCorrect entry list.

19. **Delete** the AutoCorrect entries for *lm* and *bs*.
    In order to have the correct "With" entry appear, you will need to remove the previous name from the With box before typing the next shortcut entry in the Replace box.

20. When you have finished deleting all three entries, click **OK**.

21. Click **OK** to close the Excel Options window.

22. **Save** the changes and **close** the workbook.

Apply Your Skills

Restructure an Accounts Receivable Report

In this exercise, you will insert and move columns and rows, create a formula, and apply a theme to the report.

1. **Open** the as-Accounts Receivable workbook from the Lesson 05 folder in your file storage location.

2. Use the **DATE** function to insert the the date **October 14, 2014** in **cell E4**.

3. **Delete** the empty cells in **row 8**.

4. Insert **two columns** between columns A and B. Enter the **customer numbers** and **invoice numbers** shown in the illustration at the end of the exercise. Also, enter the headings in the **range B6:C6**, and **wrap** the text within the cells. Align the data as shown in the illustration.

5. Format the entries in column D in **Currency Style** with **no decimals**.

6. Enter a formula in **cell F7** that calculates the number of days since the invoice was issued (date in row 4 minus the invoice date). Make certain to use **absolute** and **relative** cell references correctly in the formula. Use **AutoFill** to extend the formula.

7. Use formulas in **column F** to calculate the number of days the invoices are past due. Assume the terms are **net 30 days**. Your formulas should subtract 30 from the number of days since the invoice was issued.

8. Apply a **border** to the left of each column in **columns B through G**.

9. Apply the **theme** of your choice to change the formatting of the workbook.

10. **AutoFit** all data columns.

11. Increase the row height of **rows 7 through 12** to add some extra space among the entries.

12. **Rename** the sheet tab as `Aging Report` and **delete** the unused sheet tabs.
    Your completed worksheet should look similar to the following illustration. However, the formatting may be different based on the theme you chose.

▲	A	B	C	D	E	F	G
1				Green Clean			
2			Accounts Receivable Aging Report				
3							
4						*Report Date:*	10/8/2014
5							
6	Customer Name	Customer Number	Invoice Number	Invoice Amount	Invoice Date	Days After Invoice Date	Days Past Due
7	Castro Screenprinting	R202	189	$234	8/1/2014	68	38
8	Lucas Mfg., Inc.	R314	155	$980	9/1/2014	37	7
9	MAA Medical Labs	R572	130	$469	8/15/2014	54	24
10	Medina Electrical Supply	W016	246	$345	7/20/2014	80	50
11	Molly's Dance Studio	W215	228	$765	8/21/2014	48	18
12	Sosa Marine, Inc.	W264	210	$123	7/9/2014	91	61
13							

| ◄ ◄ ► ►| Aging Report 🗐 | | ◄ | ||||

13. **Print** the worksheet when you have finished.

14. **Save** 💾 the changes and **close** the workbook.

APPLY YOUR SKILLS 5.2

Vertically Align and Rotate Text

In this exercise, you will create a worksheet, create formulas, and change the vertical alignment and text rotation.

1. **Open** a new Excel file and **enter** all text, numbers, and dates as shown in the illustration at the end of this exercise. Follow these guidelines to create the large paragraph shown near the top of the worksheet:

   - Merge and center the **range A2:H2**.
   - Set the height of **row 2** to 75.00 points.
   - Turn on the **Wrap Text** option.
   - Change the **vertical alignment** to center and the **horizontal alignment** to left.
   - **Type** the text in the large merged cell.

2. Rotate the text in **F5:H5** up 90 degrees. Use ⎇+↵ to force line breaks in the **range F4:H4**.

3. Follow these guidelines to format the worksheet:
   - Merge and center each of the following ranges: **A4:A5**, **F4:F5**, **G4:G5**, and **H4:H5**.
   - Merge and center the ranges **A1:H1**, **B4:C4**, and **D4:E4**.
   - Apply the borders as shown in the illustration, including a border around the **range A12:H13**.

4. Use formulas in **column F** to calculate the number of days between the two assessments.

5. Use formulas in **column G** to calculate the point increase between the two assessment scores.

6. Use formulas to calculate the percentage increase in **column H**. The percentage increase is calculated as the point increase in column G divided by the first assessment score in **column C**.

7. Use the **AVERAGE** function to calculate the averages in **cells F12** and **H13**.

8. Format the percentage increases in **column H** as **Percent Style** with **no decimals**. Apply additional formatting to numbers, dates, and text as desired. Adjust row heights and column widths similar to those shown below.

9. **Print** the worksheet when you have finished.

10. **Save** 💾 with the name **as-Performance Assessments** in the Lesson 05 folder and **close** the workbook.

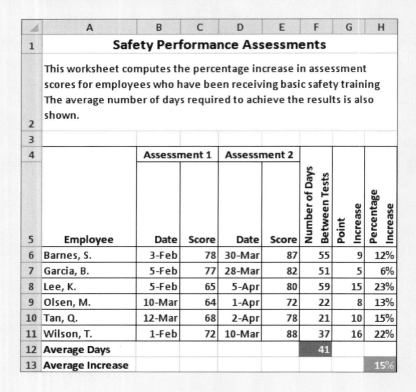

Use Find and Replace

In this exercise, you will find and replace both text and formatting in a worksheet.

1. **Open** the as-Excel Training Objectives workbook from the Lesson 05 folder in your file storage location.

2. Using **Find and Replace**, change the formatting in **cell B6** and every other cell with the same formatting so that they are no longer italicized and are blue (you choose the exact shade of blue) rather than a dark shade of red.

3. Find every instance of the word *learner* and replace it with **employee**.

4. Adjust the **row heights** as necessary.

5. **Print** the worksheet when you are finished.

6. **Save** 🖫 the changes and **close** the workbook.

Critical Thinking & Work-Readiness Skills

In the course of working through the following Microsoft Office-based Critical Thinking exercises, you will also be utilizing various work-readiness skills, some of which are listed next to each exercise. Go to labyrinthelab.com/workreadiness *to learn more about the work-readiness skills.*

5.1 Add a Column to a Worksheet

WORK-READINESS SKILLS APPLIED

- Organizing and maintaining information
- Improving or designing systems
- Thinking creatively

Open ct-Safety Training (Lesson 05 folder). Insert a column immediately to the right of the Performance column (under Exam Categories). Label the column **Team Participation** to reflect the new cooperative behaviors Green Clean wants to encourage. Indicate that there will be one item for each of the performance objectives. Adjust column widths for size and appearance. Print preview to ensure that the columns fit across one page width. Save the file as **ct-Safety Training Team** and close it. Why might Green Clean add a Team Participation category to their safety training program? If working in a group, discuss this question. If working alone, type your answer in a Word document named **ct-Questions** saved to your Lesson 05 folder.

5.2 Proofread a Worksheet and Add a Row

WORK-READINESS SKILLS APPLIED

- Applying technology to a task
- Solving problems
- Writing

While accurate data and consistent formatting help readers understand a worksheet, well written text also contributes to that goal. Open ct-Safety Training Team, if necessary. Find all instances of the characters *mix* and change them to *blend*, making certain to match the case of the original word. Add *paln* to the AutoCorrect list to be replaced by *plan*. Then, insert a new row for objective 6. Type **Create team paln** to see how Excel responds, then remove *plan* from AutoCorrect. Next, explore the use of the Spelling checker located on the Review tab of the Ribbon, and make any corrections needed. Save with the name **ct-Safety Training Plan** in your Lesson 05 folder. If working in a group, discuss why Green Clean might want to have a plan that specifies the roles for each team member. Discuss how other Microsoft Office tools can help you create and monitor a team plan. If working alone, type your answers in a Word document named **ct-Questions2** saved to your Lesson 05 folder.

5.3 Adjust Column and Row Formatting

WORK-READINESS SKILLS APPLIED

- Organizing and maintaining information
- Applying technology to a task
- Solving problems

Open ct-Safety Training Plan, if necessary. Format all column B cells identically. Delete the row containing objective 3c. Autofit the height of all rows containing data, and then review all row heights for consistency. Delete the Sheet2 and Sheet3 worksheet tabs. Save your file as **ct-Safety Training Final** in your Lesson 05 folder, and then close it.

Charting and Transmitting Worksheet Data

In this lesson, you will use Excel's charting features to create various types of charts. Charting is an important skill to have when using worksheets because comparisons, trends, and other relationships are often conveyed more effectively with charts. You will use Excel to create column charts, line charts, and pie charts. In addition, you will learn how to edit and format legends, data labels, and other chart objects to communicate data clearly. A worksheet or workbook, including its charts, can be sent via email to others who need the information or who are collaborating on a group project. Excel also allows you to copy data from a web page into a worksheet.

LESSON OUTLINE

LEARNING OBJECTIVES

After studying this lesson, you will be able to:
- Create a variety of different types of charts
- Move and size embedded charts
- Modify, format, and print charts
- Send a worksheet or workbook via email
- Import web data into a worksheet

Charting Sales Performance

Mary Wright is the vice president, sales and marketing, of Green Clean. Her company earns revenue by selling janitorial products and contracts for cleaning services. Mary has asked sales manager Talos Bouras to prepare several charts depicting revenue for the most recent fiscal year. Mary wants charts that compare sales in the various quarters, the growth trend throughout the year, and the contributions of each sales team member to the company sales. Talos will work together with administrative assistant Jenna Mann in using Excel's features to produce accurate and easy-to-understand charts that meet Mary's high standards.

green clean

A column chart that compares the sales that sales team members achieved in each quarter of the year

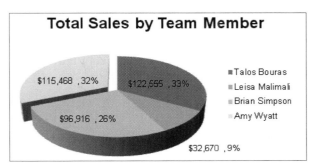

A pie chart that displays the portion of total yearly sales that each sales team member contributed

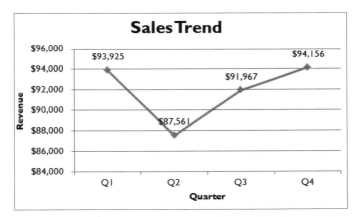

A line chart that indicates the sales trend upward or downward from quarter to quarter

6.1 Creating Charts in Excel

Video Lesson labyrinthelab.com/videos

Numerical data is often easier to interpret when presented in a chart. You can embed a chart in a worksheet so that it appears alongside the worksheet data, or you can place the chart on a separate worksheet. Putting the chart on a separate worksheet prevents the chart from cluttering the data worksheet. Regardless of their placement, charts are always linked to the data from which they are created. Thus, charts are automatically updated when worksheet data changes. Charts are made up of individual objects including the chart title, legend, plot area, value axis, category axis, and data series. You can apply options and enhancements to each object.

Integrated Chart Engine

A chart engine is integrated within the suite of Office programs. You can create a chart in Microsoft Word or PowerPoint as well as in Excel. Once you have mastered the topics in this lesson, you will be able to understand how to create charts in those other Microsoft Office applications as well! When a chart is created in Word or PowerPoint, it is actually saved and stored as an Excel chart. You can create charts in Access, but the chart engine is different.

Creating New Charts

When you create a chart, you have the option of either embedding it into the current worksheet where the data is or placing it on a separate sheet of its own. You may want to embed the chart if it can fit on one printed page with the worksheet data. A large or complex chart may display better on its own sheet. An embedded chart can be moved to its own sheet, and a chart on a separate sheet can be moved to embed on a worksheet.

Embedding a Chart in the Worksheet

Embedded charts can be created by choosing the chart type from the Insert tab of the Ribbon. If you want to see the entire list of chart types displayed before you make your choice, you can open the Insert Chart dialog box. To avoid covering the worksheet data, you can move and resize an embedded chart.

Creating a Chart on a Separate Sheet

FROM THE KEYBOARD

F11 to create a chart on its own sheet

To place a full-size chart on its own sheet, simply select the source range of cells in the worksheet and then tap the F11 key. A new sheet with a generic name, such as Chart1, will be created before the active worksheet in the workbook tab order. When you use the F11 key, the chart on the new sheet will be based on the default chart type, but you can change the type after creating the chart. You can choose the chart type while creating an embedded chart, if you prefer, and then use the Move Chart command in the Ribbon to relocate the chart from the worksheet to its own sheet.

Choosing the Proper Data Source

It is important to select the proper data on which to base your chart. In addition to selecting the basic data for the chart, you will also want to determine whether or not to select any "total" rows to include in the chart. You will not usually include both individual category data and totals because the individual data will appear distorted, as shown on the next page in the illustration to the right. You should also make certain that you select the proper row and column headings for your column and bar charts. If you notice that any of these important pieces are missing, you will need to reselect your source data.

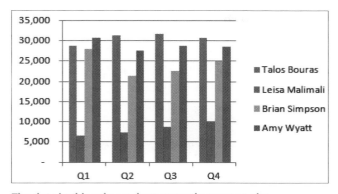

The data in this column chart correctly compare the sales among the four sales team members during each of four quarters.

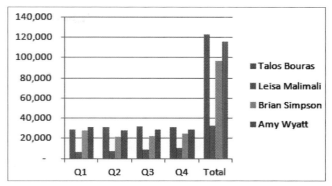

Including the total sales in the chart shrinks the columns for the individual sales team members. Comparing their data is more difficult, and their sales may seem bad as compared with the totals.

Chart Types

Excel provides 11 major chart types. Each chart type also has several subtypes from which you can choose. Excel has a chart type for most data-display needs.

Built-In Chart Types

Each chart type represents data in a different manner. You can present the same data in completely different ways by changing the chart type. For this reason, you should always use the chart type that most effectively represents your data. The three most common chart types are column, pie, and line. You will be creating all three types in this lesson.

User-Defined Charts

Excel lets you create and save customized charts to meet your particular needs. For example, you can create a customized chart that contains the name of your company and its color(s) in the background and use it as the template for all new charts of that type.

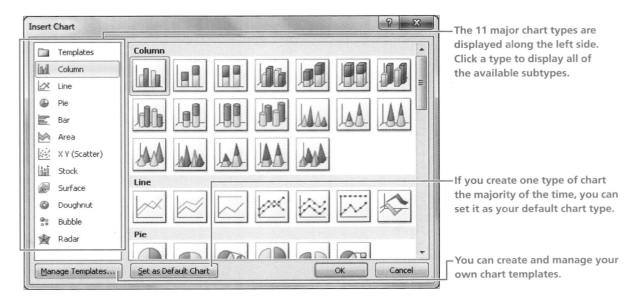

The 11 major chart types are displayed along the left side. Click a type to display all of the available subtypes.

If you create one type of chart the majority of the time, you can set it as your default chart type.

You can create and manage your own chart templates.

Column Charts and Bar Charts

Column charts compare values (numbers) using vertical bars. Bar charts compare values using horizontal bars. Each column or bar represents a value from the worksheet. Column charts and bar charts are most useful for comparing sets of values (called data series). Column and bar charts can be created in 2-D or 3-D formats.

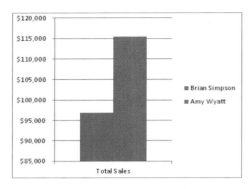 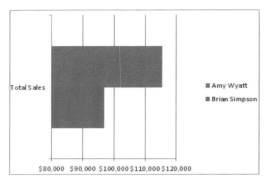

The column chart on the left and the bar chart on the right both display the same data to compare total sales for two people, but the chart types are different. The number of dollar values on the bar chart axis has been modified to accommodate the bar length.

Category Axis and Value Axis

The horizontal line that forms the base of a column chart is the category axis. The category axis typically measures units of time such as days, months, and quarters, although it can also measure products, people, tests, and other categories. The vertical line on the left side of a column chart is the value axis. The value axis typically measures values such as dollars. Most chart types (including column and bar charts) have a category and a value axis.

Legend

The box containing a text description for each data series is the legend. The text labels usually are taken from the first column or first row of the selected worksheet data.

The following illustrations show the worksheet data and one of the two column charts you will create in the next exercise. The illustrations show the objects included on most column charts and the corresponding data used to create the chart. Take a few minutes to study the following illustrations carefully.

	A	B	C	D	E	F
2		Quarterly and Total Sales - Fiscal Year				
3						
4		Q1	Q2	Q3	Q4	Total Sales
5	Talos Bouras	28,775	31,342	31,763	30,675	$ 122,555
6	Leisa Malimali	6,575	7,304	8,768	10,023	$ 32,670
7	Brian Simpson	27,850	21,471	22,634	24,961	$ 96,916
8	Amy Wyatt	30,725	27,444	28,802	28,497	$ 115,468
10	Quarter Total	$ 93,925	$ 87,561	$ 91,967	$ 94,156	$ 367,609

The following chart was created using the selected data shown here. Notice that the Total row and column were not included in the selection. The column chart compares the sales numbers for the individual quarters, but it does not include the total sales from row 10 nor column F.

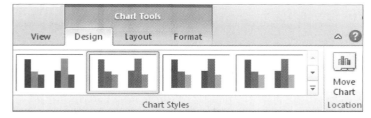

This is the vertical value axis. Excel created the numbering scale (0–35,000) after it determined the range of values included in the chart.

This is the horizontal category axis. The category axis labels (Q1, Q2, Q3, and Q4) were taken from row 4, the first row of the selected worksheet range.

Notice the chart columns. The columns represent values from the various data series. The first data series is the Talos Bouras numbers in row 5. The first column in each group of four columns represents his sales for that quarter.

The legend identifies each data series in the chart columns. The four names in the legend were taken from column A, the first column of the selected worksheet range.

Notice that the chart includes a chart title (Sales by Quarter), a value axis title (Revenue), and a category axis title (Quarter).

Chart and Axis Titles

Excel allows you to create titles for your charts as well as the value and category axes. If you choose a range of information that includes what appears to Excel to be a title, Excel will include it in the new chart. You can always edit this title if it is not correct.

The Chart Tools

When a chart is selected, various Chart Tools will be displayed as additional tabs on the Ribbon. These tabs allow you to make changes to the design, layout, and formatting of the chart.

When a chart is selected, the Chart Tools will be displayed, adding the Design, Layout, and Format tabs to the Ribbon.

These additional Ribbon tabs are called contextual tabs.

CREATING AND PLACING A CHART

Task	Procedure
Create a chart	▪ Enter the data you wish to chart into Excel. ▪ Select the data range for the chart. ▪ Display the Insert tab of the Ribbon. ▪ Choose the type of chart from the Charts group.
Move an existing chart to its own sheet	▪ Right-click a blank area of the chart and choose Move Chart from the context menu. ▪ Choose New Sheet in the Move Chart dialog box and rename the sheet, if desired.
Move a chart from its own sheet to a worksheet as an embedded object	▪ Right-click a blank area of the chart and choose Move Chart from the context menu. ▪ Choose Object In and select the desired worksheet in the Move Chart dialog box.
Add a title to a chart	▪ Select the chart to which you wish to add a title. ▪ Choose Layout→Labels→Chart Title from the Ribbon to display the title options. ▪ Choose how you wish the title to appear. ▪ Select the default title "Chart Title," and type in the title you wish for your chart.
Add axis titles to a chart	▪ Select the chart to which you wish to add an axis title. ▪ Choose Layout→Labels→Axis Titles from the Ribbon to display the axis options. ▪ Choose whether you wish to apply a horizontal or vertical axis title. ▪ Choose how you wish the title to appear. ▪ Select the default title "Axis Title," and type the title you wish for your axis. ▪ Repeat these steps for the other axis.

DEVELOP YOUR SKILLS 6.1.1

Create Charts

In this exercise, you will create two column charts. The 2-D column chart will display on a separate sheet and the clustered cylinder chart will be embedded in the worksheet.

Create a 2-D Column Chart on a New Sheet

1. **Open** the Sales Performance Charts workbook from the Lesson 06 folder in your file storage location.

2. Select the **range A4:E8** in the Sales by Quarter worksheet.

3. **Tap** the F11 key.
   Tapping F11 creates a new sheet before the Sales by Quarter sheet in the workbook tab order. The new chart fills the area on the sheet and the chart is based on the default chart type of Clustered Column. Notice that the Chart Tools display on the Ribbon; they can be used to modify the chart.

4. **Double-click** the new chart tab, type **Sales by Rep**, and **tap** Enter to rename the sheet.

Create an Embedded Column Chart

5. Display the **Sales by Quarter** worksheet and make certain the **range A4:E8** is still selected.

6. Follow these steps to create a clustered cylinder column chart:

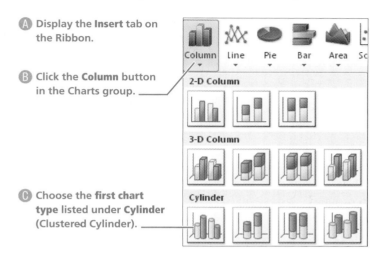

Ⓐ Display the **Insert** tab on the Ribbon.

Ⓑ Click the **Column** button in the Charts group.

Ⓒ Choose the **first chart type** listed under **Cylinder** (Clustered Cylinder).

The chart will appear embedded in the Sales by Quarter worksheet with the default properties for the clustered column chart type displayed. The data in the chart is based on the range of cells you preselected.

7. Look at the Ribbon to see that the **Chart Tools** are now displayed and the **Design** tab is active.
Notice that the chart is covering part of the data. In the next exercise, you will learn how to move charts within a sheet.

Edit the Chart and Axis Titles

8. Choose **Chart Tools→Layout→Labels→Chart Title** ▯ **→Above Chart** from the Ribbon.

9. Follow these steps to title the chart:

Ⓐ **Select** the default title, *Chart Title.*

Ⓑ **Type** the new title as shown here.

Ⓒ **Click** in a blank area of the chart to accept the new title.

10. Choose **Layout→Labels→Axis Titles** ▯ **→Primary Horizontal Axis Title→Title Below Axis** from the Ribbon.

11. **Drag** to select the default title, *Axis Title.*

12. **Type** in the new horizontal axis title, **Quarter**, and then **click away** to accept the new title.

13. Choose **Layout→Labels→Axis Titles** 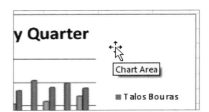**→Primary Vertical Axis Title→Horizontal Title** from the Ribbon.

14. Notice that the default title placeholder, *Axis Title*, is selected.

15. **Type** the new vertical axis title, **Revenue**, and then **click** outside the title box to accept the new title.

16. **Save** the changes and leave the workbook **open** for the next exercise.

6.2 Moving and Sizing Embedded Charts

Video Lesson labyrinthelab.com/videos

When a chart is selected, it is surrounded by a light border with sizing handles displayed. A selected chart can be both moved and resized.

Moving Embedded Charts

Charts that are embedded in a worksheet can easily be moved to a new location. A chart can be moved by a simple drag, but you need to ensure that you click the chart area and not a separate element. Regardless of whether a chart is embedded within a worksheet or moved to a separate tab, the chart data will automatically update when values are changed in the source data.

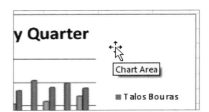

A four-pointed arrow indicates that you can drag to move this selected chart.

Sizing Embedded Charts

To size a chart, it must first be selected. You simply need to drag a sizing handle when the double-arrow mouse pointer is displayed. In order to change a chart size proportionately, hold Shift while dragging a corner handle.

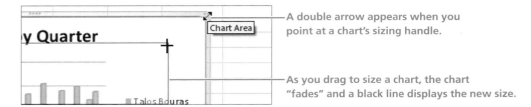

A double arrow appears when you point at a chart's sizing handle.

As you drag to size a chart, the chart "fades" and a black line displays the new size.

Deleting Charts

Deleting an embedded chart is a very simple process—just select the chart area and tap
Delete . You can always use the Undo command if you delete an embedded chart by mistake.
You delete a chart that is on its own tab by deleting the worksheet. This action cannot be
undone, so Excel warns you with a prompt to confirm the deletion.

QUICK REFERENCE	MOVING AND SIZING EMBEDDED CHARTS AND DELETING CHARTS
Task	**Procedure**
Move an embedded chart	Drag the selected chart to a new location with the move pointer while it is positioned over the chart area.
Change the chart size	Drag any sizing handle (hold down Shift while dragging a corner handle to resize proportionally).
Delete a chart	Embedded Chart: Select the chart, and then tap the Delete key.
	Worksheet Chart: Delete the worksheet.

DEVELOP YOUR SKILLS 6.2.1
Size and Move an Embedded Chart

In this exercise, you will move and resize the embedded column chart that you created in the previous exercise. You will also copy a sheet containing an embedded chart and delete the chart.

Size a Chart

1. **Click once** on the chart area of the embedded chart in the Sales by Quarter sheet to select the chart.
   Sizing handles appear around the border of the chart.

2. Follow these steps to resize the chart to be smaller:

A Place the mouse pointer over the **upper-right sizing handle** until you see the double-pointed arrow (not a four-pointed arrow).

Chart Area

y Quarter

Talos Bouras

B **Press and hold** Shift while you drag the sizing handle down and to the left.

C **Release** the mouse button about one-half inch from the corner in order to decrease the size by one-half inch; **release** the Shift key.

Notice that Excel resized the width and height proportionately because you held down the Shift key as you resized the chart.

Move a Chart

3. Follow these steps to move the chart and center it below the worksheet data:

Ⓐ Place the mouse pointer over a blank area of the chart so that a **four-pointed arrow** appears. ──────

Ⓑ Drag the chart **down and to the left** until it is just below row 11 and centered within **columns A through F.**

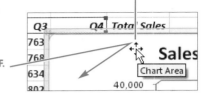

Ⓒ **Release** the mouse button when you are satisfied with the chart position.

You will see a rectangle "ghost" as you drag, showing you where the chart will land if you release the mouse button at that location.

Copy a Sheet

4. **Hold down** the ⌈Ctrl⌋ key; **drag** the Sales by Quarter sheet tab to the right and then **release** the mouse and ⌈Ctrl⌋ key.

The duplicate sheet is named Sales by Quarter (2).

5. **Rename** the Sales by Quarter (2) sheet to **Team Totals**.

Delete an Embedded Chart

6. **Click once** to select the column chart in the Team Totals sheet and **tap** ⌈Delete⌋.
Excel deletes the embedded chart.

7. Use ⌈Ctrl⌋+⌈Z⌋ to undo the **Delete** command.
The embedded chart reappears on the worksheet. You can restore an embedded chart right after it is deleted.

8. Use ⌈Ctrl⌋+⌈Y⌋ to redo the **Delete** command.
The chart is once again deleted. (You will create a pie chart here in a later exercise.)

9. Use ⌈Ctrl⌋+⌈S⌋ to **save** your workbook, and leave it **open** for the next exercise.

Video Lesson <u>labyrinthelab.com/videos</u>

In the previous section, you learned about column and bar charts. Now you will explore line and pie charts and how they can make your data work for you.

Line Charts

Line charts are most useful for comparing trends over a period of time. For example, line charts are often used to show stock market activity where the upward or downward trend is important. Like column charts, line charts have category and value axes. Line charts also use the same or similar objects as column charts. The following illustration shows a line chart that depicts the trend in quarter sales throughout the year. Data labels indicate the value for each time period along the line plotted on the chart. Take a moment to study the following figures.

	A	B	C	D	E	F
1	**Sales Department**					
2	*Quarterly and Total Sales - Fiscal Year*					
3						
4		*Q1*	*Q2*	*Q3*	*Q4*	*Total Sales*
5	Talos Bouras	28,775	31,342	31,763	30,675	$ 122,555
6	Leisa Malimali	6,575	7,304	8,768	10,023	$ 32,670
7	Brian Simpson	27,850	21,471	22,634	24,961	$ 96,916
8	Amy Wyatt	30,725	27,444	28,802	28,497	$ 115,468
10	Quarter Total	$ 93,925	$ 87,561	$ 91,967	$ 94,156	$ 367,609

The following chart was created using the selected data shown here. Notice that the data is in two separate ranges. You use the Ctrl key to select these nonadjacent ranges so that you can chart just the totals and the Q1–Q4 labels.

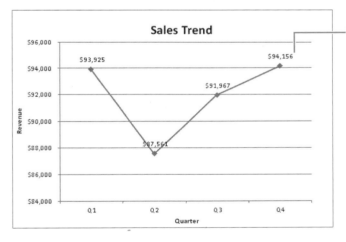

This is a data label. Data labels show the precise value of the various data points. You can use data labels with any chart type.

The line chart clearly depicts the downward and upward trend in sales volume.

Create a Line Chart

In this exercise, you will create a line chart that displays the total sales.

Before You Begin: The Sales by Quarter worksheet should be displayed.

Create a Line Chart

1. Follow these steps to select the data for the line chart on the Sales by Quarter worksheet:

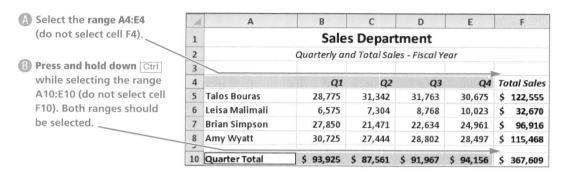

Ⓐ Select the **range A4:E4** (do not select cell F4).

Ⓑ **Press and hold down** Ctrl while selecting the range A10:E10 (do not select cell F10). Both ranges should be selected.

	A	B	C	D	E	F
1	**Sales Department**					
2	*Quarterly and Total Sales - Fiscal Year*					
3						
4		**Q1**	**Q2**	**Q3**	**Q4**	**Total Sales**
5	Talos Bouras	28,775	31,342	31,763	30,675	$ 122,555
6	Leisa Malimali	6,575	7,304	8,768	10,023	$ 32,670
7	Brian Simpson	27,850	21,471	22,634	24,961	$ 96,916
8	Amy Wyatt	30,725	27,444	28,802	28,497	$ 115,468
10	Quarter Total	$ 93,925	$ 87,561	$ 91,967	$ 94,156	$ 367,609

2. Choose **Insert→Charts→Line** 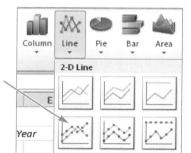 **→Line with Markers** from the Ribbon, as shown.

   Excel creates an embedded line chart in the current worksheet. Notice the light border and sizing handles, indicating the chart is selected. The Chart Tools contextual tabs are also visible on the Ribbon.

Move the Chart

Now you will move the chart to its own worksheet.

3. Follow these steps to move the chart:

   ■ Make certain the chart is **selected** (displays handles), which also makes the Chart Tools contextual tabs visible.

   ■ Choose **Design→Location→Move Chart** 📊 from the Ribbon.

   The Move Chart dialog box appears. In this dialog box, you can choose where to place the chart as well as provide a name for a new sheet if you wish to create one.

4. Follow these steps to move the chart to its own sheet:

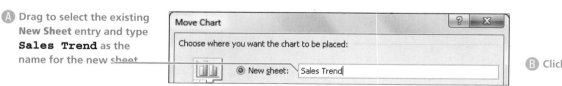

Ⓐ Drag to select the existing **New Sheet** entry and type **Sales Trend** as the name for the new sheet.

Ⓑ Click **OK**.

The chart now appears on its own worksheet.

5. Click the **Title** text box once to select it, and then **triple-click** on Quarter Total to select the entire entry.

6. Type **Sales Trend**, and then **click** another area of the chart.

7. Choose **Layout→Labels→Axis Titles**  **→Primary Horizontal Axis Title→Title Below Axis** from the Ribbon.
   Excel provides a text box below the horizontal axis with a default name of Axis Title *displayed.*

8. **Drag** to select the default horizontal axis title.

9. **Type** the new horizontal axis title, **Quarter**, and then **click away** to accept the new title.

10. Choose **Layout→Labels→Axis Titles**  **→Primary Vertical Axis Title→Rotated Title** from the Ribbon.

11. **Triple-click** to select the default vertical axis title.

12. Type **Revenue** as the new vertical axis title, and then **click away** to accept the new title.

13. Choose **Layout→Labels→Data Labels**  **→Above** from the Ribbon.
    Excel displays the values above the data points on the chart.

14. Use Ctrl + S to **save** your worksheet, and leave it **open** for the next exercise.

Pie Charts

Video Lesson   labyrinthelab.com/videos

Pie charts are useful for comparing parts of a whole. For example, pie charts are often used in budgets to show how funds are allocated. You typically select only two sets of data when creating pie charts: the values to be represented by the pie slices and the labels to identify the slices. The following illustration shows a worksheet and an accompanying 3-D pie chart with data labels applied. Notice that the worksheet has a Total Sales column.

	A	B	C	D	E	F
4		**Q1**	**Q2**	**Q3**	**Q4**	**Total Sales**
5	Talos Bouras	28,775	31,342	31,763	30,675	$ 122,555
6	Leisa Malimali	6,575	7,304	8,768	10,023	$ 32,670
7	Brian Simpson	27,850	21,471	22,634	24,961	$ 96,916
8	Amy Wyatt	30,725	27,444	28,802	28,497	$ 115,468
10	Quarter Total	$ 93,925	$ 87,561	$ 91,967	$ 94,156	$ 367,609

The names in column A will become labels in the legend. The numbers in column F will determine the sizes of the slices.

Excel calculates the percentages based on the numbers you select.

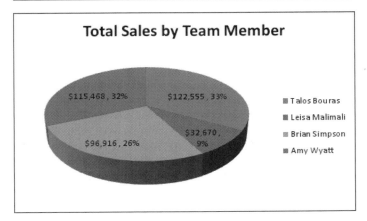

Total Sales by Team Member

$115,468, 32%
$122,555, 33%
$32,670, 9%
$96,916, 26%

■ Talos Bouras
■ Leisa Malimali
■ Brian Simpson
■ Amy Wyatt

Exploding Pie Slices

There are times when you may want to draw attention to a particular slice of the pie chart. You can make one slice explode from the chart simply by dragging it away from the other slices.

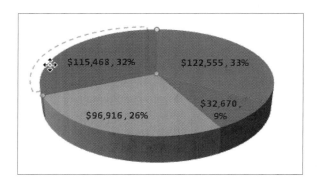

Notice that as you drag a slice out to give it an exploded effect, Excel will show with a dashed line where it will land.

Rotating and Elevating Pie Charts

You have the option to change the rotation and perspective (also known as elevation) of pie charts in order to display data in a different position or change the angle at which it is viewed. The 3-D Rotation button on the Layout tab of the Ribbon will open a dialog box that allows changes to the rotation and perspective to take place.

DEVELOP YOUR SKILLS 6.3.2
Create a Pie Chart

In this exercise, you will create a pie chart with the same data used for the line chart and leave it embedded in the Team Totals worksheet.

Before You Begin: The Team Totals worksheet should be displayed.

Insert the Pie Chart

1. Follow these steps to select the range for the chart on the Team Totals worksheet:

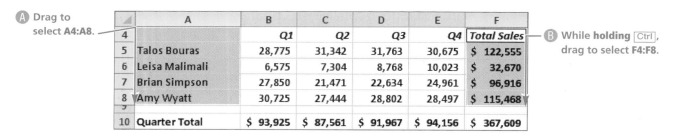

Ⓐ Drag to select A4:A8.

Ⓑ While holding Ctrl, drag to select F4:F8.

	A	B	C	D	E	F
4		Q1	Q2	Q3	Q4	Total Sales
5	Talos Bouras	28,775	31,342	31,763	30,675	$ 122,555
6	Leisa Malimali	6,575	7,304	8,768	10,023	$ 32,670
7	Brian Simpson	27,850	21,471	22,634	24,961	$ 96,916
8	Amy Wyatt	30,725	27,444	28,802	28,497	$ 115,468
10	Quarter Total	$ 93,925	$ 87,561	$ 91,967	$ 94,156	$ 367,609

2. Choose **Insert→Charts→Pie** ⬤ **→3-D Pie→Pie in 3-D** from the Ribbon.

Edit the Chart

3. Place the **mouse pointer** over the chart area so that the **four-pointed arrow appears**, and then **drag** it **down** and to the **left** until it is below row 11 and centered between columns A through F.
   Notice that the cell F4 entry, Total Sales, is used as the chart title.

4. **Edit** the chart title to read **Total Sales by Team Member**, clicking outside of the Title box to accept the new title.

5. Choose **Layout→Labels→Data Labels** 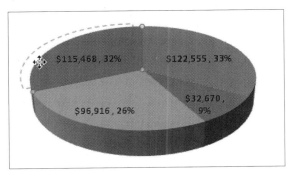→**More Data Label Options** from the Ribbon.
   The Format Data Labels dialog box appears.

6. Follow these steps to format the data labels:

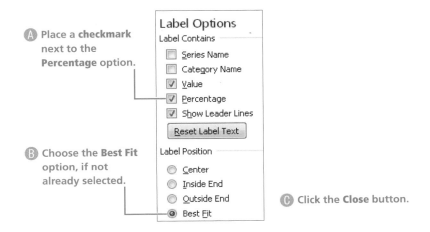

Ⓐ Place a **checkmark** next to the **Percentage** option.

Ⓑ Choose the **Best Fit** option, if not already selected.

Ⓒ Click the **Close** button.

Excel displays both the value and the percentage in each pie slice wherever they "best fit."

Explode a Pie Slice

7. **Click** the slice representing Amy Wyatt's sales, and then **pause** and **click** it again.
   The first click will select all slices, and the second click will select just the slice for Amy Wyatt.

8. Place the **mouse pointer** over the Amy Wyatt slice until you see a **move pointer**, and then **drag** away from the pie chart slightly and **release**.
   Notice that as you drag the pie slice away from the main chart, a dashed line appears where the slice will land if you release the mouse button.

9. Use ⌃Ctrl⌄+⌃S⌄ to **save** your worksheet, and leave it **open** for the next exercise.

6.4 Modifying Existing Charts

Video Lesson   labyrinthelab.com/videos

You can modify any chart object after the chart has been created. You can change the size, font, color, and placement of titles; format the numbers on the value axis; change the background color of the chart area; and more. You can also add or remove objects such as legends and data labels. You can even move an embedded chart to a separate worksheet and vice versa. These changes are made with the Chart Tools, which are grouped onto three contextual Ribbon tabs that appear when a chart is selected: Design, Layout, and Format. The following table describes the various Chart Tools available to modify your charts.

QUICK REFERENCE	USING CHART TOOLS ON THE RIBBON
Contextual Tab	**Command Groups on the Tab**
Design	■ *Type* allows you to change the type of chart, set the default chart type, and save a chart as a template.
	■ *Data* allows you to switch the data displayed on rows and columns and to reselect the data for the chart.
	■ *Chart Layouts* allows you to change the overall layout of the chart.
	■ *Chart Styles* allows you to choose a preset style for your chart.
	■ *Location* allows you to switch a chart from being embedded to being placed on a sheet and vice versa.
	■ *Mode* allows you to switch the display mode for charts.
Layout	■ *Current Selection* allows you to select a specific chart element and apply formatting to it.
	■ *Insert* allows you to insert objects into your chart.
	■ *Labels* allows you to make changes to various labels on your chart, such as the title and data labels.
	■ *Axes* allows you to choose whether to display axes and gridlines, as well as to set the properties for them.
	■ *Background* allows you to change the background formatting, such as fill color, for the chart.
	■ *Analysis* allows you to analyze the data displayed within the chart.
	■ *Properties* allows you to change the name of the chart.
Format	■ *Current Selection* allows you to select a specific chart element and apply formatting to it.
	■ *Shape Styles* allows you to visually make changes to the selected chart element.
	■ *WordArt Styles* allows you to apply WordArt to text labels in your chart.
	■ *Arrange* allows you to change how your chart is arranged in relation to other objects in your worksheet.
	■ *Size* allows you to change the size of your chart by typing in exact values.

Changing the Chart Type

There are so many chart types available that you may wish to explore other options before making a final decision. It is easy to change the type of an existing chart by using the Change Chart Type dialog box.

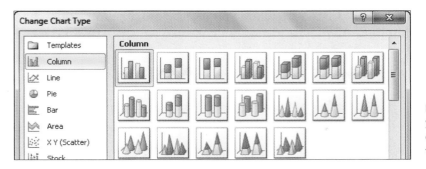

In the Change Chart Type dialog box, you can choose from many preset chart types if you wish to change the type of an existing chart.

Reselecting Data

You may decide after creating a chart that some source data is missing or data that should be excluded. The Select Data command displays the Select Data Source dialog box, where you may change the data range for the entire chart. The recommended reselection method is to collapse the dialog box and drag in the worksheet. The following illustration shows that the Chart Data Range reference =Sales!$A$4:$E$8 includes the worksheet name followed by an exclamation (!) point. You also can add, edit, or remove a single data series or edit the category axis labels. The Switch Row/Column option swaps the data in the vertical and horizontal axes of the chart. You could use this option when values display along the horizontal axis and you would rather have them on the vertical axis.

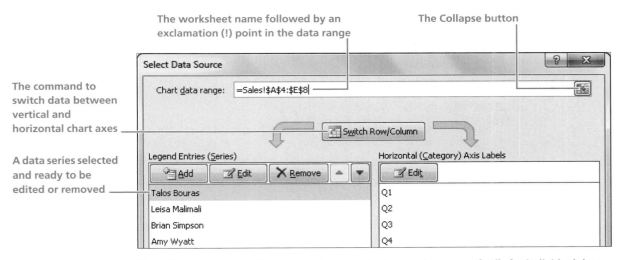

The worksheet name followed by an exclamation (!) point in the data range

The Collapse button

The command to switch data between vertical and horizontal chart axes

A data series selected and ready to be edited or removed

The Select Data Source dialog box allows you to change the range of cells for individual data series or the entire chart.

Using the arrow keys while attempting to edit a data range in a text box results in unwanted characters. For best results, reselect a data range by dragging in the worksheet.

Modifying Chart Elements

Charts are made up of various elements. For example, the legends, titles, and columns are all types of elements. You must select an element before you can perform an action on it. You can select an element by clicking it with the mouse. Once selected, you can delete, move, size, and format the element. You delete a selected element by tapping the Delete key, move a selected element by dragging it with the mouse when you see the move pointer, and change the size by dragging a sizing handle.

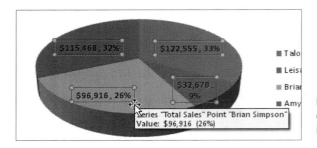

In this illustration, the data labels are the selected element, and the ScreenTip indicates that the mouse is pointing at the data label for Brian Simpson.

Formatting Chart Elements

You can modify any chart element after the chart has been created by using the visual Chart Tools on the Ribbon. As an alternative, you can double-click the chart element to display a Format dialog box with many options for that element. For example, options in the Format Data Series dialog box allow you to adjust the column bar width; change the space between bars; and apply a fill, border, or other visual effects.

Previewing Formatting Before Applying

You can preview how a formatting change would appear in a worksheet cell before actually issuing the command to apply it. The same is true with the Chart Tools Format ribbon in Excel. If you place the mouse pointer over a button on one of the options in the Shape Styles or WordArt Styles group, a preview displays how the change will look in your chart.

QUICK REFERENCE	MODIFYING EXISTING CHARTS
Task	**Procedure**
Change the chart type	■ Select the chart you wish to change to a different type.
	■ Choose Design→Change Chart Type from the Ribbon.
	■ Browse the types available and double-click the desired type.
Reselect a data range for the entire chart	■ Select the chart.
	■ Choose Design→Data→Select Data from the Ribbon.
	■ Click the Collapse ▦ button at the right of Chart Data Range in the Select Data Source dialog box.
	■ Drag in the worksheet to select the new data range.
	■ Click the Expand ▥ button at the right of Chart Data Range in the Select Data Source dialog box.

Task	Procedure
Reselect the range for a data series	■ Select the chart. ■ Choose Design→Data→Select Data from the Ribbon. ■ Select the desired item under Legend Entries (Series) in the Select Data Source dialog box and click Edit. ■ Drag to select the entire Series Name or Series Values entry in the Edit Series dialog box. ■ Drag in the worksheet to select the new range and click OK.
Delete a chart element	■ Select the desired chart element and tap ⌴Delete⌴.
Format an element on an existing chart	■ Select the chart element that you wish to format. ■ Display the Design, Layout, or Format tab of the Ribbon. ■ Choose the appropriate formatting command from the Ribbon.

DEVELOP YOUR SKILLS 6.4.1

Modify a Chart

In this exercise, you will change a chart type and then apply various formatting features to it.

Before You Begin: The Sales by Rep worksheet should be displayed.

Change a Chart Type

1. Click anywhere within the column chart on the **Sales by Rep** sheet to select the chart and display the **Chart Tools** Ribbon tabs.

2. Choose **Design→Type→Change Chart Type** ![icon] from the Ribbon.
The Change Chart Type dialog box appears.

3. Follow these steps to change the chart type:

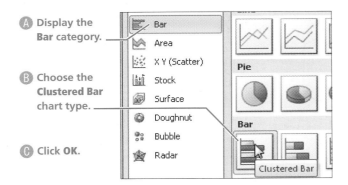

Ⓐ Display the **Bar** category.

Ⓑ Choose the **Clustered Bar** chart type.

Ⓒ Click **OK**.

Reselect Data

4. Choose **Design→Data→Select Data** 📊 from the Ribbon.
   The Select Data Source dialog box appears with the Chart Data Range as ='Sales by Quarter' !$A$4:$E$8. You want to compare sales performance without including sales manager Talos Bouras. You will reselect the range to include the labels in row 4 and the data for the other three sales team members.

5. Follow these steps to reselect the chart data range:

Ⓐ Click the **Collapse** button or drag the title bar of the dialog box, as necessary, to view the worksheet data.

Ⓑ Drag to select the **range A4:E4**.

Ⓒ **Hold down** `Ctrl` and select the **range A6:E8**.

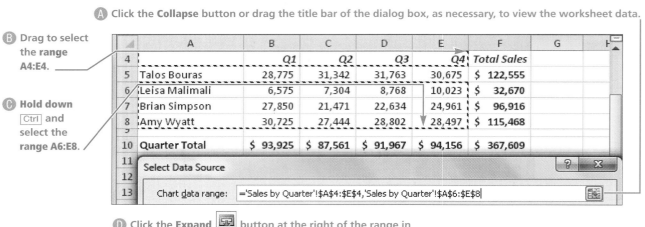

	A	B	C	D	E	F	G	H
4		Q1	Q2	Q3	Q4	Total Sales		
5	Talos Bouras	28,775	31,342	31,763	30,675	$ 122,555		
6	Leisa Malimali	6,575	7,304	8,768	10,023	$ 32,670		
7	Brian Simpson	27,850	21,471	22,634	24,961	$ 96,916		
8	Amy Wyatt	30,725	27,444	28,802	28,497	$ 115,468		
10	Quarter Total	$ 93,925	$ 87,561	$ 91,967	$ 94,156	$ 367,609		

Select Data Source

Chart data range: ='Sales by Quarter'!$A$4:$E$4,'Sales by Quarter'!$A$6:$E$8|

Ⓓ Click the **Expand** 📊 button at the right of the range in the Select Data Source dialog box if you collapsed the box.

The Legend Entries (Series) should list Leisa Malimali, Brian Simpson, and Amy Wyatt.

6. Click **OK**.

7. Select one of the column bars for Leisa Malimali and **tap** `Delete`.
   Now two data series display in the chart. Any chart element can be deleted in this way.

Format a Chart Using the Ribbon

8. **Click** anywhere within the top bar in the chart, which represents the Amy Wyatt data series.

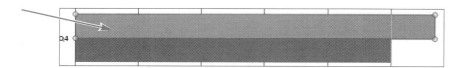

Make certain that you single-click because that selects Amy Wyatt's data series for all four quarters and leaves the current tab displayed. If you double-click, the Design tab with the current style displays on the Ribbon. In this case, it won't matter as you are already viewing the Design tab, but it could cause you to take extra steps if you were already working on the Format tab.

9. Follow these steps to apply formatting to the Amy Wyatt data series:

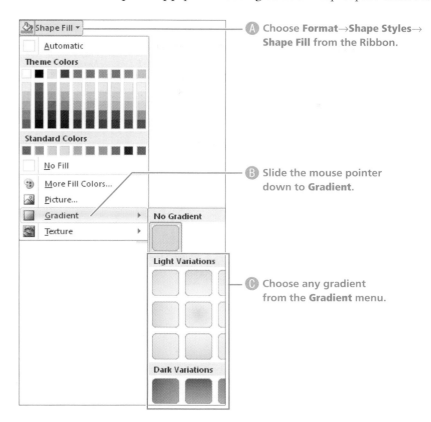

(A) Choose **Format→Shape Styles→ Shape Fill** from the Ribbon.

(B) Slide the mouse pointer down to **Gradient**.

(C) Choose any gradient from the **Gradient** menu.

10. **Click** anywhere within the chart area to select it.
    Remember that any formatting you choose will apply only to the chart element you have selected.

11. Choose **Format→Shape Styles→Shape Outline** **→Weight** from the Ribbon.

12. Point at various line weights to preview how they would look in the chart; then choose **3 pt** from the list.

13. Choose **Format→Shape Styles→Shape Outline** from the Ribbon, and then apply the color of your choice.
    A line now appears around the entire chart area. In the next few steps, you will be changing the number format of the value axis.

Format Axis Numbers

14. **Double-click** on any of the values in the horizontal axis at the bottom of the chart.
    The Format Axis dialog box displays. If the Format Plot Area or other dialog box displays, close it and again double-click a value on the horizontal axis.

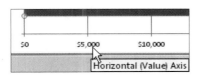

15. Follow these steps to format the axis numbers as Currency:

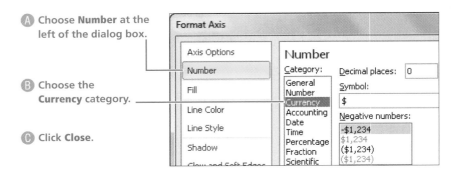

Ⓐ Choose **Number** at the left of the dialog box.

Ⓑ Choose the **Currency** category.

Ⓒ Click **Close**.

The numbers on the axis now display with dollar ($) signs.

Add a Chart Title

16. Choose **Layout→Labels→Chart Title** **→Above Chart** from the Ribbon.

17. Change the default chart title to **Sales by Rep**.

18. **Save** 💾 the changes, and leave the workbook **open**.

Sales by Rep

6.5 Applying Layouts and Styles to Charts

Video Lesson   labyrinthelab.com/videos

Chart layouts, also known as quick layouts, are designs that contain various chart elements. Choosing a chart layout saves time versus adding and formatting chart elements one at a time. Chart Quick Styles are based on the theme applied to your workbook. There are many preset styles that you can apply to charts. The layouts and styles displayed on the Design tab of the Ribbon are based on the type of chart that you currently have selected. In the figures displayed below, you can see that the layouts and styles available for column charts are different from those available for pie charts.

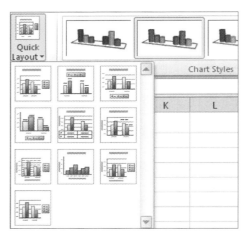

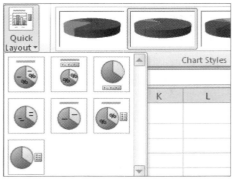

The chart layouts and styles available through Excel's Design tab of the Ribbon will change based on the type of chart you have selected.

Formatting Attributes Controlled by the Selected Style

When you choose a style for your chart, the colors and effects (such as fill effects) will change to match the style selected. Data in worksheet cells is not affected by any styles that you apply to charts. Excel does not allow you to create your own styles, but you can save the formatting from a selected chart as a template to use as the basis for future charts.

Viewing All Available Layouts and Styles for a Chart Type

The Ribbon will display just a few of the layouts and styles available for the selected chart type. To view the entire gallery, click the More button to expand the Chart Layouts or Chart Styles group of the Ribbon.

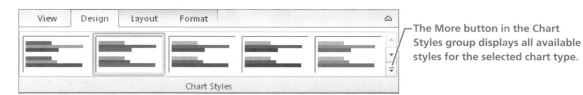

The More button in the Chart Styles group displays all available styles for the selected chart type.

QUICK REFERENCE	APPLYING A LAYOUT AND STYLE TO A CHART
Task	**Procedure**
Apply a layout or style to a chart	■ Select the chart to which you wish to apply a layout or style.
	■ Choose the Design tab from the Ribbon.
	■ Click the More ⊽ button in the Chart Layouts or Chart Styles group to display the full array of available choices.
	■ Click to choose the layout or style you wish to apply.

DEVELOP YOUR SKILLS 6.5.1
Apply a Layout and a Style to a Chart

In this exercise, you will apply a quick layout and Quick Style to the bar chart you created in the last exercise.

Before You Begin: The Sales by Rep sheet should be displayed.

Apply a Workbook Theme

1. Choose **Page Layout→Themes→Themes** [Aa]→**Origin** from the Ribbon.

2. **Click** each of the workbook tabs and view the result.
   A uniform color scheme, font set, and graphic effects are applied to all worksheet data and charts. The chart style that you apply later in this exercise will match the workbook theme.

Change the Chart Layout

3. Select the **Sales by Rep** sheet.

4. **Click** in the chart area of the **Sales by Rep** chart to select the chart.

5. Choose **Design→Chart Layouts→More** ☰ from the Ribbon.
   Excel displays all of the chart layout choices for this type of chart.

6. **Click once** to apply the layout of your choice and view the result in the chart.

7. Choose **Design→Chart Layouts→More** ☰ from the Ribbon.

8. Choose **Layout 2** in the list.
   A Screen Tip displays the layout name as you point at each layout. You will need to reenter any title that is not within the data range specified for the chart.

9. If the default chart title displays at the top of the chart, change it to **Sales by Rep**.

Change the Chart Style

10. Choose **Design→Chart Styles→More** ☰ from the Ribbon.
    Excel displays all of the available chart styles for this type of chart. The gallery styles match the color scheme and graphic effects from the currently applied workbook theme.

11. **Click once** to apply a chart style you find attractive.
    If there were data on this worksheet, the data would not be affected by the new chart style.

12. Repeat **steps 10 and 11** if you wish to apply a different chart style.

13. **Save** 💾 the changes and leave the workbook **open**.

6.6 Previewing and Printing Charts

Video Lesson labyrinthelab.com/videos

The Print command is used to preview and print charts. If a chart is embedded, you can print the entire worksheet or select and print just the chart. If a chart is on a separate worksheet, you must first display the sheet before issuing the Print command. In the preview on the Print tab in Backstage view, the chart will display in black and white or in color, depending on the type of printer selected.

Color fills and borders may not provide good contrast in charts printed on grayscale printers. Consider using shades of gray or black-and-white pattern fills.

QUICK REFERENCE	PRINTING CHARTS
Task	**Procedure**
Preview how a chart will look when printed	▪ Select the chart by either clicking it if it is embedded or displaying the sheet on which it is placed.
	▪ Choose File→Print and look at the preview in Backstage view.
Print a chart	▪ After using the above steps to preview the chart, select printing options in the Print tab of Backstage view.
	▪ Click Print.

Preview and Print a Chart

In this exercise, you will preview the pie chart you created in the last exercise and print the column chart.

Before You Begin: The Team Totals worksheet should be displayed.

1. **Click once** to select the pie chart on the **Team Totals** worksheet.

2. Choose **File→Print**.
   The pie chart appears in the preview of the Print tab in Backstage view.

3. **Tap** Esc to exit Backstage view without printing.

4. **Click** in a cell away from the pie chart to **deselect** the chart.

5. Choose **File→Print**.
   Notice that when the chart is not selected, Excel will print the worksheet along with the embedded chart.

6. **Tap** Esc to exit Backstage view without printing.

7. Display the **Sales Trend** worksheet.

8. Choose **File→Print**, select an appropriate printer, click **Print**, and retrieve the printout.
   Excel will print one copy of your chart to the default printer.

9. Keep the workbook **open**.

6.7 Emailing a Workbook

Video Lesson   labyrinthelab.com/videos

When you want to send an Excel workbook to someone by email, you have two choices. You may send the entire workbook as an attachment, or you may send a single worksheet as the body of the email message. Each method has its uses. Sending a worksheet as an email message may cause some formatting to be lost. However, if you just need to transmit a single worksheet, sending it as the body of an email message may be more convenient for the recipient to quickly view and print.

If you need to send a multisheet workbook, you must use the attachment method.

Attaching a Workbook

You may send email from within Excel if you previously set up a Microsoft Outlook or Windows Live Mail email account. After you give the Send as Attachment command, an email message window appears with the workbook file already attached. You simply enter the recipient's email address and type your message. You may edit the subject line and attach more files, if desired. You may attach Excel workbooks from within most other email programs if you do not have an Outlook or Windows Mail account.

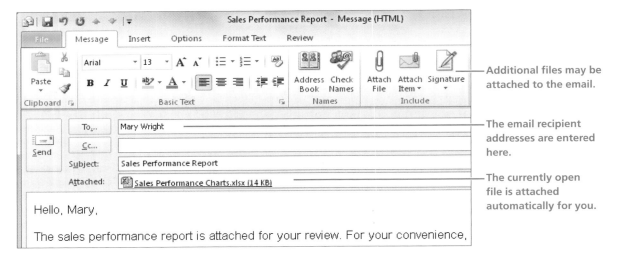

A Microsoft Outlook email message window

Additional files may be attached to the email.

The email recipient addresses are entered here.

The currently open file is attached automatically for you.

Inserting a Worksheet in an Email Message

The Send to Mail Recipient command has an option to place the currently displayed worksheet in the email message area. You fill in the email address, a subject for the message, and a short introduction to the worksheet before sending the message. The Introduction box will not be available in an email program other than Outlook.

> The Send to Mail Recipient command does not appear on the Ribbon. You must add it to the Quick Access toolbar.

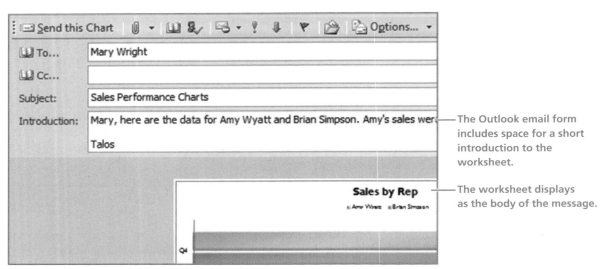

Sending one worksheet as the message body in Outlook

The Outlook email form includes space for a short introduction to the worksheet.

The worksheet displays as the body of the message.

Task	Procedure
Add the Send to Mail Recipient command to the Quick Access toolbar	■ Choose File→Options→Quick Access toolbar. ■ Choose Commands Not in the Ribbon from the Choose Commands From list. ■ Scroll down the list, select Send to Mail Recipient, and click the Add button.
Send an entire workbook as an attachment to an Outlook email message	■ Open the workbook file you wish to send by email. ■ Choose File→Save & Send→Send Using E-mail→Send as Attachment (or click the Send to Mail Recipient button on the Quick Access toolbar, choose Send the Entire Workbook as an Attachment, and click OK). ■ Address the message and revise the default subject (the document name) for the message, if desired. ■ Click the Send button on the message window. ■ Close the message window.
Send a single worksheet as an Outlook email message	■ Display the worksheet you wish to send by email. ■ Click the Send to Mail Recipient button on the Quick Access toolbar, choose Send the Current Sheet as the Message Body, and click OK. ■ Enter the email recipient(s), subject, and a brief introduction. ■ Click the Send This Sheet button on the email form toolbar. ■ Click the Send to Mail Recipient button on the Quick Access toolbar to hide the email window.

DEVELOP YOUR SKILLS 6.7.1

Send a Workbook via Email

In this exercise, you will set up a workbook to be emailed as an attachment. Because an email account may not be available on your computer, you will not actually send the message.

Before You Begin: The Sales Performance Charts workbook should be open. Outlook or another email program compatible with Microsoft Office should be installed.

1. Choose **File→Save & Send**, make certain **Send Using E-mail** is the selected category, and click **Send as Attachment** at the right of Backstage view.
   After a few moments, a new message is created in an Outlook message window (or another program set as the default email program for your computer). Notice that the Excel workbook is already attached. Its filename is visible in the Attached box.

2. Address the message to **Mary Wright** (for a fictitious person in your email contacts list).

3. Change the message **subject** to **Sales Performance Report**.

4. Click in the **body** of the message and type the following text:

Hello Mary,
The sales performance report is attached for your review.
For your convenience, charts have been created for data comparison.
Regards, Talos

A Send button may not be available in the email form. Because many computer classrooms are not equipped with email accounts, at this point you will close the message rather than send it.

5. **Close** the email program window.

6. Leave the workbook **open** for the next exercise.

6.8 Importing Data into Excel via a Web Query

Video Lesson labyrinthelab.com/videos

Many web pages are created using a table structure. Some data may change frequently, such as stock quotes on an external web page or weekly sales numbers on an organization's intranet. The From Web command is used to create a web query that retrieves this type of data into a worksheet. You can set the data to refresh once when the workbook is opened or as frequently as every minute while the workbook is open. You may add a previously saved web query to any worksheet. Excel includes connections to a few "refreshable" queries, which may be accessed with the Existing Connections command on the Ribbon.

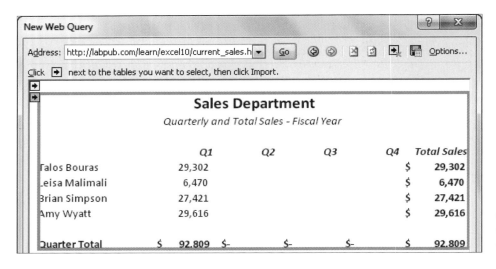

Selecting the table data from a web page to include in a web query

Task	Procedure
Create a web query and import data to a worksheet	■ Display the worksheet into which you wish to import the web data. ■ Ensure that your Internet connection is active. ■ Choose Data→Get External Data→From Web ⬚ from the Ribbon. ■ Enter the web page address and click one or more yellow arrows to select table areas on the web page. ■ Click Options, choose the desired formatting or other options in the Web Query Options dialog box, and click OK. ■ Click the Save Query button on the toolbar in the New Web Query dialog box, navigate to the desired location, and enter the filename. ■ Click Import in the New Web Query dialog box. ■ Choose a starting cell in the existing worksheet or choose New Worksheet as the destination. ■ Click the Properties button and select the desired refresh or other options in the External Data Range Properties dialog box. ■ Click OK in the Import Data dialog box.
Use a previously saved web query	■ Choose Data→Get External Data→Existing Connections from the Ribbon. ■ Choose an existing connection from the list or click Browse for More and navigate to the desired web query file. ■ Choose the desired location for the data in the Import Data dialog box.

DEVELOP YOUR SKILLS 6.8.1
Import Data from a Web Page

In this exercise, you will create a web query that places the current Quarter 1 sales from a web page into a worksheet.

Before You Begin: Your Internet connection should be active and the Sales Performance Charts workbook should be open.

Create a Web Query

1. Click the **Insert Worksheet** button to the right of the sheet tabs and **rename** the new sheet to **Current Sales**.

2. Choose **Data→Get External Data→From Web** ⬚ from the Ribbon.
   In the New Web Query dialog box, Internet Explorer connects with the web.

3. Enter **labyrinthelab.com/excel10** into the address bar and **tap** ⎡Enter⎤.
   Internet Explorer displays the homepage for your textbook.

4. From the left navigation bar, choose **Lessons 1–6** and then **Lesson 6**; then, click the **Current Sales** link on the web page.
   This page displays an Excel workbook that was saved as a web page.

5. Follow these steps to select the data on the web page:

Ⓐ Click the **second yellow arrow** at the left of **Sales Department**. (The first yellow arrow at the upper-left corner selects the entire worksheet, so do not click to select that item.)

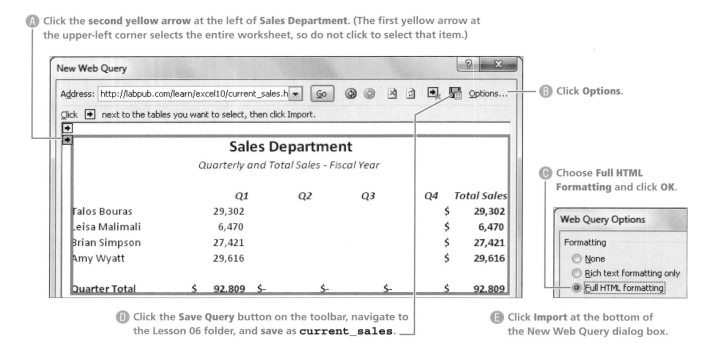

Ⓑ Click **Options**.

Ⓒ Choose **Full HTML Formatting** and click **OK**.

Ⓓ Click the **Save Query** button on the toolbar, navigate to the Lesson 06 folder, and **save** as **current_sales**.

Ⓔ Click **Import** at the bottom of the New Web Query dialog box.

Import the Data

6. If a warning appears, read the warning in the Microsoft Office Excel Security Notice dialog box and click **OK** to confirm that you trust the website source.

7. In the Import Data dialog box, verify that **=$A$1 (cell A1)** in the existing worksheet is selected, and click **Properties**.

8. Review the Refresh Control and other properties available in the External Data Range Properties dialog box; click **Cancel** without making any changes.
   You could set the data to refresh automatically with a frequency of your choice.

9. Click **OK** in the Import Data dialog box.
   The imported data displays on the worksheet. Notice that the data retained its formatting because you selected the Full HTML Formatting option. The Refresh All command on the Ribbon allows you to update the worksheet data manually if the source web page is revised. You could use the saved web query again in another worksheet.

10. **Save** 💾 the changes and **close** the workbook.

6.9 Concepts Review

Concepts Review   labyrinthelab.com/excel10

To check your knowledge of the key concepts introduced in this lesson, complete the Concepts Review quiz by going to the URL listed above. If your classroom is using Labyrinth eLab, you may complete the Concepts Review quiz from within your eLab course.

Reinforce Your Skills

Create a Column Chart

In this exercise, you will create a column chart to compare total new customers by time period. You will move and format the chart. Then you will switch the row and column data to compare the data by customer source category.

Create a Stacked Column Chart

1. **Open** the rs-Service Contracts Comparison workbook from the Lesson 06 folder.

2. Select the **range A3:E7,** taking care not to include the totals in row 8.

3. Choose **Insert→Charts→Column→2-D Column→Stacked Column** from the Ribbon.
   The chart shows a column for each quarter with the four customer source categories stacked in a column. The stacked column chart is not as cluttered as a clustered column chart, which requires 16 columns to present the same data but allows more precise comparison of single categories.

Move and Format the Chart

4. **Point** at the chart area and drag the chart down and to the left until the upper-left corner is at **cell A11**.

5. Choose **Design→Chart Layouts→Layout 3** from the Ribbon.
   ScreenTips help you to locate Layout 3 in the list. The legend is moved below the horizontal axis and a title text box is added above the chart.

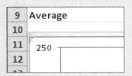

Link the Chart Title to a Cell

6. **Click** in the chart title text box.
   The entry ="Chart Title" appears in the Formula Bar.

7. Type **=** to begin a formula.

8. Click **cell A3** in the worksheet and **tap** Enter.
   You just linked the chart title to the contents of cell A3 in Sheet1. The entry =Sheet1!$A$3 appears in the Formula Bar. Notice that Customer Source now appears in the chart title text box. The chart title would be updated if you edited the text in cell A3.

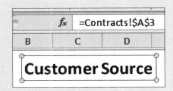

Switch Row/Column Data

Notice that the chart's horizontal axis displays the quarters of the year and the legend contains the customer source categories. Each column represents the total new customers in one quarter for comparison among time periods.

9. Choose **Design→Data→Switch Row/Column** from the Ribbon.

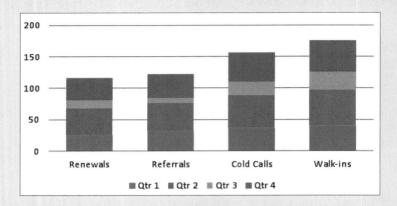

The data reverse so the horizontal category axis displays the customer source categories. Each column represents the total new customers in a customer source category for comparison among categories.

10. **Save** 💾 the changes and **close** the workbook.

REINFORCE YOUR SKILLS 6.2

Adjust a Chart

In this exercise, you will correct the data source range and convert a column chart to a line chart. The chart is formatted with a grayscale chart style suitable for printing on a grayscale printer.

Correct a Data Range

1. **Open** the rs-Chart Conversion workbook from the Lesson 06 folder.
   An embedded column chart has been created on the Service Contracts sheet.

2. Inspect the chart to locate an error in the way data are labeled.

The categories on the horizontal axis are labeled 1 through 4 rather than Qtr 1 through Qtr 4. Excel used a default number series, which indicates a common error.

3. **Select** the chart and notice that the chart data range does not include the category labels in row 3.

⬜	A	B	C	D	E
3	**Customer Source**	**Qtr 1**	**Qtr 2**	**Qtr 3**	**Qtr 4**
4	Renewals	47	37	33	44
5	Referrals	22	28	30	32
6	Cold Calls	26	17	25	22
7	Walk-ins	18	20	15	17

4. Choose **Design→Data→Select Data** from the Ribbon; drag the **Select Data Source** dialog box to view the worksheet data, if necessary.
You learned earlier in this lesson to reselect the chart data range. In the next step, you will use an alternative method to reselect just the horizontal axis labels.

5. Click the **Edit** button in the Horizontal (Category) Axis Labels area of the dialog box.

6. Select the **range B3:E3** in the worksheet, click **OK** to exit the Axis Labels dialog box, and click **OK** again.
The category axis labels are shown correctly on the chart.

Convert the Chart to a Line Chart

Suppose you are interested in seeing only the trends in customer source rather than the numbers in individual quarters. You can easily convert the column chart to a line chart.

7. Choose **Design→Type→Change Chart Type** 📊 from the Ribbon.

8. Choose **Line with Markers** in the Line category and click **OK**.

9. Choose **Layout→Labels→Data Labels** 📊→ **None** from the Ribbon.

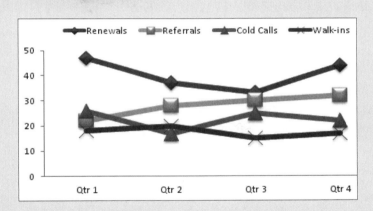

The line chart shows downward and upward trends.

10. **Deselect** the chart and **save** 💾 the changes.

11. Display the **print preview** in Backstage view, **print**, and **close** the workbook.
Both the worksheet and the chart should print on a single page.

Create Pie Charts

In this exercise, you will create two pie charts to illustrate employee salaries. The charts will show how salary cost is divided among departments and how one department's salaries are allocated. You will embed the first chart and place the second chart on a separate sheet.

Create the Company Chart

1. **Open** the rs-Payroll Expenses workbook from the Lesson 06 folder.

2. Use the Ctrl key to select the **ranges B3:E3** and **B9:E9**.

3. Choose **Insert→Charts→Pie→2-D Pie→Pie** from the Ribbon.
   If you included the totals in column F by mistake, either delete and reinsert the chart or use the Select Data command in the Design ribbon to reselect the data source range.

4. Move the chart to **row 11** below the worksheet data.

Format the Company Chart

5. Choose **Layout→Labels→Data Labels** [icon] **→More Data Labels Options** from the Ribbon.
   The Format Data Labels dialog box displays the Label Options.

6. Place a checkmark next to **Category Name and Percentage**, remove the checkmark from **Value**, and click **Close**.
   Notice that the data label does not fit inside the smallest pie slice. This is OK, but an option can make the labels look uniform.

7. Choose **Layout→Labels→Data Labels** [icon] **→Inside End** from the Ribbon.
   This data labels option causes all data labels to fit inside their pie slices.

8. Click in the legend and **tap** Delete.
   The legend is unnecessary because the department names are in the data labels.

9. Choose **Layout→Labels→Chart Title** [icon] **→Above Chart** from the Ribbon.

10. Select the default **chart title** text and use the Enter key while typing **Payroll Expenses by Department** to create a two-line title, as shown.

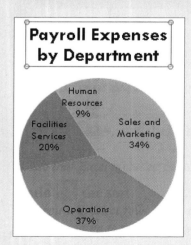

Create a Pie Chart for the Sales and Marketing Department

11. Select the **range A3:B8**.
    Using the Ctrl *key is unnecessary because columns A and B are adjacent.*

12. Choose **Insert→Charts→Pie→2-D Pie→Pie** from the Ribbon.
    Notice that the text in cell B3 is used as the chart title because B3 is the first cell in the data series.

13. Choose **Design→Chart Layouts→Layout 1** from the Ribbon.
    Layout 1 removes the legend and adds data labels with categories and percentages.

Move the Department Chart to Its Own Sheet

14. Choose **Design→Location→Move Chart** 📊 from the Ribbon.
    The Move Chart dialog box is displayed. You can move a chart to a new sheet or as an embedded object to an existing sheet.

15. Select the **text entry** (such as Chart1) next to New Sheet, type **Sales and Marketing**, and **tap** Enter to choose **OK**.
    The new sheet containing the chart appears before Sheet1 in the workbook tab order.

16. Choose **Design→Chart Styles→More** ⤓ from the Ribbon and choose an attractive Quick Style.
    You may want to choose a grayscale Quick Style if you plan to print on a grayscale printer. The styles in the last row contain a black background, which you should avoid printing to conserve printer toner or ink.

17. **Right-click** a data label to select all data labels and choose a **larger font size** from the Mini toolbar.
    Some data labels may appear outside their pie slices, depending on the font you chose.

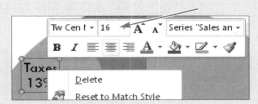

18. **Save** 💾 the changes and **close** the workbook.

Create a Doughnut Chart

In this exercise, you will create a doughnut chart. Like pie charts, doughnut charts are useful for comparing parts of a whole. However, doughnut charts can contain more than one data series. Each ring in a doughnut chart represents a data series. The chart you create will compare the quarter 4 sales with total sales.

Create the Chart

1. **Open** the rs-Sales Comparison workbook from the Lesson 06 folder.

2. Take a few moments to determine the ranges that need to be selected in order to create a chart that **compares Qtr 4 sales** with the **total product sales**.

3. Use the ⌈Ctrl⌋ key to select the **ranges A3:A7 and E3:F7**.

4. Choose **Insert→Charts→Other Charts**  **→Doughnut→ Doughnut** from the Ribbon.
   The Total data series appears in the outer ring of the chart. The Qtr 4 data series is in the inner ring. You will add formatting in the next few steps to identify the data clearly.

Doughnut

Format Data Labels and the Title

5. Choose **Design→Chart Layouts→Layout 6** from the Ribbon.
   The layout adds a default chart title and data labels with percentages.

6. **Click once** on the data label for total **Cold Calls (21%)**, and then click again to select just that label.

7. **Choose Layout→Labels→Data Labels** **→More Data Label Options** from the Ribbon.
   The Format Data Label dialog box appears with the Label Options displayed.

8. Place a checkmark next to **Series Name** under Label Contains and click **Close**.

Label Options
Label Contains
☑ Series Name

9. Select only the **Cold Calls** label for Qtr 4 (24%) and **repeat** the previous step to add the series name to the label.
   If labels were displayed for all data series names, the labels would overlap. Formatting at least one label on each ring, however, is important for identifying the time period that each ring represents.

10. Change the default **chart title** to `Sales Source` (the contents of cell A3 on the worksheet).

Move and Size the Chart

11. **Drag** the chart below the worksheet data and make certain all the data are visible.

12. Follow these steps to resize the chart width:

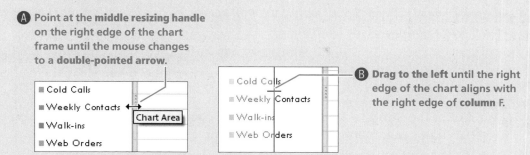

A Point at the **middle resizing handle** on the right edge of the chart frame until the mouse changes to a **double-pointed arrow**.

B **Drag to the left** until the right edge of the chart aligns with the right edge of **column** F.

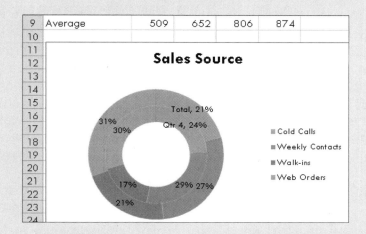

13. **Save** 🖫 the changes, and **close** the workbook.

Email a Worksheet

In this exercise, you will place a worksheet into the body of an email message.

Before You Begin: The Send to Mail Recipient command should be available on the Quick Access toolbar or you must have rights to add the command.

1. **Open** the rs-E-mail Chart workbook from the Lesson 06 folder and display the Sales by Rep chart sheet. (If a message appears about data connections above the worksheet, click Enable Content.)

2. Verify that the **Send to Mail Recipient** command is installed on the Quick Access toolbar. If it is not, follow these steps to install the command:

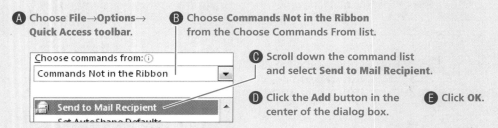

Ⓐ Choose **File→Options→ Quick Access toolbar**.

Ⓑ Choose **Commands Not in the Ribbon** from the Choose Commands From list.

Ⓒ Scroll down the command list and select **Send to Mail Recipient**.

Ⓓ Click the **Add** button in the center of the dialog box.

Ⓔ Click **OK**.

3. Click the **Send to Mail Recipient** button on the Quick Access toolbar.
A prompt appears, telling you about the two options for sending the entire workbook or a single worksheet.

4. Choose the **Send the Current Sheet as the Message Body** option and click **OK**. (If a message appears about connections, click Enable Content.)
An Outlook (or other default email program) message window appears, in which you can address the message. The active worksheet appears in the message body.

5. Follow these steps to set up the email message:

Ⓐ Type **Mary Wright** in the **To** box and assume that this name is set up with an email address in your contacts list.

Ⓑ Change the **subject line** as shown here.

Ⓒ If using Outlook, enter the **introductory message** as shown here.

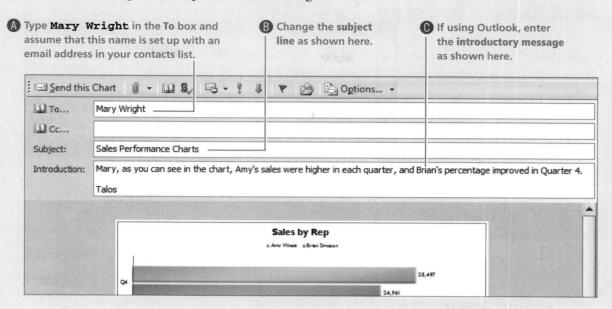

The Send This Chart button may not be available at the upper-left corner of the email form. Because many computer classrooms are not equipped with email accounts, at this point, you will close the message rather than send it.

6. Click the **Send to Mail Recipient** button on the Quick Access toolbar.
The button toggles between the email message window and the Excel workbook window when a worksheet is in the message body.

7. Close the workbook. Do **not** save when asked if you wish to save.
An email message cannot be saved in a workbook.

Apply Your Skills

Create a Line Chart

In this exercise, you will create a line chart on a separate sheet, rename the sheet tabs, and print a chart.

1. Start a **new** workbook and create the worksheet shown at right:
   - **Enter** dates for the actual previous 12 months rather than the dates shown.
   - Use **AutoFill** to expand the date series.
   - **Resize** the column widths as necessary.

2. **Format** the dates so that they are displayed as *Mar-15* without the year (your year may be different).

3. Use the worksheet data to create the following chart:
   - Set up the **axis labels** and **title** as shown (your years may be different).
   - Do **not** include a legend.

	A	B
1	Green Clean Web Orders	
2	Product Sales	
3		
4	Date	Web Orders
5	Mar-15	92
6	Apr-15	146
7	May-15	122
8	Jun-15	154
9	Jul-15	128
10	Aug-15	140
11	Sep-15	231
12	Oct-15	245
13	Nov-15	258
14	Dec-15	244
15	Jan-16	231
16	Feb-16	176
17	Total	2,167

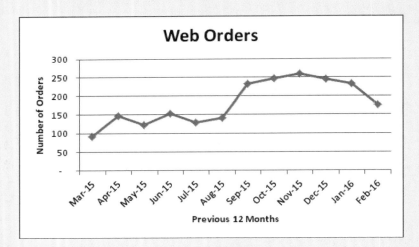

4. Place the **chart** on a separate sheet, naming it **Web Orders Trend**. *The dates will not appear slanted after the chart is moved.*

5. **Rename** the Sheet1 tab to **Supporting Data**.

6. **Print** the chart.

7. **Save** 💾 with the name **as-Web Orders** in the Lesson 06 folder and **close** the workbook.

Create a Worksheet and Pie Chart

In this exercise, you will create a worksheet and a pie chart based on the data in the worksheet. You will also apply a style to the worksheet; insert formulas in the worksheet; and move, resize, and explode a piece of the pie chart.

1. Use these guidelines to create the worksheet and chart shown in the following illustration:

    ■ **Type** all numbers and text entries as shown, but use formulas to calculate the New Balance in **column E** and the Totals, Highest, and Lowest values in **rows 9–11**. The formula for New Balance is New Balance = Beginning Balance + Purchases – Payments. Calculate the Totals in **row 9** with AutoSum, and use the MAX and MIN functions for the Highest and Lowest calculations in **rows 10 and 11**.

    ■ Use the font size of your choice for the title **cell A1**, merge and center the title across the worksheet, and then format the workbook with the theme of your choice. Apply a cell style to the cells in **row 3** and add a border around the data in **rows 9–11**.

    ■ Create the embedded 3-D pie chart shown in the illustration. The pie chart slices represent the new balance percentages of each customer. The pie chart does not represent any of the data in **rows 9–11**.

    ■ Adjust the position and size of the embedded chart as shown in the illustration.

    ■ **Explode** the largest slice.

    ■ Format all pie slice data labels as italic by using a command on the Mini toolbar or the Home tab of the Ribbon.

2. **Print** the worksheet and embedded chart on a **single page**.

3. **Save** with the name **as-Accounts Receivable Report** in the Lesson 06 folder and **close** the workbook.

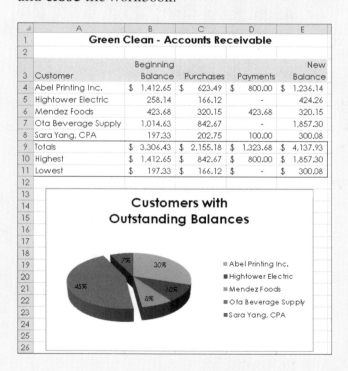

Create a Column Chart and Edit Worksheets

In this exercise, you will create a column chart embedded in the worksheet and then move, resize, and print the chart.

1. **Create** the worksheet and embedded column chart shown in the following illustration. Use the font size of your choice for the title in **cell A1** and enter the actual year instead of the words *Current Year*. Notice that the column chart is 2-D. The differences in **row 6** are simply the Revenues numbers minus the Expenses numbers. Choose an appropriate chart layout so the negative numbers dip below the category axis in the chart as shown. Move the legend to the top of the chart as shown.

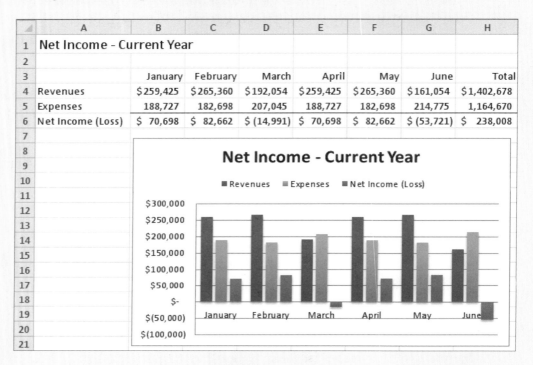

◢	A	B	C	D	E	F	G	H
1	Net Income - Current Year							
2								
3		January	February	March	April	May	June	Total
4	Revenues	$259,425	$265,360	$192,054	$259,425	$265,360	$161,054	$1,402,678
5	Expenses	188,727	182,698	207,045	188,727	182,698	214,775	1,164,670
6	Net Income (Loss)	$ 70,698	$ 82,662	$ (14,991)	$ 70,698	$ 82,662	$ (53,721)	$ 238,008
7								

2. Change the **chart colors** to shades of gray, suitable for printing on a grayscale printer.

3. Move the chart to a **separate sheet**, and **rename** the sheet tab to **Net Income Chart**.

4. **Rename** the worksheet tab to **Net Income Analysis**.

5. **Delete** the unused sheet tabs, Sheet2 and Sheet3.

6. Add the **color** of your choice to the **Net Income Analysis** sheet tab.

7. **Preview** the worksheet to ensure that it fits on one page and then **print** the worksheet and chart.

8. **Save** with the name **as-Net Income Analysis** in the Lesson 06 folder and **close** the workbook.

Send a Workbook via Email

In this exercise, you will email a workbook to yourself.

You should not perform this exercise if your computer cannot send and receive email.

Before You Begin: You must have completed Apply Your Skills 6.3. Your Internet connection should be active. You must have an email account in Microsoft Outlook or other default email program that works within Microsoft Office on your computer.

1. **Open** the as-Net Income Analysis workbook from the Lesson 06 folder.

2. Attach the entire **workbook** to an email message to yourself at your own email address.

3. Change the **subject line** to `Sending a Workbook via Email`.

4. In the **message area**, enter a greeting, a line describing the file, and a closing with your name.

5. **Send** the message.

6. Display your Inbox in **Outlook** (or other email program you used) and click the **Send/Receive** button every 30 seconds until the message you sent arrives.

7. **Print** the message after it appears in your Inbox. (It is not necessary to print the attachment.)

8. **Close** the Outlook (or other email) program window.

9. **Close** the workbook. Do **not** save when asked if you wish to save.

Critical Thinking & Work-Readiness Skills

In the course of working through the following Microsoft Office-based Critical Thinking exercises, you will also be utilizing various work-readiness skills, some of which are listed next to each exercise. Go to labyrinthelab.com/ workreadiness to learn more about the work-readiness skills.

6.1 Analyze Data Using an Embedded Column Chart

WORK-READINESS SKILLS APPLIED

- Seeing things in the mind's eye
- Reading
- Interpreting and communicating information

As part of an effort to reduce costs and environmental impact, Talos Bouras is tasked with reporting the delivery reps' driving activities. Open ct-Rep Driving Data (Lesson 06 folder). Create an embedded column chart that displays the miles driven by each driver. Title the chart appropriately. Label each driver at the base of the appropriate chart column. Use data labels to display the number of miles driven at the top of the appropriate column. Remove the legend. Create a similar chart to graph the total expenses for each driver. Save the file as **ct-Rep Driving Charts**. If working in a group, present your results. Answer questions such as: Who drove the most? Who drives the most efficiently? If working alone, type your answers in a Word document named **ct-Questions** saved to your Lesson 06 folder. Close the workbook.

6.2 Display Test Results Using a Pie Chart

WORK-READINESS SKILLS APPLIED

- Seeing things in the mind's eye
- Reading
- Interpreting and communicating information

Open ct-Test Results (Lesson 06 folder). On a separate worksheet, create a 3-D pie chart showing the percentage of contribution for each cleaner category to the overall total produced. Apply an appropriate style to the chart. Include appropriate data labels and give the chart a title. Change the 3-D rotation of the chart so the largest slice is in front. Determine whether or not to display the legend. Explode the largest slice. Change the sheet name to **Test Pie Chart** and save the file as **ct-Test Pie Chart** in your Lesson 06 folder. If working in a group, present your results. Discuss what cleaning product creates the most waste. Can you think of any alternative cleaning products that might be used? If working alone, type your answers in a Word document named **ct-Questions2** saved to your Lesson 06 folder.

6.3 Chart Sales Trends

WORK-READINESS SKILLS APPLIED

- Seeing things in the mind's eye
- Interpreting and communicating information
- Using computers to process information

Green Clean's sales results are in! Your job is to chart the sales data so that your manager can discuss the implications in a team meeting. Open the the Microsoft Word document named ct-Sales Results (Lesson 06 folder). Enter the information shown into a new Excel workbook. Type the actual current year, and calculate the totals. Review the data to determine the significant trends in sales performance. Create an embedded pie chart with appropriate labeling for one of these trends. Show other results in a columnar chart on a separate sheet. Keep in mind the data relationships that each chart type can best display. Save the file as **ct-Sales Charts** in your Lesson 06 folder. Why might you (or your manager) want to see the information displayed both ways? Type your answer in a Word document named **ct-Questions3** saved to your Lesson 06 folder.

Index

Notes

Notes

Notes

Notes